"There's so much more to golf than your score. *Golf, Naked* teaches you how to ace the rest of the game. It's flat out brilliant."
—Andrew Magee, PGA Tour golfer, host of the Golf Channel's *Big Break*

"*Golf, Naked* is a creative, entertaining, informative and very different golf book."
—Tom Perry, PGA Tour headquarters

"This book does everyone in our industry a huge favor. Every golfer, regardless of their ability or level of experience, should read this book."
—Brent Buckman, club manager, Spanish Oaks, Austin, TX

"*Golf, Naked* is an excellent reference for the newer golfer and should help educate future golfers for years to come."
—Rex Schultz, PGA head professional, Esmerelda Golf Course, Spokane, WA

"This book says the things that all Pros wish our members knew but don't like telling them ourselves. *Golf, Naked* does the dirty work for me in a way that's fun for the reader."
—Chad Stoddard, PGA head professional, Broken Top Club, Bend, OR

"Greg is a decent son. His book turned out better than I expected."
—Sandra Rowley, Greg's mom, lousy golfer and marginal cook

"*Golf, Naked* is a perfect tool for new golfer orientation. There's simply nothing like it out there—and it's laugh-out-loud funny."
—Rainer Gehres, former club manager, Riviera, Los Angeles, CA, and
Waverly, Portland, OR

"Reading *Golf, Naked* definitely helped me feel more comfortable at the local golf club that I recently joined. At first I felt like a bull in a china shop; now I feel like I really belong."
—Adam Deadmarsh, NHL star, Stanley Cup winner, and Olympic Silver Medalist

"In golf, I find much of the same satisfaction that I did as a professional skier. *Golf, Naked* puts into words something I'd only previously felt. Golf, to me, is a feeling, not the final score."
—Josh Loubek, professional skier, Winter X Games head judge

"What a great book!"
—Len Zamora, PGA director of golf, The Mirabel Club, Scottsdale, AZ

GOLF, NAKED

The Bare Essentials Revealed

GOLF, NAKED

The Bare Essentials Revealed

Greg Rowley, PGA

Pick It Up Publishing, LLC
Coeur d'Alene, Idaho

Published by Pick It Up Publishing, LLC
P.O. Box 3667
Coeur d'Alene, ID 83816
www.pickituppublishing.com

CEO: Denny Ryerson
President: Greg Rowley
Original illustrations: Jeremy Deming

Distributed by Greenleaf Book Group LLC

For ordering information or special discounts for bulk purchases, please contact Greenleaf Book Group LLC at 4005-B Banister Lane, Three Park Place, Austin, TX 78704, (512) 891-6100

Design and composition by Greenleaf Book Group LLC
Cover design by Nathan Brown and Greenleaf Book Group LLC
Initial editing by David Kilmer

All photos throughout the book have either been personally taken by the author in his travels, or have been provided by and used with the permission of the respective courses.

Publisher's Cataloging-In-Publication Data
(Prepared by The Donohue Group, Inc.)
Rowley, Greg.
Golf, naked : the bare essentials revealed / Greg Rowley. -- 1st ed.
p. : ill. ; cm.

ISBN-13: 978-0-9815319-5-3

1. Golf--Miscellanea. 2. Golfers. 3. Sportsmanship.
I. Title.

GV967 .R69 2008
796.352 2008907927

Printed in China on acid-free paper

08 09 10 11 12 13 14 10 9 8 7 6 5 4 3 2 1

First Edition

For Denny.
You've changed our lives.
Thank you for your courage and confidence.

CONTENTS

SECTION 4: On-Course Survival Guide

SECTION 5: Taking Your Game to the Next Level

Preface

I've had the privilege of working as an assistant golf professional, teaching professional, head professional, and director of golf at some of the country's most prestigious golf properties. The Quarry at La Quinta is a fixture on the Golf Digest "Top 100" list, and in 2004 The Club at Black Rock was named "America's Best New Private Golf Course."

My experiences have consistently taught me one simple, unwavering lesson about this maddening game: Preparation is no guarantee that the golf gods won't punish you on any given day—for no apparent reason. However, it's the preparation and understanding of golf as a culture, the sum far greater than its parts, that compels us all to love it so much. We're all equals because at any time, on any given course, this little mistress called golf may just knock us down, spank us, and leave us lying there with our pants around our ankles. Yet somehow we always say "thank you," and "may I please have another?"

Why is this so? Why is it that you can wander out to the local golf club on a Saturday morning (or Tuesday afternoon, for that matter), spray it all over the place for five hours, lose three sleeves of balls, get a little sunburned, cough up 30 bucks in side action to your buddies, tweak your bum hip on that shank you hit out of the rough on No. 13, and then revel deliciously over laughs and stories with a few ice-cold beverages in the clubhouse when it's all over, knowing that you just had a truly great time? I know the answer, and I believe that after reading this book, you too will better understand this feisty temptress that we all love to hate and hate to love.

I've written this book for two reasons. First, I want to share my love of the game and my experiences in working and playing with some of the most interesting people in the world. It's my hope that I can help novices and experienced golfers alike to better understand the nuances that make golf not just a game but a great game.

Second, I'm revealing these secrets so that everyone, especially my knuckleheaded buddies, will stop calling me incessantly with questions like these:

"How do I talk about golf and not sound like a rookie?"

"What should I wear to the private club this Thursday to play golf with my boss? I don't want to look and feel out of place."

"How much cash should I bring?"

"How much should I tip the good-looking beer-cart girl?"

"Shenanigans! You said we were only playing for $2! How the heck do I owe you $30? What's a press, anyway?"

"What's the best old-fashioned golf prank I can pull on my jerk brother-in-law this weekend?"

"How might I get my wife interested in the game?"

"What's an appropriate amount to pay my caddie? For that amount, what should I expect to be done?"

"How much does a lesson cost? Is it worth it?"

"Is it a penalty if I move my ball when it's sitting on a steaming pile of animal dung?"

Enjoy *Golf, Naked*. I promise you'll enjoy the game more thoroughly.

That's me at the Bally Bandon Sheep Ranch. I'm much older (and stronger) than I look!

Introduction

There's no doubt I've been blessed with a career that has presented many unforgettable opportunities. I met my wife, supported my family, and traveled the world—all because of this game!

I've played on truly hallowed ground and remember many of the most satisfying shots of my life like they were yesterday. Some were under extreme pressure in front of many, while others were witnessed by only a few Jumping Cholla cacti or Ponderosa pine trees.

I've played (typically very poorly) on every imaginable degree of golf course—from the shabby Indio Muni to the ultra-chic and impeccably maintained Quarry at La Quinta. I've played Riviera, Pinehurst, Big Horn, Ballybunion, Bally Bandon, Bandon Dunes, Whiskey Run, and Royal County Down. I've played Black Rock, Whisper Rock, Fire Rock, Red Rock, and Rimrock. I've designed a course at the Sheep Ranch one morning, and then played the Oregon Coast shoreline as a barefooted single that evening. I've played with a stick for a club and a pinecone for a ball on a sandbar island in the middle of the raging Salmon River. I've played two hundred holes in twelve hours and raised $25,000 to give to the Red Cross following the 9/11 attacks. I've even played on the surface of the moon, or at least it felt like it, amid the coastal dunes at Cairn in Ireland.

I've taught and played with men, women, juniors, seniors, celebrities, professional athletes, PGA Tour players, and beginners, and I've discovered the universal theme that's apparent at every golf course in every part of the world: Nobody wants to look stupid.

You need to be comfortable on the golf course. That's because this game can strip you bare without warning or regret—physically, mentally, and emotionally. Golf requires so much attention, and can be so utterly humiliating, that everything else must support the focused effort necessary to execute your swing. If you aren't comfortable in all of golf's language, behaviors, and preparations, then your willingness to dive into its depths will certainly suffer.

As one of 61 million golfers worldwide, you probably share the same concerns as the rest of us. Do you enjoy the game? The camaraderie? The challenge? Have you ever felt nervous or a little unsure of what to say or do—before, during, or after a round? Do you play better when you're by yourself than you do with your friends, family, clients, or boss? Have you ever been distracted while playing for a reason that had nothing to do with your next shot? Do you know someone who you'd like to help become more excited about the game? Most golfers fall somewhere in the middle of the bell curve—and if you're one of "us," then this book is for you.

Golf, Naked will give you confidence. It offers the understanding that no one cares how well you play because everyone is worried about their own actions. No one ever remembers your score (unless it's really, really good). They *will* remember how you look and act. These tips and techniques will help you master the rest of the game—the real stuff that truly demonstrates experience, comfort, confidence, class, humility, and ultimately, golfing grace.

The goal here is simple—to help you unlock the secrets of all the little things that go into the typical golf experience. When they become second nature, you'll enjoy your playing partners and the game more thoroughly—no matter where, when, or who you're playing.

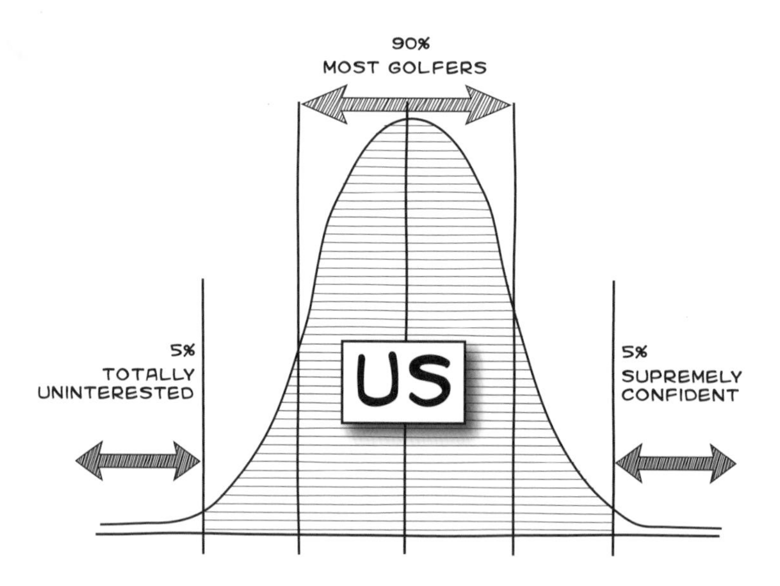

Swing Thoughts

The golf lifestyle doesn't come with a blueprint. The courses are vastly different, as are the players and the reasons why they play. To help you achieve total golf culture integration, I've drawn you a road map. Sometimes the route is short, simple, and direct, and other times it's much more circuitous, but the goal remains the same—a more enjoyable time at the course.

Golf, Naked starts with the decision to play golf. Sounds simple, right? From there we move through the golf experience: Preparing to play, arrival at the course, parking lot to the first tee, playing the game, and wrapping up everything. Then we'll get into the nuts and bolts of the game, my teaching methodology, and a practical understanding of the rules.

Here are a few recurring themes that you'll see throughout the book. They're intended to help make certain points clearer.

ROOKIE MISTAKES

Common errors I've made, seen, and heard. If you see yourself in some of these examples, perhaps a change in your customary behavior might be appropriate.

PEARLS FROM THE PRO

Wisdom I hope you'll find valuable and useful.

STORY TIME

Stories from personal experience, or others I've heard that are worth sharing.

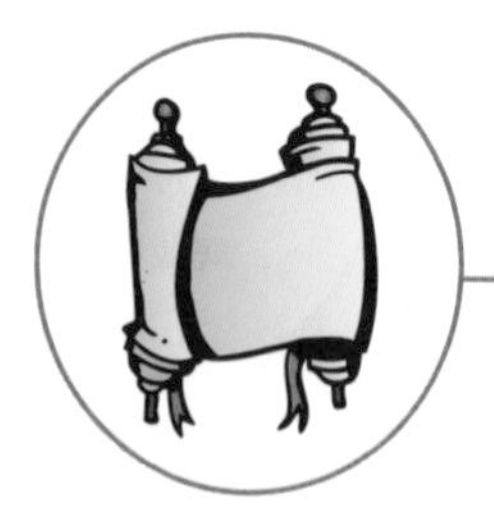

HISTORY LESSON

Perspective on the game, the equipment, and the rules.

FACE PLANTS

I've definitely fallen on my face more times than I care to remember. No matter how bad you might feel about a particular performance, someone—usually me—has done something every bit as bad, or worse.

IF I RULED THE WORLD

If it were up to me to change some of the customs of the culture, this is what I'd do. Don't mistake these for actual rules; they're just wishful thinking.

Now it's up to you. Read, learn, live, love, dog-ear, highlight, laugh, and recite. Use *Golf, Naked* to learn the real rules and customs of the game, those that your local golf pro wants you to know, and the ones that lead to comfort and confidence at the course. Regardless of your experience and ability, you'll not put down this book unchanged.

See you on the other side . . .

Off and Stumbling

CHAPTER 1

Sweat the Small Stuff

"Golf is deceptively simple, and endlessly complicated; it satisfies the soul and frustrates the intellect. A child can play it well and a grown man can never master it. It is almost a science, yet it is a puzzle with no answer."

—Arnold Palmer

Going to a golf course for the first time as a beginner, or to a new course for the first time as an experienced player, can be utterly intimidating. I've learned this lesson in many ways over the course of my career. None, however, was more poignant than my first day of work at the Hayden Lake Country Club in northern Idaho.

It was a Thursday afternoon in April 1997. A phone call to the PGA headquarters in Florida was all it took for me to officially become an apprentice professional. No fanfare, no confetti and balloons, no cheers and hugs, just a phone call. Big deal.

Shortly thereafter, the annual Men's Opening Day Tourney was starting. The golfers were scattering to their hole assignments when word reached the golf shop that one of the "A" players was a no-show. So, yours truly was quickly called into action, and before I knew it, I was being introduced by the head professional to the rest of my team: Jim, sixtyish and a 10 handicap; John, fiftyish and a 14; and Willard, ninetyish and a mostly blind 27. I was told to ride with Willard so I could help him spot his ball.

To make a long and painful story short, I was so nervous I shot a 103, highlighted by a handful of shanks, tree ricochets, and even a wayward shot that struck a passing motorist. All three of my mates beat me straight up. However, as luck would have it, our team actually won the event. Willard played a career round and carried the team to victory! There was some grousing by the other participants that the team with the "pro" had won—that it wasn't fair. But, the truth of my round was quickly exposed by my erstwhile teammates, and I was fed to the wolves.

Fortunately, this strange culture of golf has become much less intimidating since then. Not only have I personally learned the appropriate on- and off-course behaviors through instruction, modeling, trial and error, and thousands of mistakes, but I've also had to teach them to others at the beginning, middle, and end stages of their journey.

> "A journey of a thousand miles must begin with a single step."
> —Lao Tzu

You Have to Start Somewhere

In fact, a good friend of mine recently asked me to help him learn to golf. His wife had played a handful of times and he wanted to surprise her by giving it a go. Shhhhh! He visited the local golf megastore to explore and look at the fancy equipment. Whoops! Sensory overload! He staggered out in a gear-induced stupor and phoned me immediately. We met later that evening, and it didn't take me long to realize our conversation was worth recording. I immediately began to scribble with kids' crayons on the back of my paper placemat:

(Ryan) "Should I buy new clubs?"

(Me) "Maybe."

"How do you know which clubs to buy?"

"Well, when you're first starting out—see if you can borrow some. You'll want to try a few times before you buy some expensive equipment that you're not even sure you're going to enjoy using. In that regard, it's a lot like skiing."

"How do you know which golf ball to use?"

"Whichever's the cheapest—'cause you're going to lose 'em all anyway. Someday you might be able to tell the difference between expensive and cheap golf balls, but I doubt it. Certainly that day isn't today, nor is it tomorrow!"

"What is the difference?"

"You see, golf balls used to be made of balata rubber, the harvested sap from trees in the rain forest, but now balata is rare, so balls are made from compressionless cores of compacted rubbery stuff . . . Never mind, it's pretty scientific and a multibillion dollar industry."

"The guy at the store said that I should be custom fit for clubs. What's that?"

"Golf clubs can be built specifically for your body and your swing—based on your height, arm length, hand position at impact, strength, swing speed, lie angle, shot trajectory, etc."

"Does all that stuff really matter?"

"Yes, eventually."

"When?"

"I don't know. When you improve enough to feel as though you're ready to make a serious investment in your equipment."

"But how will I know that I like golf if the clubs I'm using aren't right for me?"

"Good question. For now, you can at least get a general understanding of the game and see if it appeals to you, and regardless of club fit, you should still be able to hit a decent shot every now and again."

"Sweet. Which club goes farthest?"

"Typically the 1-wood, or driver. But to start with, you won't hit it the farthest. You'll probably hit a 5-wood or 3-wood farther. They aren't actually made out of wood anymore either. Woods are the big, fat-headed, metal clubs with the socks on them."

"Huh?"

"Yeah, I know. It's confusing. Basically, until you become better, you'll need the added loft of the 3-wood or 5-wood to help get the ball into the air. When your swing speed and your ability to hit the ball in the middle of the clubface increase, then you'll be able to use the driver."

"What are loft, swing speed, and clubface?"

"Arrrgh! We'll get to that. It makes more sense when we're actually swinging a club at the range."

"What's a range?"

"Seriously?"

"Yeah."

"The practice area at the golf course."

"Does every golf course have a range?"

"No. Not necessarily."

"Then how do people practice?"

"Most don't."

"Then how do they get better?"

"Most don't."

"Then why do people play?"

"Because it's fun."

"Is it fun even if you suck?"

"Sure. But it's definitely more fun to be good."

"I've played miniature golf before. Does that count?"

"Hey, it's a start. Putting is super-important."

"Is it more important to putt good or to hit the ball way out there?"

"Well."

"Well what?"

"Putt 'well.' It's more important to putt well."

"What?"

"Never mind. Most of a player's strokes come within 50 yards of the green. So yeah, it's more important to your score to putt well. But honestly, it's more important to your psyche and to the overall enjoyment of the game to hit the ball a long ways."

"What's a green? The whole course is green."

"You've gotta be kidding?! The green is the closely mown area on each hole that surrounds the flagstick. It's where you putt on the golf course. The really short grass—like carpet."

"Is that where those sand pits are, too?"

"You mean 'bunkers.' Bunkers can be anywhere on the golf course, but yeah, they surround the greens in most cases."

"What club do you use to hit with when you're in a sand pit?"

"Bunker. You use whatever club you think you can hit the proper distance based on the length required for the shot and how deeply the ball is buried in the sand. But usually, from a greenside bunker, you'll use a wedge."

"How do you know which wedge to use? Is that like the 7-wedge or the 6-wedge?"

"No, those are called irons—but they're not really made out of iron. It depends on how far you want to hit the ball. The longer the iron, measured by length in inches, the lower and farther it goes and the lower the number that's on it. A 5-iron is longer, goes lower, and should go farther than a 9-iron."

"How will I know how far the ball goes?"

"Playing and practice."

"How far do you hit a 5-wedge?"

"5-iron. 195 yards."

"Every time?"

"No. It depends on how well I make contact, how hard I swing, and the conditions of the course and the weather. You know—wind, rain, temperature, grass length, altitude, attitude, etc."

"All of that matters?"

"Yes."

"On every shot?"

"Yes."

"Dude, one time my dog ate a bird."

"No kidding."

"I have learned that, if one advances confidently in the direction of his dreams, and endeavors to live the life he has imagined, he will meet with a success unexpected in common hours."
—Henry David Thoreau

Culture Shock

Can you imagine moving to a foreign land and instantly adapting to its culture with only a limited knowledge of the people, customs, or language? Impossible. For instance, in some countries it's customary to kiss total strangers upon introduction—on the mouth. While in others, you don't even shake hands, because it's the hand that is used in lieu of toilet paper.

Among countless other factors, proficient integration into a culture requires a complex understanding of its vocabulary. Speaking a new language is difficult enough without mastering the nuances such as context, tempo, tone, and inflection. Add to that the need to walk, dress, spit, sneeze, stand up straight, and scratch oneself in the appropriate time and meter, and the task of becoming a

competent golfer may seem quite daunting. It might take years of stumbling—or just reading this book!

The fact is, there's a huge difference in application between many of the "official" terms of the game and the "real" ones. For example:

Official: "Good heavens, Buffy! It appears that your ball in play, struck from the teeing ground with your 1-wood, has crossed the margin of the lateral water hazard, designated by the red stakes and lines, entitling you to five relief options, one of which is to measure two club lengths from that spot and drop there."

Although the verbiage here is totally correct, if you talk like this you'll sound like an idiot. Try this instead:

Real: "Honey, you snapped the big dog into the drink. Just drop up there where it went in."

Admittedly, this is less refined, but totally accurate and equally as acceptable.

Without formal instructions, it seems to take between two and three years to learn a new language, and that's when it's used daily or is necessary for survival. Anyone with children can confirm that. But when the words are only used periodically, like every other weekend for the summer months, and when the nonverbal communication carries an elevated importance, the task of cultural assimilation can seem hopeless.

I don't remember learning to talk—but watching my daughters makes me appreciate the process. I do remember learning to speak the "language of golf," and I've seen hundreds make the same transition, from goo-goo-gah-gah, "whiffs," and "dubs" to silver-tongued eloquence, "roped 2-irons," and "holes-in-one." Have faith, it can happen.

> "Faith is being sure of what we hope for, and certain of what we do not see."
>
> —Hebrews 11:1

Consider the Source

> "Men are four: He who knows not and knows not he knows not, he is a fool—shun him; He who knows not and knows he knows not, he is simple—teach him; He who knows and knows not he knows, he is asleep—wake him; He who knows and knows he knows, he is wise—follow him."
>
> —Lady Burton

Interestingly enough, practically all golf literature is written by someone without PGA credentials. This seems like a total disconnect when you consider that PGA-certified golf professionals are the only official practitioner-instructors of the sport and its culture. You wouldn't take piano lessons from your accountant just because he or she likes music, would you? You shouldn't take golf advice from any other source, either.

The golf experience encompasses so much more than just swinging a club. If a golf swing takes two seconds and you shoot 100, then only two hundred seconds are spent "golfing" during a typical round. The rest is spent talking, joking, searching, preparing, keeping score, relaxing, eating hot dogs, gambling, admiring the view, and interacting with your fellow players. These are the real meat and potatoes of the game.

Don't get me wrong; proficiency in the game is important, and we'll get to it. But if you're not comfortable at the golf course and if you're not committed to the process, you won't come back.

Every golf experience begins with a simple decision to play. It can start with a casual conversation in the locker room, a quick trip to the practice range while you're headed home from the office, or a formal invitation from your buddy to an upcoming member-guest tournament.

Every golf experience has its own set of details. Where will you play? When? Why? Who will you be with? Will you walk or ride? Do you have time to arrive early? How early? What will you do with that time—practice, warm up, eat? What will you wear, depending on conditions? Should you pay for your guest fees, or will the host pick it up? What kind of betting should you expect, and how much cash will that require? Can you write a check? What can you do to make things easier on the staff? Will you have time to hide a pound of raw hamburger in the bottom of your buddy's golf bag before you leave post-golf? Will he find it before he can smell it? Would you, if the beef was in your bag?

Contrary to the popular adage "Don't sweat the small stuff," in golf it's the small stuff that matters most. And in a game of unwritten rules and outdated stereotypes, learning that small stuff can be a daunting task.

Gozzer Ranch, Coeur d'Alene, Idaho—15th Hole.
Photo provided courtesy of Gozzer Ranch, Coeur d'Alene, Idaho

CHAPTER 2

Slicing Through a Snowstorm

"I know that you believe you understand what you think I said, but I'm not sure you realize that what you heard is not what I meant."

—Robert McCloskey

It's a commonly held misconception that the Inuit have something like thirteen different words for snow. That seems excessive to me, even as a native northern Idahoan where we get four full seasons of weather each year and there are five ski mountains within an hour's drive of my front door. Sure, I'm aware of some cold-climate subtleties. I know when snow needs to be shoveled immediately from the driveway and wiped from the satellite dish because it's the kind that will stick instead of the light and wispy kind that will quickly melt or blow away. I know not to eat yellow snow. You see, one time when I was little, a friend of mine told me that it was lemon-flavored, and I . . . well, never mind . . . it's too painful to discuss.

Although the Inuit don't really have so many words for snow, the myth makes an excellent point about the subtleties of language and culture. Golf is a culture of its own, and its terms are similarly redundant. Witness how many golf words are synonymous with "slice," the most common miss-hit shot shape: banana ball, cut, chop, block, knife, fade, fan, push, shove, wipe, carp, carve, gash, hack, slash.

Golf, too, can feel like a foreign land with a language of its own. Learn the language and you'll be that much closer to comfortably hanging out with the locals.

Nothing can be more embarrassing than totally misunderstanding what someone is trying to say, not seeking clarification, and then asking a really dumb question as a result.

STORY TIME

When my older brother, Jeff, was in the fourth grade, Mom and Dad signed him up for a summer series of golf lessons at one of the local courses. It culminated with a fun competition called Horserace in which all competitors begin on the first hole in a large group and are eliminated hole by hole. The winner is the last person (or team) remaining.

When Mom picked up Jeff after the second-to-last session, the pro greeted her with a huge grin on his face. Apparently, after the pro announced that there would be a Horserace the following week, Jeff had raised his hand and frantically squawked, "But I don't know how to ride a horse!"

Just like my brother and the Horserace, you will encounter many common golf terms that carry other real-world definitions. If you don't know any better, imagine the possibilities of what you might end up thinking or doing as a result.

Flight Spike Marks Cut APRON Flop Driver SCRAMBLE
WINTER RULES Shank Slice
SHOOT-OUT Follow Through
Impact HANDICAP SHOTGUN START CHIP
HEADCOVER HAZARD Lip Out

The Game of Opposites

> "If you're not confused, you're not paying attention."
>
> —Tom Peters

What a confusing and backward game is golf. Very little is intuitive. Every hole has a hole. A ball considered through the green can actually be on a green—but not the green of the hole being played. A player has a course handicap and every golf course has a handicap on each hole. The shorter clubs have higher numbers; they fly higher but not as far. Hitting downward on the ball projects it up into the air with backspin; swinging upward to help lift the ball into the air actually drives it downward into the ground with topspin. For a right-handed player, a clockwise spin on the ball makes it curve to the right (slice); a counter-clockwise spin on the ball makes it curve to the left (hook). The more you aim to the left, the faster it spins to the right; the more you aim to the right, the faster it spins to the left. Swinging slower can make the ball go farther.

Golf is a game of opposites, which explains why it's so complex, maddening, and addicting. It doesn't make sense for most beginners. At first, the swing seems to be an awkward contortion that looks and feels nothing like the balanced and fluid motion a good player learns to execute.

Worse yet, players finally reach a fundamental understanding of the swing, only to find their heads filled with hundreds of thoughts, most of which don't actually have anything to do with their semi-success. If you're one of those players, you wish for the days when you ignorantly flailed away without rhyme or reason.

Then alas, a breakthrough! Epiphany! An understanding of the motion, combined with the ability that comes only from practice and experience, finally produces a somewhat repeatable swing with somewhat predictable results.

Now you're golfing . . . somewhat.

Pop Quiz, Hot Shot

Here's the deal: You must know some basics of golf to make sense of the game, the culture, and certainly the remainder of this book. You beginners need to be brought up to speed or you'll get left in the dust—and we don't want that. At the same time, I don't want you "old hands" to lose interest.

Here's a little test. A passing score punches your ticket to chapter 4, but a marginal or failing score means chapter 3 is calling your name.

With two No. 2 pencils in hand, you have fifteen minutes to complete this portion of the exam:

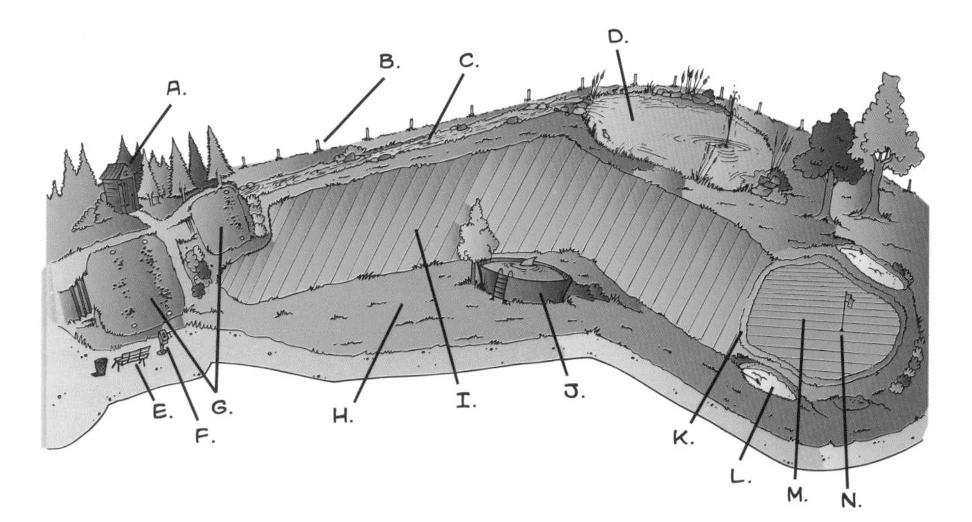

Golf Course Anatomy

1. Teeing Ground	_____	8. Outhouse	_____
2. Shark Tank	_____	9. Flagstick	_____
3. Ball Washer	_____	10. Water Hazard	_____
4. Bunker	_____	11. Lateral Water Hazard	_____
5. Fairway	_____	12. Out of Bounds	_____
6. Rough	_____	13. Bench	_____
7. Fringe	_____	14. Green	_____

15. The two categories of swing techniques are _________ and _________.
   a. Etiquette and Rules
   b. Full Swing and Short Game
   c. Driving and Putting
   d. Gripping and Ripping
   e. Swing Path and Swing Plane

16. Golf originated in what European country and by what tradesmen?
   a. Finland; bobsled makers
   b. Norway; curlers
   c. Scotland; shepherds
   d. Ireland; pugilists
   e. Germany; rifle makers

17. How many clubs are you allowed to have in your bag, per *The Rules of Golf* (published by the USGA each year)?

18. True or False: Loft is the angle between the club shaft and the clubhead.

19. A common slang term for a putter is _____________.
   a. Flatstick
   b. Magic wand
   c. Holy roller
   d. Great equalizer
   e. Billy, Billy, Billy, Billy, Billy . . .
   f. All of the above

20. True or False: A putter has zero degrees of loft.

21. True or False: The "outward half" of a golf course refers to the back nine.

22. There are _____________ types of hazards.
   a. Four—out of bounds, cart paths, boulders, and trees
   b. Three—swarms of angry bees, crocodiles, and rattlesnakes
   c. Three—water, lateral water, and bunkers
   d. Two—lightning and locusts
   e. Three—out of bounds, electric fences, and electric eels

23. True or False: Water hazards are designated by yellow stakes and lines.

24. Name the character from *Star Wars* that is also a slang term for a ball that goes beyond the parameters of a golf course. Hint: It's not C3PO.

25. Who's the best superhero ever?

Golf Club Anatomy

26. Shaft ______
27. Clubface ______
28. Butt ______
29. Grip ______
30. Hosel ______
31. Sole ______
32. Toe ______
33. Clubhead ______
34. Heel ______

Answers are on pages 21 and 22.

No peeking!

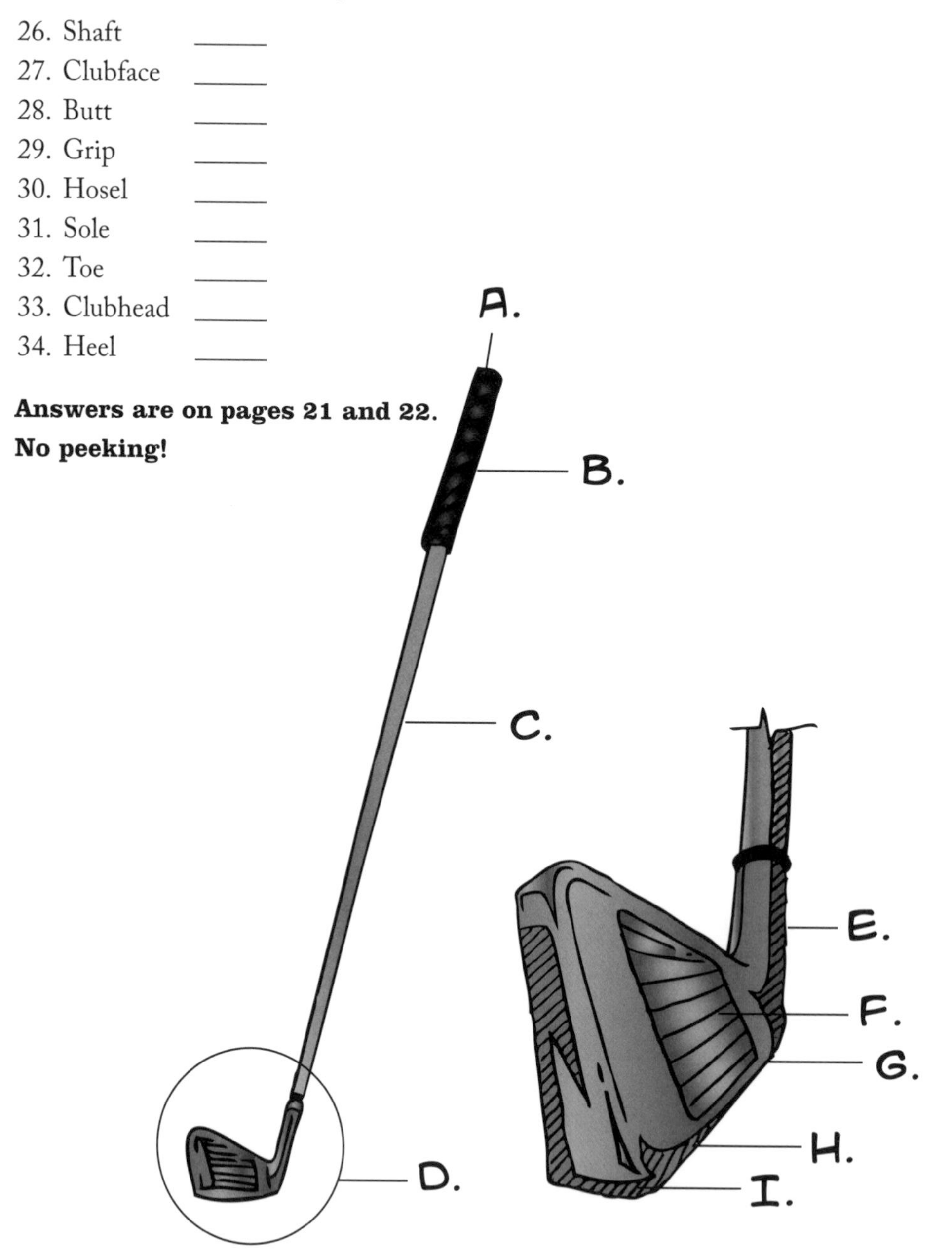

Grading Scale

0–6: With the first and second finger of your right hand, check your left wrist for a pulse. Still with us?

7–14: Speakin' English?

15–21: Get a highlighter, a cup of coffee, and enjoy chapter 3.

22–28: It probably wouldn't hurt to skim.

29–33: Do not pass Go, do not collect $200, proceed directly to chapter 4.

34: Cheater!

Answers:

Golf Course Anatomy

1. Teeing Ground: G
2. Shark Tank: J
3. Ball Washer: F
4. Bunker: L
5. Fairway: I
6. Rough: H
7. Fringe: K
8. Outhouse: A
9. Flagstick: N
10. Water Hazard: D
11. Lateral Water Hazard: C
12. Out of Bounds: B
13. Bench: E
14. Green: M
15. b: Full Swing and Short Game
16. c: Scotland; shepherds
17. 14
18. False
19. f: All of the above
20. False
21. False
22. Three—water, lateral water, and bunkers
23. True
24. Obi-Wan Kenobi (or OB)
25. Green Lantern (Come on, everyone knows that!)

Golf Club Anatomy

26. Shaft: C
27. Clubface: F
28. Butt: A
29. Grip: B
30. Hosel: E
31. Sole: H
32. Toe: I
33. Clubhead: D
34. Heel: G

StoneRidge Golf Course, Blanchard, Idaho—4th Hole.
Photo © John R. Johnson—golfphotos.com

CHAPTER 3

Golf 101

"Does the road wind uphill all the way? Yes, to the very end. Will the day's journey take the whole long day? From morn to night, my friend."

—Christina Rossetti

This chapter is dedicated to the beginner—that brave soul who stands at the precipice of the unknown, toes dangling over the edge of a journey yet begun. It's a journey sure to bring belly laughs and lousy shots, three putts and supreme satisfaction. If you're considering taking the plunge, welcome! The water's warm.

This chapter covers the elements you'll need to stay afloat—the game, the equipment, and the course.

Big Rocks

I'm reminded of the first day of a philosophy class I took my sophomore year in college. The professor held up a glass pickle jar filled to the top with golf ball–size stones. She asked us, "Is this jar full?" Naturally, we all nodded our heads and mumbled some sort of affirmation. "Uh-huh, yep, looks full to me . . ."

Next, she poured sand into the jar, which settled into the spaces between the bigger rocks. She asked again, "Is this jar full?" Again, we all blankly nodded, "Ah, yes, now I see. Yes, now the jar is full . . ."

Finally, she carried the jar over to her desk, where a pitcher of water was waiting. She emptied it into the jar, now filled to the brim. "Now is this jar full?" "Aha," we all answered in unison. "Yes, now I see. Yes, now that jar is completely full." Her point, of course, was that learning any behavior follows a similar pattern. It's essential to start with the big rocks, those fundamentals that initially take up the most space. Once those principles are understood, the sand and water can be added to fill the gaps. It wouldn't all fit in any other order.

So let's start with the basics and fill your pickle jar with some big rocks.

The Game

> "Golf is a game in which you yell 'fore,' shoot six, and write down five."
>
> —Paul Harvey

Golf courses come in all shapes and sizes and can be found in every condition and climate. Some are downtown and others are off the beaten path. Some are meticulously maintained, and others are dusty and downtrodden. Nonetheless, the game played on every course in every corner of the world is exactly the same.

The premise itself is quite simple. Starting from the teeing ground on the first hole, the goal is to get the ball into each hole in as few strokes as possible. Score is kept for each hole and, cumulatively, for the entire round.

The modern techniques used to play golf come in two categories: the full swing and the short game. The full swing is just what it sounds like—an attempt to hit the ball as far as you can. The short game is a group of three techniques—the putt, chip, and pitch—employed to control the distance and trajectory of a shot.

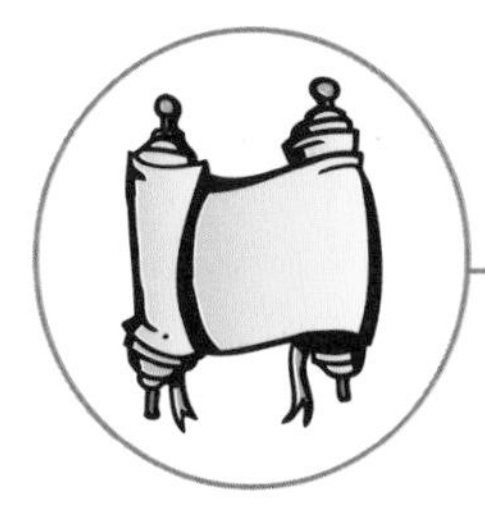

HISTORY LESSON

Although there are historical records of golf-like games dating back as far as AD 1456, the modern game originated in the late 1500s with Scottish shepherds who struck rocks with sticks as they herded their flocks from one field to the next. Predictably, as male competitiveness kicked in, they began to modify the equipment and count the number of strokes it took.

The very first golf tournament played under a written set of rules was at Leith Links in 1744. Those rules included these gems:

"If a Ball be stopp'd by any Person, Horse, Dog or anything else, The Ball so stopp'd must be play'd where it lyes."

"Neither Trench, Ditch or Dyke, made for the preservation of the Links, nor the Scholar's Holes, or the Soldier's Lines, Shall be accounted a Hazard; But the Ball is to be taken out, teed and play'd with any Iron Club."

The Ancient Golf Club at St. Andrews in Scotland is considered the home of modern-day golf and was founded by twenty-two gentlemen in 1754. In 1834, King William IV conferred his patronage on the club and it became the Royal and Ancient (R&A) Golf Club.

With the explosive growth of the game in the late 1800s, the need arose for a standardized set of rules. Other clubs looked to the R&A for their stability and leadership. In 1897, the first Rules of Golf committee was established, and the R&A became the officially recognized governing body of the game throughout the world except in the United States. Today, the R&A works together with the United States Golf Association (USGA) to set the standards and rules of the game around the world.

"The emblem on the necktie reserved for the members of the Royal and Ancient Golf Club of St. Andrews, the Vatican of golf, is of St. Andrew himself bearing the saltaire cross on which, once he was captured at Patras, he was to be stretched before he was crucified. Only the Scots would have thought of celebrating a national game with the figure of a tortured saint."
—Alistair Cooke

The Equipment

Golf Ball

The engineering of the modern golf ball is truly mind-boggling. I've sat through seminars and listened as aerospace engineers explained why the quantity, depth, and circumference of the dimples made their brand better for the weekend warrior. Honestly, all that technology doesn't matter much to most golfers. But, if it matters to you, here's what to consider: A hard outer shell will spin less and fly farther and straighter, while a soft outer shell will spin more and offer increased feel around the greens.

HISTORY LESSON

In the earliest records of golf, most of the equipment was made from wood—including the ball.

The Featherie ball, introduced in the early 1600s, was handmade from wet fowl feathers packed into a wet leather shell. As it dried, the feathers expanded and the leather shrank, creating a hardened ball. They were expensive, often costing more than the clubs. It was the ball of choice for a couple hundred years.

The mid-1800s brought the Gutta Percha ball, made from the rubbery sap of the Gutta tree found in tropical climates. When the sap was heated it could be molded into the proper shape, including the first use of dimples. The Guttie, as it was called, was much cheaper than the Featherie, and could be heated and reshaped when damaged.

In 1901 the Haskell ball, a rubber core encased in a Gutta Percha sphere, became the industry standard. The Haskell ball was produced in great quantities and was very affordable.

In 1921, the USGA set standards for the size and weight of the golf ball, which remain to this day.

Golf Clubs

> "Golf is a game whose aim is to hit a very small ball into an even smaller hole, with weapons singularly ill-designed for the purpose."
> —Winston Churchill

Let's take a quick look at your tools. In simple terms, two main variables determine the function of your golf club—the loft of the clubface and the characteristics of the shaft.

Loft is the angle of the clubface in relationship to the ground. With more loft, the ball will fly higher and roll less when it lands. Club selection (deciding which club to use for the next shot) is almost always based on loft—and an estimation of how high and far the ball needs to be projected toward the target.

The *shaft* is the steel or graphite rod that connects the grip to the clubhead. Here, two important variables influence ball flight: length and flex. *Length* is measured in inches. In general, the longer the shaft, the farther the ball will fly. It's simple physics. The shaft *flex* is its stiffness. On one end of the spectrum, a strong and tall player might choose a firm flex for accuracy. On the other, a senior female might prefer a soft flex to help her more easily project the ball into the air. Most players fall somewhere in the middle.

Clubs are numbered according to their loft. A club with a lower number (a 3-iron, for example) will have a longer shaft and less loft and will propel the ball lower and farther. A club with a higher number (an 8-iron) will have a shorter shaft and more loft and should send the ball higher and softer, but not as far.

When someone says to "take more club" or "club up," it means to use a lower-numbered club to hit the ball farther. Conversely, "take less club" or "club down" means to use a higher-numbered club.

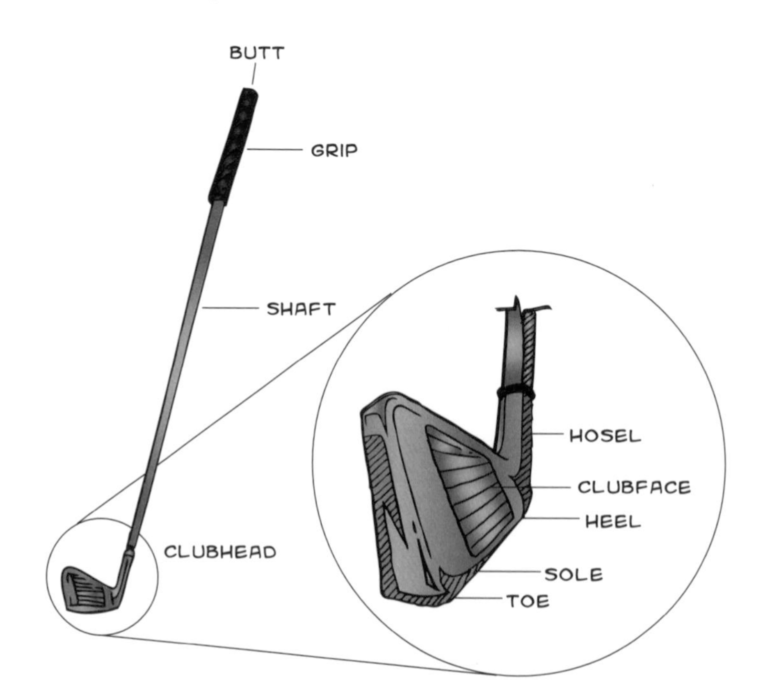

Here's a list of clubs you'll need in your bag.

Woods They're not made out of wood anymore, but they're still called woods. These clubs are the longest and have the least amount of loft (other than the putter). They're designed to hit the ball the farthest. However, they also tend to hit it the farthest in the wrong direction at times.

Irons These classic-looking metal clubs are designed to most easily project the ball into the air off the ground or from a tee.

Hybrids These clubs combine the shaft of a longer iron with the larger hollow metal clubhead of a wood. This hybrid club, also known as a "utility club," is typically easier to hit than a long iron. The hybrid also tends to produce a higher ball flight that lands softer than an iron—using less effort or clubhead speed—but travels about the same distance. In my opinion, every amateur should replace their long irons with hybrid clubs.

Wedges These are the short irons. They have the most loft and are engineered to be more versatile than longer irons, which makes them the club of choice for the short game.

Putter Also known as the flatstick, the magic wand, and the great equalizer, the putter is the shortest and least-lofted club in the bag. It's designed to roll the ball across the ground in as straight a line as possible and into the hole. Without question, putters are built with the most variety and creativity. Some look like potato mashers, while others look like butter knives. Their function is simple yet maddening. It's not uncommon for experienced golfers to have several putters in their garage or locker and regularly switch back and forth based on recent performances.

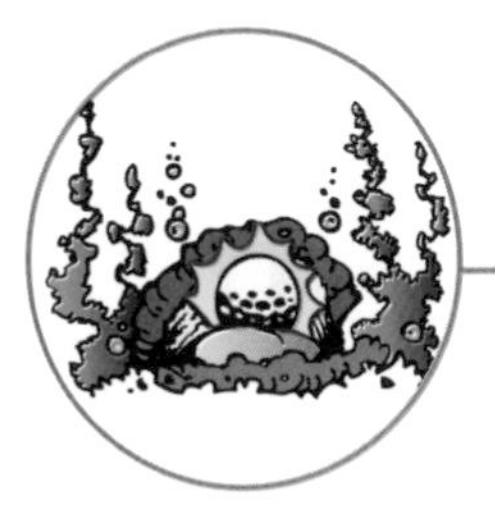

PEARLS FROM THE PRO

Cameras, computers, cell phones, and golf clubs—the big companies seem to come out with a new and improved product every few weeks. It's frustrating for consumers—and even more discouraging if you're a promoter, salesperson, or retail manager—to try to keep up with new technology. On several occasions, I've spent significant time and energy trying to sell a golf club worth several hundred dollars to a patron, only to have the whiz-bang technology be labeled as illegal or obsolete within days of the purchase.

If your clubs are fairly new (made within the last decade), then keep 'em. If not, it could be time for an upgrade. I believe that having confidence in one set of clubs—and knowing how high and far the ball can go with each of them—is more important than continually jockeying from one set to the next to keep up with TV commercials and tour pros.

Every golfer will have different results when using the same club. A tall, strong person with a technically correct swing can add thirty or more yards to each of the average club distances. Conversely, a shorter or weaker person, or a player with a lousy swing, can subtract thirty or more yards.

The Rules of Golf allows a player to carry only fourteen clubs. You can choose to include all woods or none, one putter or four. Sometimes it's difficult to decide which clubs you'd like to keep in your bag, but making tough decisions is all part of the game. Don't be one of those players who carries extra clubs—it's a blatant disregard for the rules. Build a legal set and learn to use it.

Average Club Lofts and Distances			
Club	Degrees of Loft	Distance (in yards) Men (+/-)	Distance (in yards) Women (+/-)
1-wood (Driver)	8° – 13°	240	170
3-wood	15°	220	160
5-wood	19°	200	150
7-wood	21°	185	140
9-wood	24°	-	130
11-wood	27°	-	120
2-hybrid	16°	220	-
3-hybrid	19°	200	150
4-hybrid	22°	190	135
5-hybrid	25°	180	125
1-iron	15°	220	-
2-iron	18°	210	-
3-iron	21°	200	-
4-iron	24°	185	-
5-iron	27°	175	120
6-iron	31°	160	110
7-iron	35°	150	100
8-iron	39°	140	90
9-iron	43°	130	80
Pitching wedge	47°	115	70
Gap wedge	52°	100	60
Sand wedge	56°	85	50
Lob wedge	60°	70	40
Putter	4°	-	-

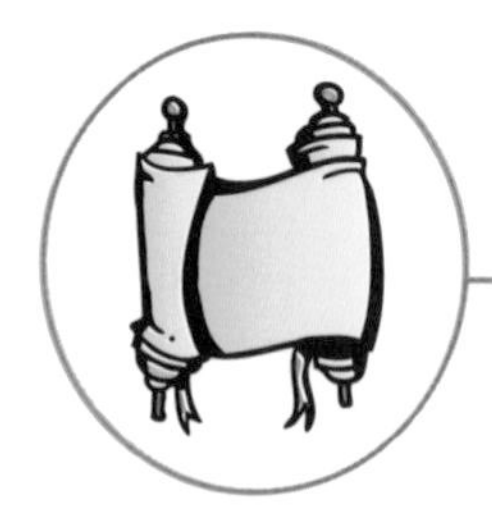

HISTORY LESSON

The first full set of golf clubs dates back to the early 1600s when a set consisted of "longnoses" for driving, "grassed drivers" and "spoons" for fairway shots, "niblicks" for wedges, and the "cleek" as a putter. Clubs were constructed from wood, with a head that was lashed to the shaft by leather straps.

During the early 1800s, hickory shafts with metal clubheads became the industry standard. By the mid-1800s, "bulgers" became popular, which most closely resemble the modern driver. In the early 1900s, grooves were added to the clubface to put spin on the ball for increased distance and accuracy.

In 1931, Billy Burke won the U.S. Open golf tournament using metal-shafted clubs, the first notable event won with such newfangled equipment. Cast metal clubheads were introduced in 1963, the process by which most clubs are now made. Graphite entered the game in 1973, becoming the industry standard for driver shafts.

The Golf Course

The playing field is made up of either nine or eighteen holes. Eighteen-hole courses are divided into two nines—the front (first nine holes) and the back (second nine holes).

Holes are assigned a par, which is determined by the length of the hole in yards and by how many strokes (attempts to strike the ball) it should take a competent player to reach the green and take two putts to get the ball into the hole from there. Usually, a golf course consists of two par 3s (one on the green plus two into the hole), two par 5s (three on plus two in), and five par 4s (two on plus two in) on each nine, but that configuration isn't mandatory.

HISTORY LESSON

Originally the front and back nines were referred to as the "outward" and "inward" halves of the course. Back then, golf courses didn't return to the clubhouse at the halfway point, or the turn (transition between the nines), the way they do now. They were played as nine holes in a row going away from the clubhouse (outward), then nine more holes returning to the clubhouse (inward).

Dazzle your friends by asking them how they played the outward half when you stop at the turn to refill your beer cooler next league night.

Here are some of the common features you'll find on most courses, along with some lingo you'll enjoy using on your next golf outing.

Teeing Ground

This is the level area of short grass from where play of each hole begins. It's also known as the tee box, tee, box, bump, or mound. The teeing ground has color-coded tee markers that correspond to a row on the scorecard telling you the length of each hole. Contrary to popular belief, the colors don't specify a gender, ability, or age—just the length of each hole and, cumulatively, the course.

This is the only place on the course where you're allowed to place your ball on a tee. However, you don't have to do that. *The Rules of Golf* requires that you start play, or tee off, between and behind (up to two club-lengths) the markers. Don't tee up your ball in front of the tee markers. That's a penalty and it reveals inexperience. The extra three inches won't help—I promise.

Fairway

The fairway is the area of maintained grass where you want your tee shot to come to rest. It's also known as short grass, short stuff, runway, landing strip, or position "A."

Rough

The longer, thicker grass that flanks the fairway is the rough, also known as the hay, gack, hoopla, or crud. Typically, the rougher the rough, the more challenging it is to play. That's why hitting the fairway from the tee is so important.

Fringe

The fringe is the narrow strip of fairway-length grass that surrounds the green. It's also called the apron, skirt, frog hair, or collar.

Green

The area of very short grass that surrounds the hole is the green, also known as the dance floor, hardwood, or carpet.

Hole

You try to hit your ball into the opening in the ground called the hole, also known as the cup, can, jug, jar, dish, or clown's mouth.

Natural Obstacles

Many times, the golf course designer has used natural features—trees, big rocks, canyons, swamps, herds of wildebeest, etc.—to require strategy, create drama, or enhance the aesthetics of each hole. You may be forced to hit your ball over, under, around, or through them. Good luck!

Hazards

A hazard is a defined land feature where you don't want to hit your ball. These menaces come in three variations: water hazard, lateral water hazard, and bunker. Water and lateral water hazards can exist without water in the case of a ditch, canyon, or gully.

Water Hazard A body of water a player must go over or around, perpendicular to the intended direction of play. Water hazards are designated by yellow stakes or lines.

Lateral Water Hazard Typically a body of water a player must play alongside parallel to the intended direction of play. Lateral water hazards are designated by red stakes or lines.

Bunker A collection of sand strategically positioned about the golf course to stop the forward movement of the golf ball and cause a player difficulty in playing the next stroke. A bunker is also known as the beach, kitty litter, sand trap, or trap.

Bunker

Out of Bounds

All golf courses have parameters usually defined by white stakes or white lines, fence posts, or the inside edges of paved roads that might border the course. The area outside of these markers is out of bounds, or OB, Obi-Wan Kenobi, or Oscar Bravo.

ROOKIE MISTAKES

My parents' house sits alongside a fairway at a local golf course. It's hard to believe the behavior of some of the golfers who hit balls into the yard. We've seen people stomp around and tear up Mom's flower beds looking for a ball. Others have actually hit their ball, complete with divots, right from the lawn!

Those who live beside golf courses expect wayward balls and perhaps the occasional broken window. But there's no excuse for doing further damage to personal property while retrieving your ball. Leave it—it's your tax for hitting it OB.

You have to crawl before you can sprint. For example, you now know to tee off with a driver because it has the least loft and goes the farthest, and you know that you're required to start each hole between and behind the tee markers. That's a good start.

The next step is to understand the nuances. Such as, it's best to tee it low into a headwind, or high in a tailwind. Or to tee it up on the far right side of the box if your typical ball flight is left-to-right, or vice versa. There are so many fascinating layers to this journey. Let's take a few steps together—from learning the A-B-C song to writing your own chorus.

Now that you have some big rocks in your jar—the game, the equipment, and the course—the rest of this book will add the sand and water to fill all the spaces around them. We'll make a golfer out of you yet.

Class dismissed.

The Coeur d'Alene Resort, Coeur d'Alene, Idaho—5th Hole.
Photo provided courtesy of Quicksilver Photography, Coeur d'Alene, Idaho

Prepare Like a Pro

Chapter 4

Prepare Like Crazy

"The will to succeed is important, but what's even more important is the will to prepare."

—Bobby Knight

You've made a decision to play. Perhaps it's the first time ever, or perhaps it's the seventh time this week—and it's only Thursday morning. Either way, good for you!

Here's something you need to know. Preparing to play golf is almost always more important to the ultimate success of each experience than actually playing golf. The good news is it's also the easiest to manage. Every golf experience starts long before your arrival at the course. The quality of your preparation can ultimately determine the success or failure of the round, regardless of your score.

Most common mistakes are easily preventable—such as not paying attention to a weather report, forgetting to bring a few bucks in cash for tips and wagering, or neglecting to call in advance to clarify club policy or to be sure that the course is even open.

As a golf pro, I've faced guests who showed up in jeans and T-shirts, then argued with me when I asked them to change into something more appropriate. I've dealt with groups that arrived twenty minutes late for their tee time, yet still demanded to play immediately. Some golfers forget to bring their shoes or an umbrella, a mild inconvenience. Others forget their clubs altogether, a significantly greater problem. There's a lot that can, and regularly does, go wrong.

I truly believe most golfers want to do the right thing. The problem is that many times we just don't know the difference between right and wrong, especially in a new environment. Unfortunately, this brand of ignorance can easily lead to embarrassment at the golf course.

"We never forgive those who make us blush."

—Jean-François de La Harpe

So many parts make up the sum of each golf experience, and only a few are within your control. Consider how much influence—or lack thereof—you have over some of golf's essential elements:

1 = A Candle in the Wind · 5 = Master of Your Domain					
Weather	1	2	3	4	5
Rules, regulations, and restrictions of the facility	1	2	3	4	5
Condition of the golf course	1	2	3	4	5
Who you'll play with	1	2	3	4	5
Their ability	1	2	3	4	5
Their behavior	1	2	3	4	5
Appropriateness of your attire, per club policy	1	2	3	4	5
Your expectations	1	2	3	4	5
Your golf swing	1	2	3	4	5
Amount of money you've agreed to wager	1	2	3	4	5
Your attitude when you're playing well	1	2	3	4	5
Your attitude when you aren't	1	2	3	4	5
Capacity of your bladder	1	2	3	4	5
Time and effort devoted to preparation	1	2	3	4	5

Your only chance is to prepare like crazy for those things you can control, which includes WHO you'll play with, WHERE and WHEN you'll play, and usually—most important of all—WHY.

If confidence at the golf course comes from comfort, what creates comfort? I believe it starts when you can convince those around you that you've been there previously. In the absence of experience, demonstrating poise in all situations comes from preparedness.

Most of the decisions that ultimately influence the outcome of every golf experience are known prior to the round—or at a minimum, they can be reasonably predicted. The key is to find out as much as possible in advance and control the factors you can. Preparing like a pro requires effort, but ultimately it's worth it when you find yourself sharing a memorable golf experience.

Speaking of Crazy . . .

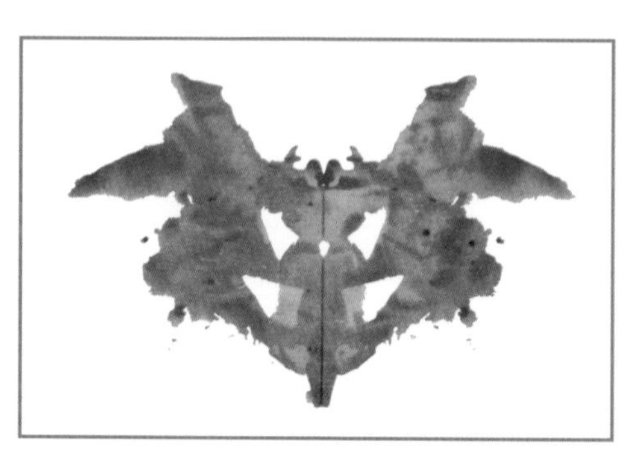

The Rorschach inkblot test is an old-school, yet still commonly used, method of psychological evaluation intended to determine our underlying feelings and to differentiate psychotic from nonpsychotic thinking. There are no correct answers—just subjective interpretations of our responses to the abstract images. The picture to the right is the first in the classic series. I think it looks like two witches pulling the legs off a cat. Obviously.

Similarly, the game of golf is open to interpretation. Golf can be anything to each of us—a hobby, a hopeless distraction, relaxation, work, frustration, a passion, a pebble in our shoe, a social activity, solitary confinement, a fling, a first date, a worthy adversary, or a soul mate. The extent to which you're willing to prepare for every golf experience reveals the underlying depth of your commitment.

So, how crazy (about golf) are you?

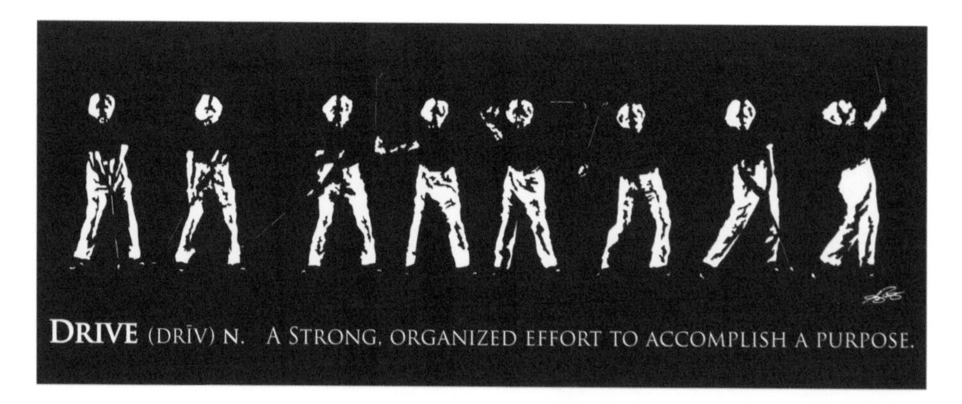

The Club at Black Rock, Coeur d'Alene, Idaho—10th Hole.
Photo provided courtesy of The Club at Black Rock

Chapter 5

If the WHO Fits . . .

"Give me golf clubs, fresh air, and a beautiful partner, and you can keep the clubs and the fresh air."

—Jack Benny

Whether you're hosting the most important game of your life or just knocking it around solo, preparing for the WHO is essential. For example, when hosting clients at an exclusive resort, you may want to dress to the nines, shine your shoes, arrive early, rent the carts, stock them with beer, have a friendly competition arranged with teams predetermined and the scorecards prepared, and pay the guest fees ahead of time. Then again, if you're just planning to whup your jerk brother-in-law at a course you've played together hundreds of times before, it may not be necessary to show up until the last minute.

Family

As many of us have found, the decision to play with family can sometimes be depicted rather accurately by this graph. Regardless of how you intend to enjoy your time on the course with your wife, kids, parents, grandparents, siblings, or in-laws, consider these things before you tee it up:

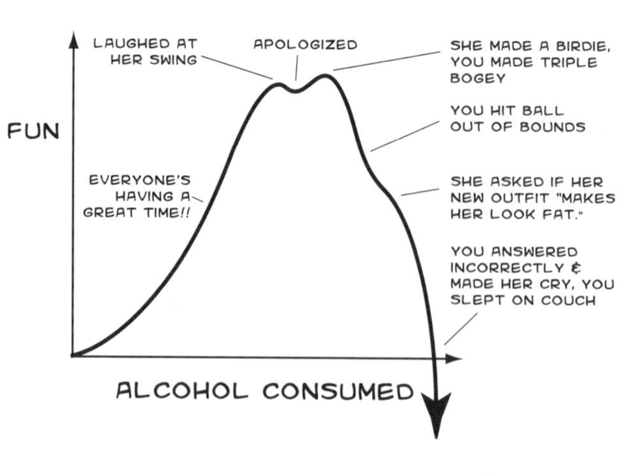

- *Course Restrictions*: Most courses have no gender or age restrictions. Others are so strict that it feels as if they might require you to pass an IQ test and provide a DNA sample prior to play. When you plan to golf somewhere new, it's a good idea to call in advance and confirm availability for all genders and ages.
- *Junior/Senior Discounts*: Some courses will offer different guest fee rates depending on age. When reserving a tee time, ask for the junior or senior rate and the corresponding qualifications.
- *Family Rates*: Many private and semi-private courses offer a family rate to members. However, the definition of "family" can differ. It might be limited to adult kids and parents, or extend to siblings and their spouses; your two drunken fraternity brothers and their Uncle Mike may not qualify. Either call in advance to ask about the rate, or refer to the club policies manual (if you're the member). From the pro's perspective, it's never comfortable to have to inform patrons of a policy that they should already know, or to haggle at the counter over the rate, especially in the presence of the guests.

Friends or a Regular Group

A regular golfing group doesn't have to be comprised of friends, and friends don't necessarily have to regularly play golf together. However, when the stars align and you find a regular group with which to play, comprised of similarly able golfers with mutually agreeable gambling and drinking preferences, at a time and place that works well with the schedules of each—magic!

Appoint a Leader

If one of the group members doesn't naturally assume leadership, appoint someone to that position. It will make things much easier if one person is in charge of making tee times, travel plans, pairings, or inviting others. You don't want to have three different people trying to fill a foursome and end up with six players and only one tee time. Put just one player in charge of logistics, and eliminate uncomfortable situations.

Name That Group

Once it's official that you have a group, give it a name. It can be descriptive, such as the Chicks-n-Dicks couples group, or totally irrelevant, such as the Grizzlies or the Goats (all actual names of groups from my work experiences). Here's a fun starter kit to facilitate the golf group naming process. Take one word from the first column and add it to a word from the second. Then get it tattooed on your bicep. (For some immediate street cred, you can end things with a *Z*.)

Shaft	Squeezerz
Birdie	Boyz
Bumps n'	Runz
Ball	Washerz
Hitz n'	Gigglz
Rough	Riderz
Two-Bit	Hookerz
Deep	Lip-Outz
Shag	Ballz
Jail Yard	Shankerz
Tee	Galz

STORY TIME

I've only been fortunate enough to be part of one golf group with a name. The Ancient Secret Social Holy Order of Links Experts was founded at Murphy's Pub in Killarney, Ireland, in October 2006. We even have our own crest.

When you play regularly with the same group, you have an opportunity to turn golf into something much more meaningful. Small talk and customary pleasantries are no longer necessary. You'll already know the answer to the surface-level questions such as, "What's your name?" "What's the game?" "What's your handicap?" and "Where do you usually play?" Time spent with friends on the golf course becomes more relaxing and enjoyable than being randomly paired in the same group with strangers. Real conversations can take place. I've even found that my game improves proportionately to the frequency by which it's executed with the same people. Comfort breeds confidence, both on and off the golf course.

> "Be who you are and say what you feel, because those who mind don't matter and those who matter don't mind."
>
> —Dr. Seuss

Playing as a Single

I enjoy golfing alone. It can be therapeutic. But when you play as a solo and intend to stay a solo, then consider doing so at a time when the course isn't likely to be very busy. A single has no standing on the golf course when playing among multiple foursomes. It's a real pain in the tail feathers for every group on the course to have to allow one golfer to continually play through.

At some courses, you may not even be permitted to play as a single on certain days and at certain times. Instead, the staff may require you to join with another non-foursome. Not only could you potentially be a nuisance, but it costs the course money. It makes sense if you think about it—the course will lose money selling one green fee and one cart rental to a single, instead of two carts and four green fees to a foursome at a premier weekend starting time.

While on the course as a solo, you might be invited to join up with another group. You don't have to, but you might consider it if the pace of play is slow and larger groups are waiting on you, or you're waiting on them. Either way, always thank the person who invited you.

> "Solitary trees, if they grow at all, grow strong."
>
> —Lord Byron

Looking for a Game

Sometimes it's nice to head to the golf course without a game plan. Maybe practice, hit some putts, grab a cup of chowder, or see if you can join up with another group. However, finding a game (joining another player or group) can be challenging or even uncomfortable. It's kind of like asking a cutie to dance. And certainly, nobody likes rejection. Here are some tips to help you consistently find a game.

Use Your Resources

Tell the staff—from valet attendant to the golf professional—you're looking for a game. The guys and girls working the practice range are usually the best matchmakers, since they generally have their ears closest to the street (and first tee). Try searching, too. The best places to drum up a game are the practice range, putting green, and locker room—not the golf shop or grill.

HISTORY LESSON

Master professional Dan Hill taught me to refer to it as a "golf shop" rather than a "pro shop." He said to make that distinction because the latter was an old-school expression for a brothel. Apparently to some, the expression "going to check in at the pro shop" has a totally different meaning than anticipating a game of golf!

Don't Take Rejection Personally

Most of the time you're going to get shot down because the other groups are prearranged. That's okay. Just cast as many lines as possible, and hope to get a nibble. Don't take the rejection personally, because it rarely is.

However, if you do keep getting denied by obvious threesomes in need of a fourth, ask yourself the following questions:

- Have I had a haircut and shave this decade? A decent teeth cleaning?
- Am I wearing deodorant? Pants?

> "Adventure is just discomfort in retrospect."
> —Evelyn Mundell

Tread Lightly

Don't put any pressure on others to change their plans. Perhaps the other group has a standing game that's foursome-specific and they don't want a fifth wheel. Or perhaps it's a threesome of purists and they've noticed the 30-pack of cheap beer under the towel in the back of your cart.

Don't be picky if you do catch an invitation to join. Holding out for something better is an inconvenience to the players who invited you to join them. They'll want an answer right away.

Be gracious when you are invited to join a game. Thank the other players before and after the round for allowing you to participate. You just might get a return invitation in the future.

Client and Guest Hosting (Part I)

You really don't want to screw this one up. You've invited a potential customer, or perhaps your soon-to-be father-in-law, the hot chick who works in the snack shop, or the VPs of your multibillion-dollar empire. You must impress. You're the director and they're the cast. Get everything set up correctly, so when you (inevitably) play like a baboon, nobody will notice.

> "The sport of choice for the urban poor is basketball. The sport of choice for maintenance-level employees is bowling. The sport of choice for frontline workers is football. The sport of choice for supervisors is baseball. The sport of choice for middle management is tennis. The sport of choice for corporate officers is golf. Conclusion: The higher you are in the corporate structure, the smaller your balls become."
>
> —Unknown

Three factors ensure a successful hosting:

- *Plan ahead.* Triple-confirm the reservations, including breakfast, lunch, dinner, golf tee time, carts, caddies, club rentals, and massages.
- *Be thorough.* Make sure everyone has directions to the golf course and an itinerary of events. It can be written or verbal—but be clear exactly where and at what time everything is happening. Your demonstration of preparedness will be sure to impress.

- *Be informative*: Make sure everyone has the information they'll need to do their own preparations. If you don't know, find out. Tell your guests the dress code, whether you'll walk or ride, whether you'll take caddies or a forecaddie, who else is playing, the facility's tipping policy, how much cash to bring, if plaid is permissible, and the weather report.

PEARLS FROM THE PRO

The granddaddy of all guest hosting has to be the private club men's member-guest tournament (also known as an "invitational"). Participating in one, either as the host or the guest, comes with serious financial considerations—some obvious, like the entry fee, others not so obvious, like the cash required for a "closest to the pin" contest or the obligatory locker room dice game.

I've been asked many times, by both hosts and guests, just exactly who should pay for what. As a rule of thumb, I've always held that the host should be responsible for the items that can be charged to his or her membership account. This includes, but certainly isn't limited to, the tournament entry fee, cart rentals, and all drinks and meals at the course. The guest should be willing to cover the tournament-related expenses requiring cash, such as the caddie fee, tipping, team contests (like daily skins), and any other form of cash wagering. I say that the guest should be "willing" because, in some cases, the host will insist on paying for everything. At other times, the host will be very thankful that you've shared some of the burden.

If you're the host, and if it's comfortable for you to do so, then plainly tell your invitee of the costs and how much you're planning to pay for. It may influence the guest's decision to play. If you're the guest, and the inviter wasn't very clear as to what you should expect to pay, then ask. If, however, you're not totally comfortable asking the host, call the golf shop for answers. They may not tell you the exact amount of the entry fee, nor should they, but they should be willing to give you an estimate of the likely cash considerations.

Member-Guest Tournament estimated costs:

Host:

Tournament entry fee:	$300–$3,000 (facility dependent)
Food and drinks:	$50–$200/day (how much do you drink?)
Cart rental:	$25/day
Entertainment:	$? (something to consider)
Bail:	$500

Guest:

Dinner out "on the town":	$200ish
Caddie:	$100/day (including practice round)
Wagering:	$50–$5,000 (format dependent–find out in advance)
Entertainment:	$?
Travel expenses:	$?
Thank-you card and gift:	$50–$100 (a bottle of wine and this book!)

Often in golfing, as with many of the best things in life, what's important is not what you're doing, but who you're doing it with. By planning ahead and knowing the common pitfalls in advance, you can easily ensure that those with whom you choose to play will enjoy their time with you—as much as you enjoy your time with them.

The Quarry at La Quinta, La Quinta, California—10th Hole.

Chapter 6
Lost Under WHERE

"Some of us worship in churches, some in synagogues, some on golf courses."

—Adlai Stevenson

Most of the time, the answer to where is an easy one since you'll be playing your favorite course more often than not. However, should you be invited to play elsewhere or decide to spread your wings and give another course a look, you'll need to do some research.

There are three basic types of courses: public, private, and resort. To prepare for—and behave properly at—each, you need to know the difference. Thus, the second step of pre-round preparation is to determine the WHERE.

Public Golf Courses

These are courses open to anyone who reserves a tee time, and where most golfers play. In the United States, 75 percent of all rounds are played at public courses.

Just because anyone is permitted to play doesn't mean you can act like an idiot. Despite what the actions of many might otherwise suggest, you're not golfing in your own backyard. Someone still owns the course and reserves the right to send you home for being disorderly or destructive.

There are city- and county-owned or contracted courses, also known as municipals. There are semi-private courses, which offer special privileges and rates to patrons who purchase a membership or a season pass for the family. And sometimes there are privately owned public courses, run by large management companies that operate dozens of properties.

Private Golf Courses

A private course is typically restricted to members and their guests only. Fees to join can range from reasonable to jaw-droppingly exorbitant. Generally, the golf course is only one of many amenities available to members. Others might include food service, social activities, tennis courts, spa and fitness centers, and swimming pools. (Baby Ruth? It's no big deal . . .)

There are two types of private golf courses: equity and non-equity.

Equity

An equity course is owned by its members, who purchase a stock share of the club that can be sold at a future date for a profit (or loss). Members pay monthly or annual dues. A predetermined number of memberships are usually available. When they're sold out, the club creates a waiting list.

Equity courses are usually governed by a board of directors and several committees. The books are intended to break even every year. Funding for major projects, such as a new irrigation system, is approved by the membership and the cost equally shared by all.

Non-Equity

A non-equity club is designed to generate revenue for an owner or a group of owner/investors. Patrons pay a deposit that is refunded at the purchase value, or a percentage thereof, if the patron decides to leave the club. Like equity clubs, the members pay monthly or annual dues. Non-equity clubs are usually governed solely by the owners of the facility or an appointed manager.

As a pro, I found non-equity clubs to be the most enjoyable places to work. I liked to answer to one person who made the final decisions, or allowed them to be made, rather than deal with the politics of an equity club and answer to every single member.

Resort Golf Courses

Resorts are built for profit, and the golf course is the bait to hook guests into staying in the hotel. Rooms are often available as part of a package that includes a round of golf or two, and both amenities are also typically available separately from the other. Because of a resort's lodging and convention facilities, its bread is usually buttered by hosting corporate golf outings or tournaments.

IF I RULED THE WORLD

Here's an idea for a new holiday. What if one day a year every golf course in the country opened its gates and allowed anyone to play for a predetermined, reasonable, and standardized rate? Can you imagine how cool Golf Day would be? We would need some sort of lottery or limitation to who could play where depending on age, state of residence, years on a waiting list, or something. Whatever. Someone else can work out the details. I'm just the idea guy.

A nationwide day for golf would be awesome. It would allow each of us to live out our dreams of playing courses that have filled the pages of history books and hosted epic tournaments—most of which we'd never otherwise have a chance to see.

Imagine knowing that during the next decade you're going to play Cypress, Congressional, Medina, Merion, Baltusrol, Oakmont, Augusta National, Pine Valley, Pebble Beach, and Cherry Hills. Wouldn't that be incredible?

I believe it would have a massive impact on the entire golfing industry. Playing golf at a premier facility, even only once a year, would give millions of golfers a reason to keep their games in tip-top shape. Merchandise sales would go through the roof (at least for the day). Rounds, lessons, and range ball sales would all increase, everywhere. Think about it—if you knew you were going to play Augusta National next year, I'll bet you wouldn't travel all that way to lay a big fat egg. Rather, you'd work hard on your game, and go there in hopes of posting a respectable score. Wouldn't you?

Golf course owners and private club members everywhere—come on, unite. For the good of the game, you can do this!

Money Matters

Find out in advance what forms of tender are acceptable at the destination golf course. Some courses don't take cash. Some don't take checks. Others won't accept anything from guests—and everything, including merchandise, must be charged to a member's account.

Most courses allow tipping and even expect it. Others discourage the practice; in some cases, they will even terminate an employee for accepting a gratuity. Whatever the policy is, find out in advance, or immediately upon your arrival, and adhere to it. If you aren't certain, be ready for either. Usually a buck or two is appropriate for most situations. If, however, someone really goes out of their way to help you, then adjust your tip amount proportionately. (See "The Art of Tipping" in chapter 16.)

Dress Code

Let's get one thing straight from the start—sometimes it matters how you dress. As a guest at a private club, don't put your host or the professional in an uncomfortable position by ignoring the dress code. At a resort, you'll definitely want to wear conforming clothes, because the prices in the shop can be higher than other facilities due to the "logo factor." If you are asked to change, you can end up overpaying for a new shirt you might not have needed in the first place. The policies can vary drastically from public course to course—so don't get caught dressing to the lowest level of acceptable attire for one facility, only to discover after it's too late that your tank top and basketball shorts aren't considered appropriate at another.

I'm not saying you need to wear name brand or expensive clothing. I'm saying you need to plan ahead and wear clothes that conform to club policy.

Men's Wear

As a pro, the most common mistake I had to correct was the "no-collared-shirt guy." Seriously, how difficult is it to wear a shirt with a collar when you visit a new course? Just assume that it's required. If you're wearing a T-shirt that you really, really want to play golf in, hang a collared shirt in your car—just in case.

The second most common error I've seen is the "inappropriate-shorts-or-pants guy," specifically jeans and cargo pants (baggy bottoms with big pockets on the outside). This can be remedied in precisely the same manner—don't wear them unless you're absolutely certain it's allowed. Wear khakis or throw some standard pleated golf shorts in the trunk. I do have to admit I like to wear jeans and cargo pants myself. When they're allowed, those are what you'll find me in.

Ladies' Wear

For ladies, the items most often worn in error are short shorts and skirts. Most facilities require shorts to be mid-thigh in length. Believe me, there's nothing more challenging for a pro than asking a lady to change her shorts or skirt because she's showing too much leg. Anger often follows, because the shorts probably matched the blouse, socks, shoes, belt, visor, hair ribbons, fingernail polish, and lipstick. Changing a fundamental garment can have a cataclysmic effect on an entire ensemble—and can dig the pro into a hole so deep it might take several seasons to crawl out.

At Home on the Range

All these rules apply at the practice range, too. Think about it: if another group sees you in cut-off camouflaged cargo shorts, a T-shirt, flip-flops, and backwards ball cap, are they going to know you're only practicing, or is it reasonable for them to think you intend to play golf as well? It's just like my grandpa always told me—"If a jockstrap and shower shoes aren't appropriate attire for the course, they aren't appropriate for the range either." Or something like that . . .

Please understand, I'm not some snobby golfing elitist saying you must always dress your best to honor the game and respect its rich traditions. I'm a realist saying if you wear the wrong thing at the wrong place you'll look and feel stupid, embarrass your host, and put the professional in a difficult situation. Don't do it!

STORY TIME

One of our very prominent club members once wanted to reward the guys who had built his new home, so he invited them as guests for a round of golf. However, he made the mistake of not informing them specifically of the dress code, assuming they would know better.

The builders showed up in jeans and T-shirts. We all thought surely they had brought clothes to change into—but no. They had every intention of playing in the clothes on their backs. Desperate, the host asked if there was anything we could do. He didn't want to buy each guy a whole new outfit, but he didn't want them to have to buy new clothes either. I reluctantly dug up a handful of left-behind garments that had accumulated in the locker room over the past decade. It looked more like a heap of dust rags than it did golfing duds.

The club member apologized to his posse, took full responsibility for not informing them of the policy in advance, and handed them the old clothes.

When they emerged from the locker room, time stood still. It was absolutely hilarious—like a scene out of a movie, or better yet, one of those hidden camera TV shows. Everyone stared at the three large men who stood before us, each stuffed into a combination of skintight shirts and shorts, none of which matched, and none of which would have fit even an average-sized man, let alone these brutes!

The guys looked dumb, and they were required to play that way. To their credit, they were all good sports about it, and everyone ended up having a great time. Frankly, they would've looked better in their original attire, but rules are rules. The member understood that, and he certainly wouldn't have expected me to make an exception for him. Fortunately, those involved were gentlemen who were willing and able to turn a bad situation into a fond memory.

> "Human beings are the only creatures that blush—or need to."
> —Mark Twain

Greg's Golf-Fashion Rules

Some guys simply have no idea how to dress for golf. Finally, in writing, here are a handful of rules that should help.

Match the color of your shoes, belt, and socks. The only exception to this rule is with white shoes, because white belts are risky. You're either a white-belt-guy (waist less than 36 inches) or you're not (waist more than 36 inches). Any colored belt and socks work with white shoes—but the belt and socks should then match. Never wear white socks with black shoes.

Wear long socks with pants. Again, the only exception is with white shoes. Low-cut socks and white shoes work with jeans, but not slacks.

Wear low-cut socks with shorts. No exceptions here.

Shine your shoes. If you can afford them, it's nice to have at least two pairs of comfortable golf shoes, one white and one dark (solid black or brown). Keep them clean and shiny.

If you don't have a pair of golf shoes, nor the time, inclination, or means to acquire them before an upcoming round, then athletic shoes will suffice. Avoid wearing any shoes with an aggressive or knobby tread, since they will damage the surface of the greens and tees.

As for golf sandals, I don't have much of an opinion, provided they aren't worn with socks. I wouldn't suggest wearing them to a private facility, since they might be in violation of the dress code.

Iron your shirt. When you're done with that, can you come iron some of mine, too?

Don't mix patterns. Plaid shorts are cool, no doubt, but not with a striped shirt. Anytime one garment (shirt, shorts, or pants) has a pattern, the other(s) should be a basic, solid color.

Don't mix textures. A nice double-mercerized (thin and shiny) golf shirt doesn't look right with standard khaki pants. It goes much better with a nice pair of microfiber slacks. Conversely, a pique (thicker, fuzzy standard cotton) shirt looks just fine with chinos, but not with silk trousers. Khakis or chinos aren't slacks or trousers—there's a big difference. Either is probably acceptable, but they aren't the same.

ROOKIE MISTAKES

It's no exaggeration that golf professionals spend more time with our coworkers than with our families during the peak season. If we're lucky, those coworkers become our close friends. This was certainly the case with Troy Blood.

He's a fascinating guy—in a ditzy, lovable, cartoon-character sort of way. His interests include everything, and he's good at them all. He's a riverboat gambler with a heart of gold, charmingly shallow most of the time—because his fly is down or there's a booger half-hanging out his nose—then deeply sincere when you least expect it. He can't make it through the day without ripping his pants or staining his shirt with some hot sauce that squirted out of a week-old taco he found under the driver's seat in his car but ate anyway. He'll three-putt from two feet when he's your partner—then make a birdie from the trash can to kill you when he isn't. To know Troy is to love him. And I was lucky enough to have him as my right-hand man.

You may find it nice to know that rookie mistakes aren't limited to amateurs. Shortly after I hired Troy at the private club, a venue in which he had no prior experience, he confessed that he didn't know much about golf fashion and asked for some pointers. I obliged, suggesting we start with the basics (Greg's Golf-Fashion Rules you've read in this chapter). Easy enough, right?

On the following Monday I showed up to the Pro-Am tournament and was promptly greeted in the parking lot by another golf pro who inquired whether I'd seen Troy yet.

"No, why?" I said.

"You'll see," was the response. Great.

This continued throughout my pre-round preparations, as pro after pro approached me and asked if I'd seen Troy . . .

Finally, while I was walking down the 4th fairway, I spotted him coming toward me up the 17th and saw immediately why everyone was snickering. There was Troy, in a near see-through white hard-collared 1981 Seattle Seahawk coach's shirt—unbuttoned to midsternum, with haystack plumes of black chest hair billowing out—a camouflaged hunting cap, mangled khaki cargo shorts, a brown belt, knee-high black socks, and black shoes. Wow! He looked ridiculous. Surely it was a joke on me, wasn't it?

I stormed over to see just what in the world he was thinking, and to remind him that he was publicly representing our brand-new facility for the first time. He saw me coming and could tell that I was furious. From across the fairway, he started shouting, "You said black socks with black shoes! You said black socks with black shoes!" Somehow, he'd omitted almost all the other rules. Honestly, I can't believe that at some point he'd looked in the mirror before leaving his house and decided what he was wearing looked good.

His outfit was awful, plain and simple—and everyone who saw him knew it, including the members of my team, who each had something to say about it throughout the round. Sometimes golf fashion does matter!

But, as always, it was Troy who had the last laugh. He shot 67 and won the tournament.

Sometimes the "where" isn't just one of the factors in planning a golf outing, it's the reason itself. Getting to play a new course can be a quest as rewarding as painting "kills" on the side of your fighter plane, hanging animal heads on the walls of your den, or carving notches into your bedpost. But beware! If you don't make your plans based on the expectations at the facility you're visiting, it can leave you looking as ridiculous as if you were wandering in the woods—lost—in your underwear.

Bandon Trails, Bandon, Oregon—8th Hole.

Chapter 7

Breaking WHEN

"I get up every morning determined to both change the world and to have one hell of a good time. Sometimes, this makes planning the day difficult."

—E. B. White

Successful preparation comes from gathering information and making decisions. Sometimes predictable, other times not at all. Giving detailed attention to the time and season of your next golf game will reap dividends.

Timing

Time of day and season of the year can influence your play on the golf course. Pay attention to timing when gauging how busy the course will be and note climate changes that can affect the temperature and course conditions.

Beginners should avoid the busy times. If you're a beginner, inform the person who's taking your tee time, and ask if there's a time they would prefer you to play. Playing in front of faster players can be intense and you'll feel pressured (see chapter 15).

Conversely, experienced players can avoid the slow times. If you like to play at a quicker pace, or if you're only a twosome, ask the person who's taking your tee time if there's a group in front that might slow you down. Playing behind slow players is excruciating. Asking the question gives you an opportunity to take control of the situation and possibly adjust your plans.

When the time or season hands you less-than-perfect climate conditions, use common sense. Fog, frost, and dew can saturate a golf course, and slogging through any of that can leave your trousers soaked from mid-shin down. Golfing all day with cold, wet feet or pants is absolutely no fun. To combat this, first and foremost wear waterproof shoes. Another trick is to tuck your pants into your socks to keep them dry. It'll look like you're wearing knickers, which is a really cool side effect.

HISTORY LESSON

The famous tour player Ben Hogan is responsible for that trail of short grass connecting the tee boxes to the fairways on each hole of every golf course.

During an epic U.S. Open final round, the ground was soaked. Hogan played perfectly. It's still considered to be one of if not *the* greatest major tournament performances of all time. He didn't miss a fairway or a green in regulation all day. But at the end of the round his pants, shoes, and socks were wet anyway. He made mention of it publicly, and forevermore that pathway of cut grass was adopted, giving us "The Hogan Trail."

Three other common-sense precautions on the course:

- *Stay warm*: Temperature changes drastically in some climates. For example, when the evening sun goes behind the mountains in the Palm Springs desert, it can get cold in a hurry—dropping from 100 degrees to 50 degrees. It's important to account for these common temperature swings and to prepare accordingly. Nothing ruins a good round of golf like an episode of hypothermia.
- *Stay hydrated*: If you know it's going to be a scorcher, drink lots of water. Beer and other alcoholic drinks don't count. Alcohol is a diuretic; it can make things a lot worse instead of better. Nothing ruins a good round of golf like an episode of heatstroke.

- *Keep the bugs away*: In the heat of summer, mosquitoes tend to swarm in the evenings. If you're going to play late in the day at a course with swamps, ponds, or other forms of stagnant water, keep some spray in your bag—and use it! Nothing ruins a good round of golf like an outbreak of West Nile fever.

> "Fair insect! That, with threadlike legs spread out, and blood-extracting bill and filmy wing, dost murmur, as thou slowly sail'st about, in pitiless ears full many a plaintive thing, and tell how little our large veins would bleed, would we but yield to thy bitter need."
> —William Cullen Bryant

Course Availability

Keep a close eye on the calendar of events at your local course. If you don't have one for where you regularly play, get one. If you're planning to play a course you don't typically play, call in advance to make sure it's open. Don't just show up. You might get sent right back home.

Pay attention to these types of changes in the course's schedule:

Routine Maintenance Periodically, vital maintenance procedures shut the course down for several days, and it can take an even longer time for it to fully recover thereafter. Especially when you've invited guests, make sure major maintenance hasn't occurred recently. Playing shortly after these procedures, while the course is still recovering, can be distracting and frustrating.

- *Aerification*: This process removes small "cores" of earth, which look like goose turds. It's customary for courses in the colder northern climates. This ensures future grass health by relieving compaction and getting much-needed oxygen to the roots of the fragile greens.
- *Overseeding*: This process plants new grass seed on top of existing grass. It's customary in warmer climates where the course has summer or winter grass depending on the season.

Tournaments These events offer an exciting challenge for players and a significant financial boost for the course. However, they're not so wonderful to the golfers left unable to play as a result. Pay special attention when a tournament is announced, whether in a pre-season club calendar, an ad in the local newspaper, or a front-door flyer. If club officials have gone through the trouble to inform you, make a note of it to avoid future frustration.

STORY TIME

One time I had to deal with a player who showed up to play golf on a day when the course was closed for a large tournament. After some heated debate, he ultimately left in a rage because he wasn't permitted to play. The course was full. There just wasn't anywhere for him to play, but he didn't like our explanation. Subsequently he resigned his membership—a very drastic move that could have been easily avoided simply by reading the calendar of events. In high-level insider golf jargon, this guy is what we call a "jackass."

Weather

> "Sunshine is delicious, rain is refreshing, wind braces up, snow is exhilarating; there is no such thing as bad weather, only different kinds of good weather."
> —John Ruskin

There's not much to worry about when the sun is shining. You'll need ample water, some sunscreen, and your golf sunglasses. However, when the weather threatens to turn lousy, there's a lot more to think about. Proper planning, adequate gear, and a willingness to get wet can still salvage what others might consider a disastrous experience, or a reason to not even bother.

Building a Bad-Weather Golf Wardrobe

Having a functional wardrobe makes it possible to quickly prepare for all conditions—heat, wind, rain, and cold—and doesn't require closets full of gear. There are, however, a few essential components that make it easier to play in unpleasant weather.

- *Get good rain gear*: It can be expensive, but it's usually worth every penny. There's a big difference between "water repellent," which will keep you dry for a little while in a sprinkle, and "waterproof," which will keep you dry all day in a monsoon. Having both is nice.
- *Wear comfortable and waterproof shoes*: It's nice to have at least two pairs. If you're on a trip or playing on back-to-back days and one pair gets wet, you can wear the other.
- *Get a lightweight windjacket or vest*: A lightweight item engineered to block wind is essential. It's handy because it can easily be stuffed into a golf bag, yet it still provides warmth.
- *Layer your gear*: Start with the skintight turtleneck base-layer shirts worn under regular golf shirts. They can be worn in any combination with your other gear, including a short-sleeved golf shirt, long-sleeved golf shirt, vest, light jacket, warm jacket, or heavy-artillery rainwear.
- *Back in black*: Buy all your foul-weather gear to match, so you can mix and match as needed. I suggest buying everything in black—it's the most common and easiest to find in the right size, and it's slimming, which is really important in a rainstorm!
- *Keep it together*: Keep all your golf gear together in a section of your closet so you'll know exactly where it is should you be in a hurry to prepare for a last-minute golf opportunity.

FACE PLANTS

In order to become a PGA-member golf professional, the first of many challenges is to successfully negotiate what's known as the Playing Ability Test, or PAT. It's a one-day, 36-hole test of ability against par. It's not a competition against the other golfers, just the course. Historically, it's the primary roadblock that keeps would-be professionals from advancing to the education portion of the program.

I passed the PAT on my fourth try. Considering how the first three attempts went, that was nothing short of miraculous. I relate my other attempts further on in this book, but rest assured, they weren't pretty. Here's how PAT attempt number two went.

It was the late 1990s, and I'd been working feverishly on my game all summer. Still somewhat gun shy after the first disaster, I finally bit the bullet and decided to give it another stab. I'd been playing relatively well in the weeks leading up to it, and my expectations of a passing score were realistic, or so I thought.

Come test day, I was ready. I won't lie to you—I looked really good that day, too. Sweet pants, cool shirt, matching hat, shiny new shoes, and a brand-new hooded navy blue jacket. The problem with my attire, however, was that it was totally wrong for the conditions. It was cold and windy, and if you've ever tried to play golf in a hooded lightweight jacket in a windstorm, you know exactly what happened next.

I started out with a par—four strokes better than my first test. But on the second tee box, I made up for the good start. At the top of my backswing, a gust of wind kicked up and whipped my hood around the club shaft. As I started my downswing, I could feel the tangled resistance. I wasn't sure what had happened, and instinctively finished the swing. But, as I did so, my jacket was pulled up over my head at the same time—like a hockey player getting the bad end of a beating.

Somehow I contacted the ball. It dribbled exactly 9 feet forward and tumbled off the elevated tee box and into the thick rough on the downslope. I didn't actually see the result of the shot, as my cool new jacket wasn't equipped with a window. But I'll bet it looked pretty impressive.

There aren't many times this can actually be true—but it would've been better had I whiffed. At least I could've hit the ball from the tee again. As it was, I had to go back to my bag and get the lob wedge, then slash my ball out of the thicket. Luckily, I advanced the ball into the fairway, but the psychological damage was done. It's tough to rebound from something like that—especially when my co-competitors were laughing hysterically at me.

The gale blew all day, and it actually started to snow at one point. Perfect. I finished dead last (again) by a million, but I actually completed the rounds and posted a score, which at that point in my career was a major accomplishment in itself. I came home frozen, embarrassed, and defeated, but with a story to tell and an important lesson learned about preparing to play tournament golf.

Rain Strategies

When you walk in the rain, use a trolley (pull cart) to lug around all your gear. The trolley not only takes the weight but also makes it much easier for you to stay warm and dry because you are not strapping a soaking wet golf bag across your back.

Umbrella management is important when playing in the rain. When you carry your bag or use the trolley, stuff the handle end of the umbrella into your golf bag every time you leave it to go hit your next shot. Having the handle anchored prevents it from blowing away and keeps your gear as dry as possible. You can hang extra towels, gloves, or clothes from the umbrella spokes to help keep them dry.

> "Let a smile be your umbrella, and you'll end up with a face full of rain."
>
> —George Carlin

For some, the only good time to golf is Sunday afternoon from May to August, and then only if it's sunny and 72 degrees. However, those fair-weather golfers are missing out on possible moments of greatness. Sometimes the reward is found not at the destination, but in the obstacles overcome along the way. With proper preparation and careful consideration of the elements, you can have an excellent round no matter when you make a break for the course.

Chapter 8
The Mile WHY Club

"It's better to know some of the questions than all of the answers."

—James Thurber

I mean really, how many options are there? You go to the course to play, to practice, or to take a lesson. Some of you can add "compete" to that list, but it's really just a subcategory of "play." Yet, grabbing a cup of soup and practicing for thirty minutes after work will require different preparations from playing in the final round of a televised major championship. Each has its own protocol of preparation.

Practice

Although practice is a relatively simple part of the game, try these tips to make every session count.

Ensure Availability Just like you do when determining WHEN to play, check the time of day, or season, or the club's calendar of events before your practice session.

Be Prepared Keep some gear in your car just in case a practice opportunity presents itself. It doesn't have to be your entire set of clubs. Typically, I keep two wedges, a pair of golf shoes, socks, a hat, a jacket, and a shag bag in my Jeep at all times. This way I can make the most of every urge to practice. It's just like my grandpa always told me—"You should keep a pair of balls in your pants to play with, just in case you need the practice." Or something like that . . .

Take Lessons

Taking lessons is an essential component in the improvement process, and it's considerably different from practice. In short, a lesson determines what and how to practice. (For more on lesson taking and developing an effective student/teacher relationship, see chapter 18.)

Be Ready on Time The pro probably has a busy schedule. Assume he or she teaches a lesson before and after yours. Do your part and show up when you said you would so you don't impact the rest of the day's schedule for the teacher and all subsequent students. Give yourself time to warm up before the lesson so your teacher won't have to watch you do it. If you aren't ready to fully engage in the lesson on time, you're late. Being present is not the same as being ready.

Don't Be Nervous Golf pros have seen it all. You can't do much to surprise us. Really, only a handful of things can go wrong before or during the golf swing, and every golfer simply has a unique combination and severity of the same swing flaws.

STORY TIME

Talk about seeing it all! One time I was giving a lesson to a married couple when the wife hit a low screamer that struck and wounded some sort of brown bird—a grouse, chicken, pheasant, or something. The poor grouse/chicken/roadrunner didn't die; rather, it flopped and flailed away for several minutes. We were all fairly rattled, but we decided to ignore the dying mystery bird and continue. Then, on the very next shot, the husband struck the same bladed screamer and killed it!

Play

> "I have spent most of my life golfing . . . the rest I have just wasted."
>
> —Unknown

Here's the most common—and the most fun—reason to show up at your favorite golf course.

Know Where You're Going Make sure you know where you're going and how long it'll take to get there. Nothing is worse than scrambling to check in and tee off on time if you're running late. Call ahead, ask a friend, or find a map online to get directions.

Make Reservations Reserve the essentials—tee times, carts, and sometimes caddies—as far in advance as possible. Carts can be in real demand on busy days. Caddies are typically independent contractors and should be scheduled at least twenty-four hours ahead of time.

Investigate Understand and adhere to the club's policies on such matters as dress code, personal golf cart usage, and acceptable forms of tender. Never assume that you know the policy of a course that you haven't played regularly or recently.

Compete

Side effects may include sweaty palms, a racing heartbeat, mild vertigo, nausea, shortness of breath, numbness, dry mouth, and periods of extended memory loss. Nope, I'm not talking about the latest prescription pill—I'm talking about competing in a golf tournament! The physical manifestations of playing in a serious golf event can feel as severe as those of a drug overdose—and leave the participants wondering why they chose to subject themselves to such scrutiny and humiliation in the first place. Sounds fun, eh?

Preparation is even more important for the things you can control. The rest of the competitive experience will be ratcheted up tenfold: the intensity of the competitors, the adherence to the rules, the management of your pace of play, and, oh yeah, your game.

Competing can leave you in a whirlwind of emotions and end with shattered hopes and dreams, or worse, an empty wallet and a hangover. In some cases, it does get better with time and experience. Unfortunately, there's no pill you can take for that (although I do know several players who insist a beer or two does help). The only way to get better at playing in tournaments is to play in more tournaments.

You've got enough to worry about. Here are a few things you haven't thought of, perhaps.

- *Discovery*: Just like any other time you plan to play golf, find out everything you need in advance—from directions to dress code to tipping policy.
- *Know the rules of the event*: Find out the format and tournament-specific rules that might influence preparation—such as scoring method or the schedule of events—so you can plan to participate fully in the tournament, as well as all of the ancillary activities and contests.
- *Add some time to your normal warm-up routine*: Whatever your pre-round habits may be, add at least a half hour on the first day of any large event. There'll be an inevitable buzz at the course. Parking lot congestion, registration tables, tee gift distribution, pin sheet examination, lines in the restroom, cash wagering with other competitors, a crowded range, and the general conversations and smack-talk that occur every step of the way from parking lot to starting hole. All of these require more time than usual. Factor accordingly. (See chapter 9 for tips on how to develop an effective pre-round warm-up routine.)
- *Know your starting time*: Some tournaments utilize shotgun starts while others assign specific tee times. Either way, know your start time, which should be made available to you several days in advance of the first round.

They may seem like obvious questions, but careful consideration of WHO, WHERE, WHEN, and WHY in each situation can make all the difference in the success or failure of any golf experience. Now that your homework is done, we can confidently head to the course . . .

The K Club, Straffan, Ireland—7th Hole.

Now You're Getting There

Chapter 9

Connecting Dots—Practice Range and Parking Lots

"Employ in everything a certain casualness which conceals art and creates the impression that what is done and said is accomplished without effort and without its being thought about. It is from this, in my opinion, that grace largely derives."

—Baldassare Castiglione

When you get to the golf course, rubber finally meets road and all your best preparations are put to the test. Here you partake of this timeless truth: To do something better, you must do it often.

Luckily enough, getting better at golf is an enjoyable journey. Shot by shot, game by game, the beast begins to yield. Repetition builds confidence, experience brings growth, and one fine day, that rookie terror turns to the enthusiasm of a seasoned hand.

A predictable pattern always helps. And the soothing routines of golf, when repeated faithfully, do marvels for your comfort and your ability in all matters of the game. So make a tee time and dust off your clubs. It's go time, and it starts now.

On Arrival

Even before you reach the course, be sure that golf etiquette—and common sense—prevail. Don't speed between the entrance and the golf course parking lot. You could embarrass your host, kill the pet of someone whose home adjoins the course (yes, it has happened), or wipe out a golf cart. Turn down your car stereo, and resist the urge to honk at your friends on the putting green. There's no need to start distracting others before you even set foot on the course.

STORY TIME

During the 1999 Hayden Lake Country Club Men's Member–Guest Horserace, the marquee event of the summer, my wife, Jillian (then my fiancée), laid on her horn to get my attention and waved as she drove by. What she didn't realize was she also immediately got the attention of all twenty participants and several hundred spectators. She just didn't know any better; she was so excited to see me (who could blame her, really?) that she hadn't considered the potential disaster had a player been startled mid-backswing. Fortunately no such foible occurred, and the result was just a very embarrassed, but flattered, assistant golf pro.

Valet Stand or Bag Drop

As you approach, look for one of these signs: Valet Stand (an employee will park your car for you) or Bag Drop (you, or an employee, will get your clubs out of the trunk near the clubhouse, then you'll park your own car). If you don't see either, just go park.

If club unloading service is offered, use it, since more than 75 percent of all golf injuries occur in the parking lot when players lift their clubs out of the trunk. Seriously.

There's a right way to put your golf clubs into your golf bag. When the bag is being held parallel to the ground, the woods and the putter (because it's special) go into the spaces at the top. The next row down is for long irons and hybrid clubs. The bottom row is for short irons and wedges. This way, the clubheads from the shorter clubs won't dangle and damage the shafts of those that are longer (and usually more expensive).

If you keep your clubs on your own cart, this really doesn't matter—put the clubs in whichever slot you want. But if you walk, or your clubs are regularly transferred from the trunk or bag storage room to the cart, then it does matter, because every time they're lifted and moved, they'll rattle around.

A properly loaded bag.

When to Arrive

Like most things in life—work, the airport, your wedding, court—it's appropriate to get to your destination before you're expected to be there. However, arriving too early to a private club is generally considered bad form. You don't want to get there more than an hour before your tee time, or before your host.

This is because at some private courses the amenities you'd pay for elsewhere—such as snacks, tees, divot tools, ball markers, and range balls—are available free of charge. It's tacky to get there well in advance of your tee time and stuff your bag with free trinkets, then grind out a two-hour practice session at the range. In fact, it's common at many private courses for unaccompanied guests to not be allowed to use the facilities until the host arrives.

Check-In

Now you've arrived on time—not too early as a guest, and not too late if you're the host or playing in a tournament. It's time to competently apply your preparations and to casually, yet confidently, convey your intentions to the staff and the rest of your group. Your immediate goal is to check in at the golf shop, which requires that you negotiate a few hurdles along the way.

Cell Phones

If you don't know the facility's cell phone policy, find out by asking the very first employee you see. It's important to not have to be told to put it away by another member or your host. Just don't use it until you're certain you can.

STORY TIME

A professional athlete played as a guest at the Black Rock Men's Invitational a couple of years ago. Not only was he supremely foul-mouthed and rude to the staff, he was awful to the other members and guests. The worst of his transgressions wasn't the $10,000 that he lost playing cards in the locker room and subsequently refused to pay. It was his egregious cell phone use, which wasn't permitted per club policy, but lasted all week nonetheless. He was on the phone nonstop, genuinely offending every golfer unfortunate enough to be paired with him.

His host should have handled the situation, but didn't (and even made excuses to justify it). The staff tried, but couldn't. Even another member made an attempt, but was told to take a flying leap. The boorish guest used his physical size and celebrity status to intimidate anyone who attempted to enforce the rules. He was a jerk and made everyone uncomfortable—exactly the kind of guest that you should never bring, or be!

Locker Room (Private)

Think about heading to the locker room prior to the golf shop. Carry your shoes in a shoe bag and change inside, instead of in the parking lot. The locker room is also the first place to begin the search for your playing partners.

The men's locker room at Black Rock.
Photo provided courtesy of The Club at Black Rock

Locker Room (Public)

Change your shoes in the parking lot at resort and public courses—simply because lockers aren't always available and it's easier just to leave your valuables in the trunk. If the facility does have a locker room, people will be in and out all day, and some of them might never return. It's not always the safest place to store your stuff.

Golf Shop

Next, visit the golf shop to let the staff know your identity and your intentions. You might say something like this:

- "Hello. My last name is Rowley, and I have the 12:15 starting time. It might be reserved under the name Ryerson."

- "Have any of the others in my group checked in yet?"
- "I'm going to pay for my green fee and one other. The other two fellas are on their own—and should be here shortly."
- "I think we'll walk, but if we change our minds, I'll let you know right away. Are there enough carts should we decide to ride?"
- "Are you running on time? Will you call us to the tee, or should we just keep an eye on the clock?"
- "I'd like to hit a small bucket of range balls. Do I purchase or pick them up here, or at the range?"
- "Is there anything else we need to know or pay attention to out there?" (Conditions include frost delay, unusual maintenance, cart usage policy, angry bees, wet slopes, the average pace of play, etc.)

The First Time

Checking in at the golf shop the first time is reminiscent of another of life's memorable "firsts." You'll be nervous. Your face will flush. It's difficult to find a rhythm, and you'll wonder if you're even doing it right. Don't worry: checking in—just like the other—will likely be over quickly and without major incident.

Just keep in mind that as soon as you know your way around, and can confidently get from bag drop to parking lot, from car to clubhouse, from clubhouse to range, and from range to the first tee without looking like a lost tourist, you'll go completely unnoticed by all other more experienced players.

Walk or Ride?

Golf was intended to be a game played on foot. I try to be a traditionalist as much as possible, but honestly, there are times I'd rather ride in a cart, particularly if the round is more social than serious. It's easier to experience camaraderie when you share a ride. And let's be honest, it's also nice that a golf cart can easily hold so many delicious icy beverages.

But when the gloves are off and I'm trying to post a decent score—and I'm not concerned with making close friends, impressing a prospective new member, or closing a deal—then I'll almost always hoof it. I like to have time to myself between each shot to deal with my swing thoughts and my game plan. It's difficult for me to shift gears between friendly conversations about work or the kids and my focus on the next shot. Some players can handle both. I'm just not one of them, and I know I'm not alone.

A recent study determined that the average American golfer walks approximately 900 miles and drinks about 22 gallons of beer per year. That's about 41 miles to the gallon. Not too shabby, eh?

Warm-Up

An effective warm-up routine is vital to a good game. Warming up is the act of preparing to play golf by loosening up your muscles and joints, testing the golf course conditions (green speed, fairway grass firmness, and bunker sand density), and hitting the unique shot types that will be required under the conditions (weather, topography, rough length, and grass type). All of this happens at the practice range.

Warming up prior to the round is not the same as practice. Nor is it a last chance to groove your swing, a time to listen to swing advice or consider a technique change, or a time to work up a sweat and wear yourself out before heading to the first tee. Your warm-up needs two equally important aspects: full swing and short game.

Full Swing

Start by hitting ten to fifteen shots with your most-used wedge. Check the scorecard and hit a few shots with each club you think you'll use on the par 3s.

Hit a few drivers. Finish every warm-up with a perfectly executed shot with the club that you'll hit on the first tee. Plan to hit forty to fifty balls.

Short Game

Chip and putt at the practice green to get comfortable with the green speed and undulation. Look at a variety of shot shapes, including left-to-right breakers, right-to-left breakers, uphill, downhill, and flat.

Hit a few bunker shots to test the sand since it's different at every facility. Even sand from the same quarry takes on different characteristics due to precipitation, compaction, filtration, and depth. Get a feel for it in the practice bunker before you start your round so you won't have to guess the first time you find the beach on the course.

ROOKIE MISTAKES

Pitchers in the bullpen don't start warming up by throwing 100 mph fastballs. They stretch, get loose, throw some slow pitches, and then gradually turn up the heat. The same principle applies to golf. Don't go to the range and immediately reach for the driver and whale away. If I've seen it once, I've seen it a thousand times. Too many rookies think the best way to get ready is to start by chucking fastballs.

Divots

There's definitely a right way and a wrong way to make divots at the practice range. It's something players of every level routinely get wrong. Rather than make a new divot several inches apart for each ball, take one divot for the first and position every subsequent ball so they expand it. Every divot should touch, and should eliminate all the usable grass in the smallest area possible.

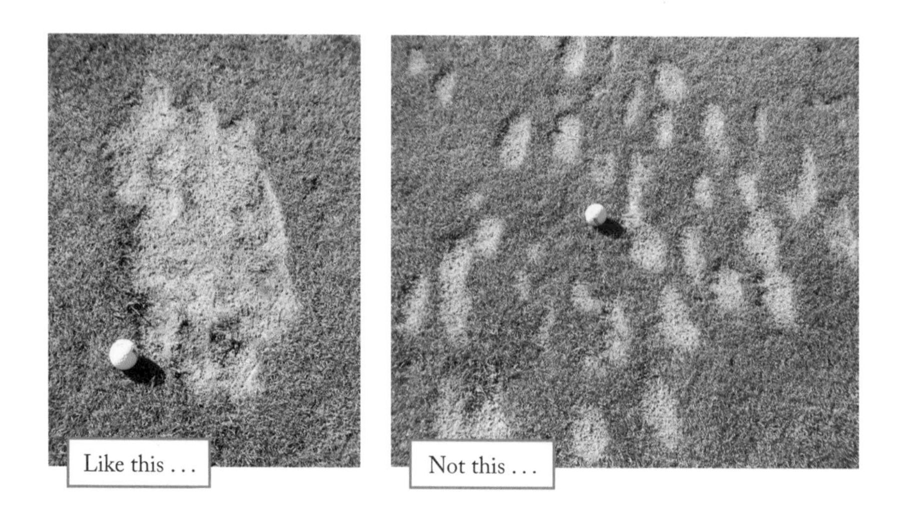
Like this . . .

Not this . . .

Obey the Other Range Rules

Hit your range balls from designated places. Most courses use ropes to indicate where they would like you to be. They might even use bag stands, 2-by-4s, buckets, baskets, or bags. Believe it or not, it really matters. The management and rotation of quality turf is monitored closely by the superintendent and golf professional.

Rake the practice bunker when you're done—even if it wasn't raked before.

Don't chip or pitch to the putting green. If signs indicate "No Chipping," then don't do it. Pay attention and demonstrate experience.

If a range is designated as "Irons Only," then hit only your irons. Some courses might ask you to do so to keep the range balls from leaving the yard and possibly damaging surrounding buildings, homes, and vehicles. Moreover, the cost to replenish range balls can add up quickly. Just do what you're told: nothing more, nothing less.

An important side note here is that it's always acceptable to hit golf balls at the range-picker cart. It's just like my grandpa always told me—"It has a cage around it, right?" Or something like that . . .

Client and Guest Hosting (Part II)

"Great things are not done by impulse, but by a series of small things brought together."
—Vincent Van Gogh

To create the best memories, your goal is to exceed expectations. You'll be amazed at how easy it can be. Try these tips to turn your next hosted outing from ordinary to exceptional.

Arrive Early Doing all the organizing can make it difficult to warm up. Hosts usually scurry around to ensure that everyone else is happy, and they don't have time to pay attention to their own game. Do your best to get there early enough to check in, stock the coolers, and execute a sufficient warm-up.

Welcome Wagon Guests shouldn't ever have to search for you as their host. Hang around and be ready to greet them upon their arrival. The putting green is the place for this. You can warm up and watch for them at the same time, and it's usually easier to get on and off the practice green to direct your guests than it is to hustle back and forth from the range.

Be the Director Have a plan, and politely and respectfully take charge. Tell your guests what to do and where to go and for how long. Don't make everything a group decision. Reasonable people never mind being told what to do as long as it makes sense. The fewer questions your guests have to ask—or worse, quietly try to figure out on their own because they're too embarrassed to ask—the better.

Decide Who's Paying This can be a tricky situation that makes members and guests alike uncomfortable. Make your intentions clear. If you're the host and you'd like your guests to pay, then don't hesitate to tell them so.

"Hey lads, they'll take your money in the golf shop for the guest fee."

"Girls, I'll get the carts and caddie. You each get your own green fees."

If you're the host and you wish to take care of guest fees and other expenses, then pay for everything in advance or tell the staff not to charge the other players. The person behind the counter should make note of it and alert the rest of the staff not to accept any payment from your guests.

If you're the guest, you should expect to pay—and always offer to do so. If the host plans to pick up the tab, or has already done so, then you'll find out when you offer. Don't expect or assume that the member will pay for everything. If they didn't plan to, believe me, they'll be thankful you offered.

"Where can I pay for my guest fees?"

"How should we settle up for golf?"

Check Your Gear and Go to the First Tee

If it looks like it might rain, bring your umbrella and rain jacket. If it's smokin' hot, buy an extra bottle of water or two and slather on some sunscreen. Check your golf ball, divot tool, tee inventory, and the freshness of your glove. Check your bag and cart for anything you might need out there on the golf course. Missing items can be a distraction.

Your ability to efficiently get checked in and situated for the upcoming round demonstrates experience. It's like a child's "connect-the-dots" game. The rookie will make abrupt moves from one stopping point to the next, without seeing the big picture in advance. The experienced hand sees the whole thing, and makes smooth transitions from point to point along the way. The results are always obvious.

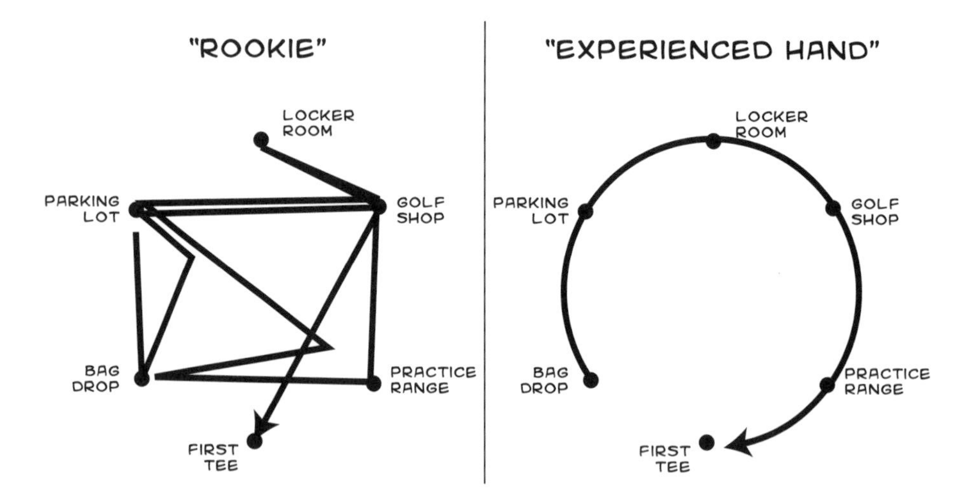

Chapter 10
The Usual Suspects

"I wish to goodness I knew the man who invented this infernal game. I'd strangle him. But I suppose he's been dead for ages. Still, I could go and jump on his grave."

—P. G. Wodehouse

There are places we go where the responsibility of the staff is obvious—like the lifeguard at the community pool, the collector of our trash, or the driver of the bus. Other times, the exact responsibility of the employee isn't quite as clear. It could be the hygienist at the dentist's office, the person at the do-it-yourself megastore who's wearing an orange apron like the other three thousand employees but doesn't work in the gardening department, or the person behind the counter at the local golf course.

At some courses there's always a golf professional in the golf shop. At others, the pro is rarely on the shop floor; more likely, he or she will be found on the lesson tee, on the golf course, or in a meeting somewhere. At yet others, there are so many employees it's practically impossible to determine the responsibilities of each.

Confidence at the golf course demands that you know where to go and what to do when you get there. It also requires you to know who you'll see there, and what they do. Here's a list of some of the characters you might meet.

The Golf Professional

Other than magician, I don't think there's an occupation more misunderstood than that of the golf professional.

"Do you know Tiger Woods?" No.

"Will I see you on TV someday?" No.

"Are you rich?" No.

"Do you just play golf all day?" I wish!

I've been asked each of those questions about a thousand times. And honestly, the fact that I used to perceive being a golf pro as somewhat glamorous is one of the reasons I chose the profession. But perception, in this case, isn't always reality.

STORY TIME

There certainly were times when being a golf professional felt fairly glamorous. I'll miss the standing ovations that occasionally followed well-run tournaments and award ceremonies. Being the guest on the local sports radio program didn't hurt the ego either. I've even been the subject of an article or two in the local newspapers and the keynote speaker at a handful of community luncheons.

The truth, however, is that the not-so-flattering times seemed to be more frequent, or at least, left more lasting impressions. I've had to bury a dog. I've had to unclog toilets. I've had to change tires. I've had to clean the stinking grass-sludge that collects at the bottom of the range ball washer—weekly. I've even had to wear a clown costume.

The PGA members responsible for my training, some of the best in the business, can tell even more humiliating tales. I've seen Dan Hill suddenly submerged in a dunk tank. George Van Valkenburg rode into an awards presentation on horseback, which wasn't so bad—but Tony Gill had to follow along holding a bucket! Chad Stoddard had to go to a ladies luncheon as Hercules, dressed in a diaper-like loincloth that nearly let it all hang out.

But nothing I've ever seen, heard, or done can match what happened to my sidekick Troy. We decided to incorporate remote-controlled boat races and a fishing derby with a Fourth of July golf tournament. Troy was out on the course supposedly learning how to use the boats, when a voice crackled over my radio. "Greg, get out here as fast as you can. Hurry. It's hilarious!"

History had taught me not to miss these moments, so I dropped what I was doing and sped away—as fast as my golf cart could take me. When I got to the huge water hazard near the 6th hole I was greeted by another employee who was red-faced and in tears, but still no Troy.

"Where is he?" I asked.

"In the water," was the reply.

"What!?"

It turns out Troy had somehow capsized the toy boat and decided to go in after it. So in the middle of a busy golf course on a holiday weekend, Knucklehead stripped down to his drawers and took a dip.

After several attempts, the salvage mission was a success, and he surfaced with the sunken vessel! While watching him dry off with the little hand towel found in the golf cart, and listening to the applause of the crowd that had gathered, it was apparent I'd just seen something I'd never forget.

Here are a few questions I've never been asked as a golf pro, but they are much more realistic:

"Have you had a day off from Memorial Day to Labor Day in the last decade?" No.

"Have you seen your wife or daughters this week?" No.

"Is it true that you have the worst-looking yard on your block?" Absolutely!

"How was the Fourth of July parade last year?" Parade? What parade?

When you hear the term golf professional, an image of Jack Nicklaus, Tiger Woods, Arnold Palmer, Ben Hogan, or Annika Sorenstam comes to mind, I'll bet. Nothing could be farther from the truth. Tiger Woods doesn't have the training to do what a golf pro does. Fortunately for him, he doesn't need it. He's such a talented golfer, he can translate his playing ability into millions—and soon billions—of dollars, and won't ever need to take a turn behind the counter at the local club.

"Mt. Golfmore"

Don't get me wrong—golf pros like me are good players, too. We've all had to be to become PGA members. In fact, we're required to be among the best 0.01 percent of all golfers in the world! That's why most club pros ended up in the profession. But on the PGA Tour, there's only room for approximately 150 players. Quadruple that number to factor in the other worldwide professional tours where a player can make a living—and it's still a miniscule number of golfers who can support themselves (and a family) by playing this game full time.

Golf pros, like cowboys, drink their coffee black. Most manage the staff at their golf facility. They create, promote, and run all the tournaments, leagues, clinics, camps, lessons, and associated social activities. Most golf pros buy, sell, ship, receive, and neatly display merchandise. Golf pros are greeter, host, rules expert, handicap manager, event promoter, staff manager, fashionista, teacher, coach, maintenance man, janitor, lackey, accountant, food and beverage manager, chef, bartender, pit boss, counselor, player, and all-around hail-fellow-well-met.

Golf pros come in all ages, genders, shapes, and sizes, but they share the same training. As I mentioned on page 67, the PGA requires that we pass its PAT, a rigorous training and education program (which takes between two and six years), and have a minimum of two years' work experience to be elected to membership. We learn skills to manage a successful small business, as well as specifics of the game such as teaching, tournament operations, and *The Rules of Golf*.

At times it can be supremely rewarding. But it's a brutal profession with an exhausting schedule and insane demands.

STORY TIME

I reached a crossroads in the summer of 2006 and made a decision to get out of the profession while at the pinnacle. I was the Director of Golf at "America's Best New Private Golf Course" (*Golf Digest*, January 2004), and was named as having one of the "50 Best Jobs in America" (*Men's Journal*, November 2004). I was right behind Tom Brady—quarterback of the then world champion New England Patriots—a swimsuit model photographer, a jet fighter pilot, and a beer taster. Why would I walk away from such a perfect job? Simple—my family.

I hadn't seen my daughters while they were awake in weeks, and my wife was fed up with being a single parent. I could stay at the perfect job, work the exhausting hours, and perpetuate the myth, or leave it behind and try to reconnect with the ladies in my life. Ultimately, it wasn't a difficult decision to make, and one that I don't regret for a millisecond. Life on this side of the counter is good. No—it's great!

Aiding and Abetting

Besides the golf professional, here are the other usual suspects you probably will meet at the golf course.

- *Golf shop attendant*: The nonprofessional guys and gals who work the counter or clothing racks in the golf shop and regularly handle player check-in.
- *Buyer/merchandiser*: At some courses, these employees manage, purchase, ship, and display the clothing sold in the golf shop. Merchandise sales can be the primary source of revenue for the course, which requires detailed management.
- *Marshal/ranger*: The marshal monitors pace of play, acting as the on-course eyes and ears for the professional staff. Some courses try to soften the perception of this job by calling it a "player's assistant" or something else quasi-helpful in nature. The role remains the same. Your pace of play matters, and a person will be driving around the course to make sure you're keeping up, and not doing anything stupid or destructive while you're at it.
- *Starter*: Occasionally, it's possible for players to park their car, go to the range, hit some balls, and then play golf without paying or checking in at the golf shop. To prevent this, a starter is sometimes positioned near the first tee to check each player's green fee receipt. No ticky, no golfy. The starter also manages the initial spacing of the groups, helping prevent backups on the course.
- *Superintendent*: As the leader of the grounds crew, the superintendent is responsible for maintaining the condition of the course. Be gracious and thank the grounds crew employees whenever you get the chance—they're the unsung heroes of the whole operation.
- *Locker room attendant*: Courses with a large locker room usually have an attendant, or attendants, to handle the details. Some might shine shoes, while others take food and beverage orders or serve as the course concierge. At private clubs, the locker room manager can arrange transportation, an afternoon massage, some aspirin, or some new spikes in your old shoes.
- *Outside services*: These foot soldiers help create your first and last impressions of the facility. They pick range balls, stand post at the bag drop, carry

and clean your clubs, and tidy the carts before and after every round. It's their job to make sure every golfer gets the same VIP treatment.

- *Beverage cart girl*: The beverage cart girl is essential. She can be found driving around the course offering liquid refreshment to weary warriors in the heat of battle. It's important to note that some backwards, deviant courses will actually try to sneak by with a beverage cart guy. Unless it's Ladies' Day, the practice of employing these imposters should definitely be discouraged.

Caddies and Forecaddies

Although these job titles are often thought to be synonymous, each has quite different responsibilities. These staff are paid by the golfers—usually to the tune of $100 minimum per round. With that investment, it's important for you to understand their roles and put their services to proper use.

Caddie

A caddie carries the bag, walks with the golfer, and assists an individual or a twosome in the play of the course. This person offers advice on club selection, strategy, and putting. A good caddie can improve your score by several strokes, particularly on a course you haven't played before.

A Caddie's Responsibilities

- Carry your bag—or push it on a trolley.
- Be your "partner" throughout the round by helping with strategy, club selection, and green-reading.
- Provide occasional levity or inspiration, as needed.
- Do all of the housekeeping.

STORY TIME

A good caddie really does become part of the team and is emotionally attached to your performance. This was evident at Ballybunion during a recent trip to Ireland.

Apparently, the caddies had side action among themselves, wagering on us, their horses. As it turned out, each had bet half of his potential tip money. Once we all learned of the bet, it added a new level of intensity to the round and our individual performances. Not only were we playing golf at one of the most spectacular courses in the world, we were each fighting for the honor and livelihood of our loopers. We formed a genuine partnership with our caddies—and it was a blast!

Shamus and Lesh at Ballybunion.

Forecaddie

A forecaddie works for the entire group to watch for wayward shots, manage the housekeeping chores, and help maintain an acceptable pace of play. Don't expect a forecaddie to improve your performance. Instead, a forecaddie should enhance your enjoyment of the course by handling most of the on-course etiquette responsibilities, so you don't have to.

A Forecaddie's Responsibilities

- Hustle and stay ahead of the group.
- Watch wayward shots and help find the lost balls.
- Provide yardages to the pin and other landmarks.
- Clean all clubs periodically throughout the round, but not necessarily after every shot.
- Clean all of the golf balls once they've been marked on the green.
- Repair pitch marks and divots, and rake the bunkers.
- Give brief descriptions of each hole to golfers who haven't previously played the course, such as: "Dogleg left par 4, hit your driver at the barn on the hill" or "downhill par 3, it plays a club shorter than the yardage."
- Tend the pin and provide general advice, when asked, on the green. The forecaddie might say: "It moves right to left" or "It's into the grain and tends to play more uphill than it appears." A forecaddie can also give other broad advice, without offering specific targets.

A forecaddie shouldn't

- Tell every player which club to use.
- Read every putt. There simply isn't enough time for one person to competently read the putts of all four players on every hole.
- Strategize.
- Attempt to be the life of the party.
- Offer stories of their own experience and ability.
- Give lessons.

PEARLS FROM THE PRO

I've seen players get so frustrated with their caddie that it ruins their round. The caddie becomes a convenient scapegoat for a poor performance. Remember that when caddies read a putt or offer advice on club selection, they are offering an opinion—not making a statement of fact. It's probably a more educated opinion than yours, and is usually worth trusting, but human opinion is also subject to human error.

If this happens, allow yourself to be briefly frustrated, sure, but understand that caddies truly want you to play your very best. They're probably every bit as unhappy about the bad read or bad club selection as you. Shrug it off, regroup, and determine how much trust you'll give their opinion the next time. Always be willing to disagree and go with your gut.

One of the members at The Quarry used to wear a hat with the letters "C.F.E." embroidered on the front. They stood for "Caddie Friggin' Error" (but he didn't say friggin'). Whenever his caddie would give him bad advice, he'd just point to his hat. Everyone got the point. Still, he always employed a caddie. To him the good advice definitely outweighed the occasional mistake.

During one of our ladies club championship tournaments at Black Rock, one of the participants could have benefited from better knowledge of the caddie's role. After the opening round, she complained to me (nearly in tears) that the caddie in her group had ignored her all day and seemed to offer assistance only to one of her co-competitors. What she didn't realize was that the caddie was employed by the other player. She thought the caddie was a service provided by the club, intended to be shared by all.

As her frustration grew, her focus shifted from her own performance to the perceived lack of fair treatment. She played herself right out of contention on the first day of the two-day competition. Bummer.

Playing with a good caddie or forecaddie enhances the golf experience. Feeling stuck with a chatty or lazy one, however, can suck the life right out of the group. Remember, you're paying for the service. Confidently take control of the situation and inform your employee if you'd like to see more or less of a particular behavior. Believe me, they want you to be happy and will gladly adjust their focus to suit your expectations.

A golfer was about thirty strokes over par by the 10th hole. He'd already sprayed, shanked, pulled, pushed, and topped the ball all over the front nine, when his caddie accidentally coughed during a very short putt. The golfer missed, and then angrily exploded. "You've gotta be the worst caddie in the world!" he screamed. "I doubt it," replied the caddie. "That would simply be too great of a coincidence."

Caddie Speak

Keep in mind that your caddie might need to deliver bad news. It helps to be able to quickly sift through the nonsense customary to caddie-speak and decipher the true meaning of the message being sent. Here are some examples.

Caddie: "Oh shucks! I'm not sure, but it looked to me like the ball just didn't spin. I thought you caught it clean. Did you? I'm afraid it may have scooted past the flag, and might have even gone near that sneaky bunker back there."

Translation: Grab a wedge. You skulled it into the trash.

Caddie: "Nice drive. It started right-center and was cutting."

Translation: You fanned it, hack. Way right. Off the map even. I'll be lucky to find it. If I'm not back in five minutes, send a search party.

Caddie: "Swing smooth. Think tempo. Make a good pass at it here."

Translation: Control yourself, man! Slow down. The only thing that didn't move during that last swing was your bowels, and even that's questionable.

Caddie: "This hole tends to play long for some reason. Why don't you take two extra clubs and make sure to get it there?"

Translation: You've been short all day, and obviously don't hit it as far as you think. Let's try a new strategy.

Caddie: "Oooaahh, nice putt. It looked good the whole way. That's my fault for the bad read. You gave it a good run, though. Good on ya."

Translation: Textbook jab. It never had a chance. You missed the mark I gave you by 3 feet, and it was only a 5-foot putt. How's that possible?

Caddie: "Here it is! Found it. A pretty clean lie, too. You were playing a Titleist 2, right?"

Translation: I found a Titleist 2 and kicked it out into the clear. I know it's not yours, but if you wanna claim that it was, I'll go along with it . . . wink, wink.

When you're not quite sure where to go, what to do, or who does what, then ask someone for help. It's their job to make sure you have an enjoyable time—trust them. You might ask questions like these:

- "Which one of you sixteen people behind the counter here is the pro? I'd like to schedule a lesson."
- "Who can help me get my clubs re-gripped?"

- "Is there a starter I should give this receipt to? Or can I wad my gum up in it and throw it away?"
- "After I change my shoes, will I find my clubs here at the bag drop, or will they be on a cart? Where will the cart be staged?"
- "I've got some guests showing up here in a bit and I'd like to pay for everything. Who should I see about that?"
- "I'm recovering from a recent knee replacement. Is it possible to get special permission to drive my cart nearer to some of the greens and tees?"

As you can see, when you make a trip to the course, it's not just you, your partners, and the other players on the field; there are countless people working behind the scenes to make sure your outing is a success. From the ringleader head pro to some of his loyal henchmen—that is, the outside services guys and gals—knowing who's responsible for what will make it easier for everyone to have a great day at the course. Just don't ask anyone to bury your pet (or your partner).

Circling Raven Golf Club, Worley, Idaho—4th Hole.
Photo provided courtesy of Circling Raven Golf Club

Chapter 11

Dirty Rotten Stinking Low-Life Sandbaggers

"It's better to deserve honors and not have them, than to have them and not deserve them."

—Mark Twain

Basically, there are two types of people in this world: dirty rotten stinking low-life sandbaggers, and the rest of us. Those who fall into the first category know who you are—and yes, I just called you out.

Sandbagging at golf is cheating. It's the complete antithesis of the virtues and values the game was built upon. Even uttering the word, and thinking of the countless examples I've had to deal with during my career, gives me flashbacks.

Cheating at golf isn't always as blatant as counting the wrong score, improving a bad lie, or miraculously finding a lost ball. Cheaters can be much more refined than that. I've seen pillars of the community turn in phony scorecards. I've seen barons of industry tank a hole or two in order to purposely score higher than their best effort. I know players who brag about keeping an inflated handicap in order to fleece their friends and perhaps get their name in the paper for scoring well in local tournaments.

I believe I can speak for most golf professionals when I say we're wise to your tricks. We know who you are, we know how you cheat, and we think you're disgusting. The only person you're fooling is yourself.

Sandbagger: \'san(d)•, bag•ger\ *n*

1. Generally, any golfer who misleads others about his/her ability level, claiming to be worse than he/she actually is.
2. More specifically, a golfer who artificially inflates his/her handicap index in order to better his/her chances of winning tournaments or bets.
3. See "Cheater."

Think about it—if sandbagging is cheating, then doing so to win money or prizes is stealing. Is that really the recognition you want? Do you want to be known as a liar, a cheat, and a thief? Then by all means, continue to manipulate your handicap and disgrace yourself and the game. Ah, catharsis!

"Honesty is the first chapter in the book of wisdom."
—Thomas Jefferson

IF I RULED THE WORLD

Although it may seem like it, I'm not advocating that we shoot the sandbaggers dead. That's a little harsh. But maybe tarred and feathered? Embarrassing and painful, but not permanent. Yeah, let's go with that. New rule: Tar and feather all known sandbaggers!

There are two types of sandbaggers: cheaters and reverse sandbaggers. Don't be either.

Cheaters

A sandbagger will find an infinite number of ways to manipulate the system. Here are some of the most common that cheaters have used. They will:

- "Forget" to post their good scores.
- Intentionally miss short putts, or poorly execute other short-game shots when in a situation in which it won't count for the team score. For example, stubbing a chip when a partner is already on the green, closer to the hole and more likely to make a better score.
- Play poorly coming down the home stretch. Once the sandbagger has mopped up all of the bets (mid-back nine), a double-bogey, double-bogey, double-bogey finish is sure to follow.
- Post higher scores when they're not in a game or competition. I've seen players repeatedly post lousy scores when playing with their spouse on the weekend, or when playing recreationally—then rationalize the maneuver by saying they play better in tournaments or money games because they concentrate more.
- Post a score from the wrong tees. A player who shoots a score from a longer and more difficult course, then posts it to a shorter, easier one, just stole the difference in course rating between the two—possibly a few strokes.

> "When dealing with people, remember you are not dealing with creatures of logic, but with creatures bristling with prejudice and motivated by pride and vanity."
>
> —Dale Carnegie

Reverse Sandbaggers

Also known as a "vanity handicap," these players don't bother me nearly as much—unless they're on my Pro-Am team! Really, the only player they're hurting is themself. But hey, they can tell their friends, guests, and clients that they have a single-digit handicap. Neat.

Essentially, these players willingly give everybody else a several stroke advantage prior to teeing it up. Why anyone would do this is beyond me, but it's very common.

Reverse sandbaggers will:

- Neglect to post their bad scores. Usually the player will say something like: "It's not going to count toward my handicap anyway." They're missing the point. The handicap will factor those higher scores if there are enough of them.
- Regularly give themselves short putts. Short putts are often missed—it's an inevitable part of the game. Avoiding them only hurts in the end.
- Take occasional mulligans—other than the customary "breakfast ball" on the first tee.
- Write a poor start off to a "practice day," and quit keeping score.

Walk a Mile in These Shoes

On behalf of golf pros everywhere, allow me to appeal to your inner sandbagger. Have you ever considered the position you put us in?

Imagine you've been told all year that a particular player's ability isn't exactly congruent with his handicap. You check his scores. They seem pretty realistic. You might even arrange to play with him. He doesn't play well. But come tournament time, he's leading his flight after the first round. People start grumbling. After all, he won the same event last year. Following round two, he's got such a big lead that everyone else is playing for second. The grumbling turns to accusations and name calling. Round three—he laps the field and wins by twenty. The membership demands his head on a platter. And all eyes turn to you, the pro. What are you gonna do about it?

Really, what can you do about it? Throw him out of the tournament? He paid. Lower his handicap by five strokes? He posted his scores all year. Tell him he's not welcome back next year? He's friends with the owner. Punch him in the neck? He hasn't got one. You're between a rock and 1-iron for sure.

As if it's not challenging enough, let's add some complexity to the situation. What if the guy's just playing better than ever? Maybe you've even given him some lessons recently (and he's paid you well in the process). Maybe you take him with you to an occasional Pro-Am, and he's helped you win a little money in the past. You might even really like the guy. There's no rule that says sandbaggers are jerks. In fact, he might be the life of the party. Here's the kicker. At the end of the week he delivers an envelope stuffed with cash for you to spread among the staff—obviously a portion of his haul for the week. Is it hush money? You (the pro) feel helpless to do anything about it.

Ultimately, it can have even greater negative ramifications other than discomfort for you and disgust from some of the other players. Rampant sandbagging causes tournaments to fail. When the majority of participants feel like the winner will be one of only three or four players or teams prior to the practice round, it creates a "why even bother" attitude, which is contagious. When tournaments die, courses lose money. When courses lose money, golf pros lose jobs. Capisce?

It's important to make it clear that not every person who plays well or wins a tournament does so dishonestly. In fact, that's usually not the case at all. I choose to believe that most golfers are honest people. Certainly it's possible to have a great round or catch fire at just the right time. But if the same person or team repeatedly wins the same event, week after week, year after year, or if rumors continually abound, then perhaps there's some validity to the whispers. It's up to you, the player (not the pro), to do something about it.

It only takes one rotten fish to make things really start to stink.

> "In looking for people to hire, look for three qualities: integrity, intelligence, and energy. And if they don't have the first, the other two will kill you."
>
> —Warren Buffett

Dude, Abide

Sandbagging is cheating. Not following the rules is cheating. Some might think that sandbagging is a "lesser offense." It's not. They are two sides of the same coin: a lack of respect for the game and your fellow competitors. It's simple, really—abide by the rules. Nothing more, nothing less.

STORY TIME

I was told of a time when a guest at a men's invitational was caught cheating, and he paid a dear price—humiliations galore.

Playing in a team match play tournament, this guest launched his tee shot on a par 3 in the direction of some boulders that surrounded the green. After a lengthy search he proclaimed he'd found his ball—in a location that seemed unlikely. It was sitting up nicely, too. Hmmm . . . ?

He chipped up near the flag, and was in position to make a remarkable comeback. But when the opponent member removed the flagstick, he discovered a ball in the cup. No way! It was the guest's real tee shot. Talk about getting your hand caught in the cookie jar.

The host partner of the not-so-lucky hole-in-one maker politely retrieved the ball, apologized, returned the ball to the cheater, forfeited the remainder of the match, and withdrew from the tournament.

Good night and good luck. No cocktails and high fives in the grill. No excited phone call home to sweetie. No photos and memories of the once-in-a-lifetime shot. Just a slap in the face to the member and a scarlet "C" forever emblazoned on the guest's chest.

Another offense that's equally appalling is that some people intentionally inflate their handicaps.

> "We tell lies when we are afraid—afraid of what we don't know, afraid of what others will think, afraid of what will be found out about us. But every time we tell a lie, the thing that we fear grows stronger."
> —Tad Williams

Golf Handicapping Made Clear(er)

Here's how all of this chicanery affects the golf handicap, one of the most important—and least understood—aspects of the game. To best explain the concept, I'll start with some fundamental definitions.

- *Handicap Index*: A calculation of a player's ten best scores from his/her twenty most recent. The handicap index is a number with a decimal point that's then converted via a course handicap conversion chart (see page 108) to determine a course handicap. The handicap index travels with you from course to course, and will likely convert differently at each.
- *Course Handicap*: A whole number—the converted handicap index.
- *Course Rating*: An assessment of what a scratch golfer should shoot at a given course.
- *Course Slope*: An assessment of the difficulty of a course.
- *Gross Score*: A player's actual score.
- *Net Score*: A player's score minus the course handicap.

Now I'll try to answer the most common questions about a handicap.

Q: Why is all this stuff so important anyway?

A: The golf handicapping system creates a standardized method for players of differing abilities to fairly compete against one another.

Q: Who's in charge?

A: There are a handful of handicap associations around the country (GHIN, AZGA, and SCGA, to name a few) that all use a similar method of assigning a handicap to amateur golfers.

Q: Who keeps the golfers honest?

A: The handicap system is intended to be self-governed. Every player's scores are easily accessible (to view, not change!), from either the golf course handicap computer or the Internet. It's every player's responsibility to monitor the honesty of the scores posted by his/her playmates.

The golf professional is not the handicap police. That responsibility must fall to the fellow players.

Q: How is a handicap determined?

A: In short, a handicap is an average of a player's ten best scores out of the twenty most recent.

A handicap index is derived from the differential, which is a calculation between each score and the course slope and rating, not par. A total differential is then calculated by multiplying the difference between each score and the course rating by the value of the course slope, times the USGA base slope of 113, then totaled and divided by 10 (the number of scores). Did you get all of that?

The final result is the player's handicap index—a two- or three-digit number with a decimal point in it (9.0, 10.3, or 26.7, for example)—which is the number of strokes that the player will then reference on each golf course's handicap conversion chart. The conversion is the player's course handicap, which is the number of strokes that he/she will ultimately subtract from the gross score to make a net score at the completion of the round.

It makes sense if you think in simpler terms. Say a player might get ten strokes (course handicap = 10) on a 6,000-yard course with no out-of-bounds or hazards. That same player needs more strokes to compete fairly on a 7,000-yard course with out-of-bounds on every hole, 6-inch rough, and pot bunkers surrounding every green. It's much like the difference in the car-driving skills required for backing out of your driveway and for navigating rush-hour traffic in an unfamiliar city.

SAMPLE HANDICAP CONVERSION CHART

Flooded Meadows Golf Club											
Men's Brown Tees											
Front Nine				Back Nine				Eighteen			
Slope Rating – 123				Slope Rating – 118				Slope Rating – 121			
½ USGA Course				½ USGA Course				USGA Course			
Handicap Index			HDCP	Handicap Index			HDCP	Handicap Index			HDCP
.45	to	1.3	1	.45	to	1.4	1	.5	to	1.3	1
1.35	to	2.2	2	1.45	to	2.3	2	1.4	to	2.3	2
2.25	to	3.2	3	2.35	to	3.3	3	2.4	to	3.2	3
3.25	to	4.1	4	3.35	to	4.3	4	3.3	to	4.1	4
4.15	to	5.0	5	4.35	to	5.2	5	4.2	to	5.1	5
5.05	to	5.9	6	5.25	to	6.2	6	5.2	to	6.0	6
And so on . . .				And so on . . .				And so on . . .			

Q: Is my handicap affected by every score I post?

A: Yes, sort of. The calculation of a player's handicap is based on the ten best scores. Thus, occasional blow-up rounds, although posted, aren't factored into the equation. If, however, higher scores become a trend, then the players' handicap will gradually rise and reflect it.

Conversely, if a pattern of improvement exists, the handicap index will go down.

Q: Do I have to post every score?

A: Absolutely. A fundamental expectation exists that all players actually attempt to perform their best on every shot, throughout every round, and then post every score. (Unfortunately, this isn't always the case.)

Q: Why do I rarely shoot my handicap?

A: Handicaps are based on potential. A player with an honest handicap should be able to shoot a net score that's equal to, or slightly better than, the course rating (not par) only one-quarter of the time.

Q: I've been taking lessons and working on my game. Recently I've been drubbing my buddies and they've started calling me "sandy." Am I?

A: Not necessarily. It's certainly possible for golfers to show improvement and to play better than what their handicap suggests. After all, what's the point of practicing, taking lessons, and buying new equipment if those things don't help? But your handicap should catch up to your ability fairly quickly.

I've heard players say they'd like to be called a sandbagger someday. What they're really saying is they wish they could play well enough on occasion that people might question their handicap. But believe me, nobody wants to be called a cheat.

Q: Some guy in our club championship shot a net 65 three days in a row. Is that possible?

A: Not really. The chart on the top of page 110 shows the mathematical improbability of that happening. As you can see, if a player consistently records scores that are outside the realm of realistic probability, then it brings his/her integrity into deserved question.

Exceptional Score Probability Table					
	Course Handicap				
Net Score (to par)	0–5	6–12	13–21	22–30	31–up
0	5:1	5:1	6:1	5:1	5:1
-1	10:1	10:1	10:1	8:1	7:1
-2	23:1	22:1	21:1	13:1	10:1
-3	57:1	51:1	43:1	23:1	15:1
-4	151:1	121:1	87:1	40:1	22:1
-5	379:1	276:1	174:1	72:1	35:1
-6	790:1	536:1	323:1	130:1	60:1
-7	2349:1	1200:1	552:1	**229:1**	101:1
-8	20111:1	4467:1	1138:1	382:1	185:1
-9	48219:1	27877:1	3577:1	695:1	359:1
-10	125000:1	84300:1	37000:1	1650:1	874:1

In this example, the chances are 229 to 1 that a player with an honest handicap between 22 and 30 will shoot a net score of 7 under the course rating. If it happens three days in a row, then it seems you've got a legitimate concern.

Q: My girlfriend told me that she can't take a score higher than an 8 on any hole. So after she hits her eighth shot, wherever it is, she picks up. Is that right?

A: No. Equitable Stroke Control (ESC) is the method of "limiting" the score that can be posted for any one hole. The actual score that's made on each hole should be recorded on the scorecard and counted toward the total of the round—and the game du jour. However, when it's time to post the score to the handicap computer, ESC requires that hole-by-hole scores be adjusted per the following chart:

Equitable Stroke Control (ESC)	
Course Handicap	Maximum Score on Any Hole
9 or less	Double bogey
10 – 19	7
20 – 29	8
30 – 39	9
40 or more	10

Again, it makes sense if you think of it in simpler terms. If the ESC limits didn't exist, a player could make seventeen pars in a row and a 22 on the 18th hole to shoot a score of 90. Although the golfer played 17 holes of scratch golf, his/her handicap would end up being an 18. That's just not fair—and unfortunately there are many players out there who'd gladly take advantage of that loophole.

Q: How do I get started?

A: When you're ready to get started with a handicap of your own, simply go to your local golf shop and tell the professional of your desire. There's an annual fee, and you're then entered into the system and instructed how to use the computer. It's not too difficult. Thereafter, it's your responsibility to faithfully abide.

So go ahead—establish and maintain an honest handicap. It helps determine your ability compared to others and monitor your improvement. When you feel confident enough to start wagering on golf or playing in a competition or league, the handicap becomes the essential tool to do so equitably. More than anything, it's just nice to be part of the culture and to have something in common with almost all other golfers on the course.

Golf is a game that's played against the course and yourself. At the end of the day, if you don't post your scores or you intentionally manipulate the system, who's really getting cheated? We're all on our own to do the best we can with what we've got. The one thing that holds it all together is the integrity of the players. Your score is your score. Play hard, play by the rules, and post it.

Hayden Lake Country Club, Hayden Lake, Idaho—18th Hole.

On-Course Survival Guide

Chapter 12
Assume the Position

"What other people may find in poetry or art museums, I find in the flight of a good drive."

—Arnold Palmer

The first tee is the point of no return. It's where preparation and experience inevitably meet demonstration. Whether you're teeing it up for the first time ever, or you're a retired desert-dweller playing your 10,000th round, you'll need effortless execution of these pre-round practices.

Here, for example, is your first chance to strike fear into the hearts of your opponents with the proper golf pose. Leave nothing to chance. It's time to use all of the weaponry at your disposal and deal a crushing blow from the start. So iron your shirt and shine your shoes, 'cause you mean business today. You're playing to win—and you're not afraid to look good doing it.

Strike a Pose

Tripod

This is the essential pose: Place your left hand on your left hip, or if you're feeling sassy, with your thumb tucked into your front left pants pocket instead. Position the club in your right hand, butt end in your palm, clubhead on the ground. Lean to the right and support your weight with the club. Cross your right foot in front of your left, toe pointing downward.

I hate to brag, but I make "Tripod" look easy!

Finally, turn your head to the left. (This provides the best silhouette, should passersby happen to notice you from afar.)

You now have three points of contact with terra firma, like a plug in a socket: drawing power, gaining strength, yet grounded. No one will beat you today.

Modification Once you're on the green and tending the pin, the same position can be assumed using the flagstick. However, grip it with your hand at shoulder height, approximately one-third from the top—as if you're hunting bullfrogs with a spear.

Caution Don't lean too heavily on a driver or 3-wood in wet grass. The club might slip out from beneath you, which would completely ruin the image you're striving to achieve. Don't lean too heavily on your club or the flagstick on a green, either. The pressure can cause damage to the grass.

Young Guns

This more advanced pose is an important part of high-level gaming and psychological warfare—another lethal weapon to add to your arsenal, like the bayonet at the end of your Tripod-musket.

Start with your feet slightly wider than your shoulders. Next, position the clubhead on the ground in the middle of your stance with both hands resting on the butt end, arms extended but not locked. Finally, and this is important, lift your chest and chin, spine straight, and squint your eyes as if scouring the horizon for your next victim. Purse your lips to create extra effect. You'll look cold, hardened, out for blood.

Are you trembling? Me, too.

Modification One-Armed Young Guns. To achieve this look while doing Young Guns, remove either arm from the club, look down at your shoes, and rub the sweat off the back of your neck while vigorously flexing your bicep (and listening for your opponents to crumble under the pressure).

Caution If you don't have a respectable bicep to flex, One-Armed Young Guns can have the reverse effect.

For starters, Tripod and Young Guns should suffice. If, however, you find that these poses don't enhance your strengths, then give Slugger, Bouncer, Billy the Kid, or Sniper a try, perhaps. You can find instructions for these advanced techniques at www.pickituppublishing.com.

"Ladies with an attitude/Fellows that were in the mood/Don't just stand there, let's get to it/Strike a pose, there's nothing to it."
—Madonna

Taking the Tee

Seriously, though, there's a certain protocol that should be thoroughly understood and effortlessly executed on the first tee. Although this list might seem like a lot to remember, it's all worth it. Done right, all these habits will go unnoticed. Done wrong, you'll be the center of attention for reasons you'd rather not be.

Take the Tee When It's Your Turn

Your group must be ready to take the tee and begin play when you're supposed to. A late group has a cumulative effect on all subsequent groups and makes it nearly impossible to catch up. A last-minute dash to the golf shop for a fresh glove, a trip to the grill for a turkey wrap, or an attempt to hit every last range ball are all time-consuming, and usually avoidable. Each should be considered and dealt with in advance.

If it's obvious your group won't be ready on time, inform the starter. Perhaps another group is willing to switch tee times. However, the other groups may need to finish their warm-up, so don't expect them to be eager to trade. Don't make your poor planning their problem. If all the players in your group aren't ready to go on time, and neither is the group behind you, then it's your obligation to tee off anyway. The tardy player(s) should willingly skip their first swing and join the group in the fairway. That's the appropriate price to pay for not thinking ahead.

Don't Hover Around the First Tee

Try not to make the group in front of you feel hurried. Every player deserves to make the very first swing without feeling you breathing down their neck. Pay attention to what's happening on the tee—from a reasonable distance. Hit putts on the practice green, stretch, or sit patiently in your cart, near enough to quickly move onto the tee when it's your turn, but far enough away not to cause performance pressure for the golfers in front of you.

If the path to the first tee is wide enough for only one cart at a time, make sure yours is out of the way so those in front of you can pass without swapping paint or driving off the path—which would make them mistakenly look like the jerk, instead of you.

> "One of the most fascinating things about golf is how it reflects the cycle of life. No matter what you shoot—the next day you have to go back to the first tee and begin all over again and make yourself into something."
>
> —Peter Jacobsen

Mark Your Ball

You should get into the habit of marking your golf balls with a permanent marker exactly the same way every time. Golf is a game of routine. And consistency in the little things will eliminate variables that otherwise occupy thought and create extra effort.

Once your group takes the tee, tell the other players what type of ball you'll be starting with and how it's marked. This shows that you've done this before, that you intend to abide by the rules, and that you expect the same from them. I promise they'll reply with their specs, too. Mention the brand, the number, the color of the number, and how you've marked it, such as:

"Hey boys, I've got a Titleist 3, red, with two blue dots . . ."

"Today I'll be starting with a Super Nuke 'em Triple Titanium 2, with a big smiley face on it, a star over the number, and the name of my dog written in green . . ."

This is mandatory in a formal competition. It's important to clearly identify your golf ball should a rules situation arise because someone accidentally hit the wrong ball.

Prepare Your Pockets

Good golfers are precise—sometimes to the point of superstition—about what, and how many of each, is in their pockets. I use a 3-2-1 method: three tees, two ball marks, and one divot tool. Having too much crammed into a pocket is distracting and makes it difficult to find things efficiently. Since I'm right-handed, I keep that stuff in my front right pocket to avoid having to fish it out with my glove-wearing left hand. Getting a gloved hand in and out of a pants pocket can be a real chore. When I walk I keep the scorecard in my front left pocket since I take my glove off to putt and then record the scores while I'm ungloved. Everything else should go in the golf bag—keys, cell phone, brass knuckles, wallet, flask, taser, lucky rabbit's foot, and loose change.

FACE PLANTS

My first attempt to pass the PAT was memorable for all the wrong reasons. Although I'd played other sports on much larger stages, I was more nervous than I'd ever been. Other than an intramural golf tourney in college, it was my first official golf competition. I felt like I was about to hurl.

At the first tee I shook hands with my playing partners and exchanged pleasantries and scorecards, per usual. I tried to make small talk and crack a joke or two, but my brain was whirling. There was a small crowd gathered around the first tee, mostly just families of the participants, a rules official, and the host golf professional who called the competitors to the tee, but it felt like a wave of humanity, all gathered to witness my imminent spontaneous combustion.

". . . Next on the tee, from the Hayden Lake Country Club in Hayden Lake, Idaho, Greg Rowley . . ."

Here we go! Do I wave to the gallery? Should I tip my hat? Will I see anyone I know? I can't believe I chose to do this. I hope I don't embarrass myself. Think positive, dummy—think positive. But what if the members find out if I play lousy? I have to pee.

I stepped to the elevated tee, driver in hand, pocket perfectly prepared with three tees, two ball markers, and my lucky Duke Blue Devil divot tool . . . but no ball! Whoops.

How did I forget a ball? Seriously? A ball? Idiot! Where's my bag? Will I be penalized for slow play? Everyone's watching! Is it too late to fake an injury? Help!!!

After shaking off the urge to curl up in the fetal position and suck my thumb, I left the first tee and scrambled through the spectators to my bag. I tried to laugh about the blunder. I think my playing partners and the crowd were even more uncomfortable than I was. It had to be like watching a comedian bomb onstage—or slowing down to catch a glimpse of a car crash on the highway. Nobody wanted to look, but nobody could look away.

I hustled back up to the tee. All in one frantic motion I teed the ball and slapped it down into the fairway. I'm not sure I made a backswing, or even actually put my left hand on the club. The ball traveled all of about 60 yards, leaving me 400 more yards to go on the opening par 4.

When I finished the first hole, 7 agonizing strokes and thirty minutes later, I had already blown my chance of shooting a passing score. Yet, there were still thirty-five more holes to play.

The next seventeen holes were a blur. Honestly, I don't remember anything about the golf course, my game, the weather, my co-competitors, or what I was wearing. All I know is that I barely kept it under 100 strokes, because at the scoreboard I was mortified to learn that our scores were posted, hole by hole, for all to see. 8-6-5-7-6-8-4 . . . Posting my score in that fancy calligraphy was an act of total futility—like putting lipstick on a pig. I had posted the worst round of the day—by far. There was only one thing left to do at that point. Get drunk.

So, I had two or three beers with my lunch, and bought twelve more little aluminum caddies to help me get around the second eighteen. Apparently, I had grossly underestimated my needs and had to replenish—at the turn. So, much like the first round, I remember very little of the second, but for an entirely different reason.

I woke up the next morning in the backseat of my car, still wearing my golf shoes and—thankfully—still in the parking lot. As I tried to piece together just what had happened, it occurred to me I had no idea what I'd shot in the second round, or frankly, if I'd even finished.

In a fog of beer breath, sunscreen, and sweat, I bumbled my way over to the scoreboard and discovered that I had actually improved my score by 14 strokes from the first round. Hooray for me! If only they'd given a most improved award . . .

And, yes, I know exactly what you're thinking . . . impressive!

Define the Game

Whether your group plays a standard game, or you're introducing a new one with strangers, it's important to clearly define the details, the amount of the bet(s), and all the associated rules before you begin. (You'll learn how in chapter 13.)

PEARLS FROM THE PRO

I like to be the scorekeeper. It's nice to have that information readily at hand instead of relying on occasional updates and the risk of getting pencil-whipped. Knowing the score and the standing of the game can create a strategic or psychological advantage.

Even if I'm walking and others are riding (and can use the steering-wheel clip to hold it), I still prefer to keep the scorecard. Here's a handy way to fold your scorecard, with a built-in pencil holder, so the tip doesn't break off, jab your leg, rip your shorts, or scribble all over the inside of your trousers.

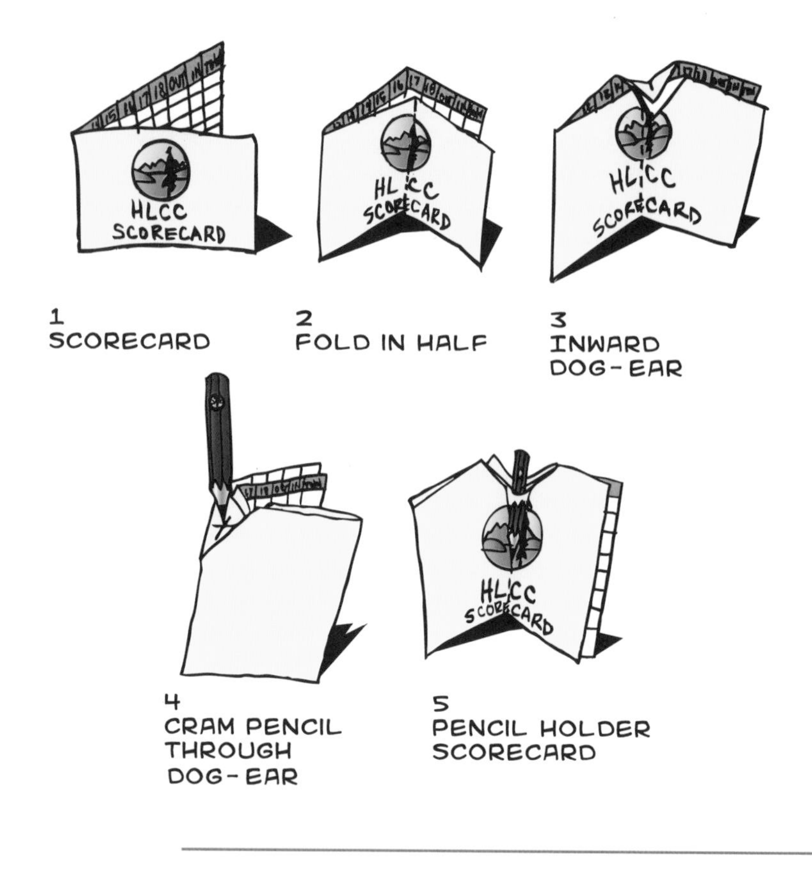

Tee It Up Properly

This is a perfect example of one of those things that, when done properly, goes totally unnoticed. When it isn't, you'll look like a moron.

Single-Handedly The ball should be teed with just one hand, and in one swift, graceful motion to the turf. Here's how: Hold the tee between your first two fingers, cigarette style. Position the ball in the cup at the top and hold it in place with your thumb. Then, while leaning on your golf club for balance, bend down and push the tee into the ground. (Skirt-wearing women may need to execute a more demure curtsy-style, bent-knee stoop, for obvious reasons.)

As with drinking afternoon sweet tea, you've got two options: pinky-in or pinky-out, shown on the opposite page.

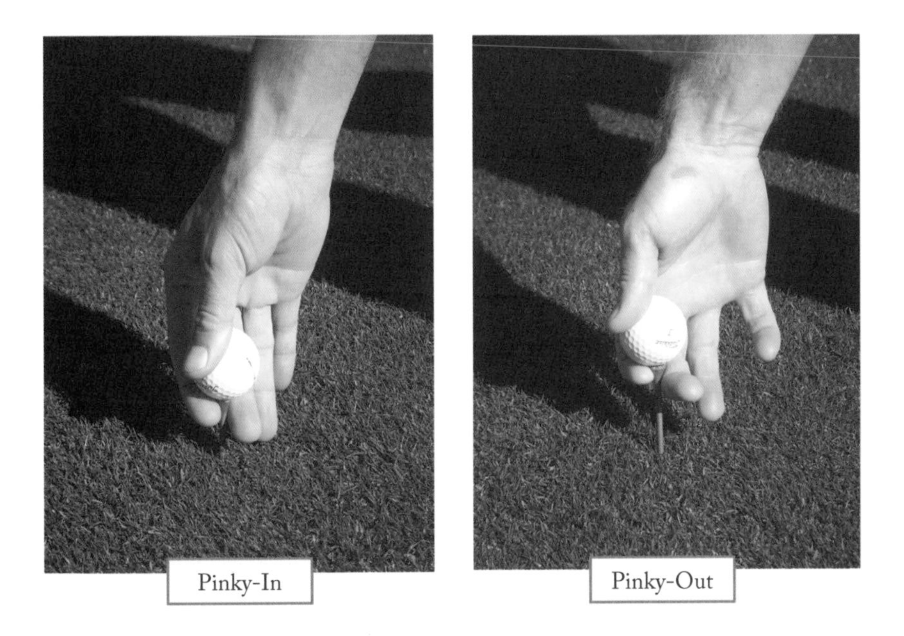

Pinky-In

Pinky-Out

The Right Height With a driver resting on the ground, tee the ball so that half of the ball is above the top of the club. With a fairway metal or a hybrid, the same principle applies. With an iron, however, the ball should be teed barely above the ground, because your goal will be to hit the ball first, the ground second, and make a divot.

Driver

Fairway Metal/Hybrid

Iron

The importance of teeing the ball the right height is twofold. Obviously, it's a critical component to hitting quality shots. But it also prevents embarrassing "sky marks."

A sky mark (also known as an idiot mark) is a scrape or scratch that's made to the top of the clubhead by the bottom of the golf ball. Sky marks happen when the ball is teed too high and the clubhead slides underneath it, popping it straight up into the air. Not only will most experienced players refuse to use a club with sky marks on it (because the constant reminder of a terrible shot is distracting), but it's fairly common for them to immediately discard the club if it's ruined this way. This also explains why many players won't loan their equipment to others, and might say something like "if you sky it, you buy it" to discourage someone from even asking.

Traction Versus Distraction Tee your ball in a location that won't require you to stand in old divots, loose sand, or uneven turf when you take your stance. Tee your ball in an area free of other visual distractions, such as divots angled in the wrong direction or too near to the tee markers.

Mulligans, Anyone?

A mulligan is a "do-over." Although it's never mentioned in *The Rules of Golf*, it's a well-known golf term. A mulligan is also called a breakfast ball, brunch ball, or lunch ball (depending on the time of day), or druthers. The most common use is the custom of hitting two drives off the first tee and selecting the best one. The spirit of the custom is to give all players a chance to begin their round with a good drive.

I discourage this practice on a busy golf course, especially if other groups are waiting to tee off behind you. But when a mulligan is appropriate, here are a few things to consider.

- The first player to take the tee should always ask for permission prior to teeing off. Mulligans? Druthers? Breakfast ball? If you wait and ask after a lousy drive, you'll look like you're begging.
- Keep the extra ball in your pocket and hit it while it's still your turn. Don't wait until after all of the other players have teed off to start your pre-shot routine all over again.
- If your first tee shot is good, then don't hit a second. It's a waste of time. Also, needing only one drive shows confidence when everyone else needs two. It's best not to get greedy. The golf gods never forget and will—I'm dead serious about this—inevitably reclaim the stroke later on during the round, always at a most inopportune time.
- In some cases, such as a short dogleg hole, there can be a strategic advantage to putting a ball safely in play and then attempting a more aggressive shot with the second ball, or vice versa. That's allowed, but you should

never change clubs to hit a mulligan. That's a gross misinterpretation of the custom.

> "The term 'mulligan' is really a contraction of the phrase 'maul it again.'"
> —Unknown

IF I RULED THE WORLD

Not only would I add a first tee mulligan to *The Rules of Golf*, I'd enforce it like this:

If a first tee mulligan is permitted and taken, it then automatically becomes the ball in play, and the original ball is abandoned.

I don't mind the breakfast ball. It seems part of the culture that's here to stay. It's also typically based on habit, not necessity. It can be time-consuming and make the first tee look more like a practice range than a golf course when every player in a fivesome hits two drives.

I just think that a mulligan should come at a higher price. Per this new rule, if a first tee mulligan is taken, it must be used. There's no choice. Doesn't that seem like a fair trade-off for the free swing and opportunity of an improved start?

Client and Guest Hosting (Part III)

When hosting guests, inform them on the first tee of local customs and policies.

- Divot and golf cart policies (chapter 14)

- Local customs, such as the "lateral rule" (chapter 15)
- The average length of time for a round (chapter 15)
- Any local rules (official rules, specific to the golf course, usually listed on the scorecard) that might regularly come into play (chapter 22)

Unless a game is being played that requires a specific order of play, the host should always tee off first. Thereafter, honors or "ready golf" (see chapter 15) should determine the order.

Playing with Strangers

When you're paired with strangers, pay attention to a few particulars prior to the start.

Nice Putt, Sport

After the introductions, write down everybody's name on the scorecard and a one-word description of each player, such as "blue" for the woman in the blue shirt, or "tall" for the tallest guy in the group. Do this even if you have no intention of recording their scores, because it's embarrassing to forget someone's name. If you do, there are ways to discreetly find out without asking. You can hang around their cart and take a peek at their scorecard or their bag tags—or simply pay attention to their conversations and hope to overhear a name. If still no luck, apologize and ask again. Admitting you forgot is a much better option than calling someone Bud, Sport, Pal, Dude, Man, Chief, Boss, Captain, Sister, Honey, Sugar, Girlfriend, or Sweetie all day long.

Which Tees?

Determine which set of tees to play—and be willing to play a shorter course. A group of strangers should always default to the shortest set of tees that's comfortable for everyone.

Who's Driving?

I prefer to be the passenger, but I'm always willing to drive the cart when paired with a player who hasn't played the course before. I was always taught that the player who knows the course best should drive.

Nonsmoking Section

I try to ascertain if the other player is a smoker before I'll agree to share a cart. I simply can't tolerate cigarette or cigar smoke. Frankly, I'd rather walk than smell it. If I'm unable to detect any clues, I have no problem asking. I'd rather ask and risk being offensive than suffer quietly for the rest of the day.

Classic Golf Pranks

Any chance to pull a good prank on a buddy should never be passed up, and there are usually a few golden opportunities prior to teeing off. These are tried-and-true golf pranks guaranteed to get a laugh. I'll issue a word of caution here: these ideas should be reserved for very close friends—not your boss, and certainly not your host or someone who's paid for your round. If you're straddling the fence of appropriateness, it's probably best to err on the side of caution. However, if you've been the subject of a prior prank or you know the target well enough, then the gloves are off! Here's how to give your friend(s) a real kick in the crotch when they least expect it.

Turn Key This is an easy one. After your playing partners have met you at the range or the first tee (and have already operated their cart), just turn their key to the "off" position. It will take them a while to figure out why the cart isn't working. Repeat.

Bag Strapped Either at the practice range or near the first tee, simply loosen the vinyl strap that holds a player's bag to the back of a cart. When the cart lurches forward, the clubs will fall off the back. Yeah, I know, it might damage the equipment—but it's hilarious. The player whose gear falls off gets embarrassed because it's loud, and they'll think it was their fault. Do this repeatedly throughout the round until the sucker catches on. Eventually they will.

Loud Speaker If a player in your group has an embarrassing nickname or is sensitive about a common mispronunciation of his or her name, give the person in the golf shop a buck or two to announce your group to the first tee using the nickname.

Sandbagged This is an adaptation of the age-old salt shaker gag. At a course that has sand-n-seed containers on each cart, simply unscrew the tops so that when the container is picked up the contents will spill everywhere. Childish, I know, but funny.

Dead Weight If you're walking, try to sneak something heavy into the bottom of your playing partner's golf bag. Maybe a five-pound weight, a handful of rocks, a sand-n-seed bottle, seven beers, or a human head . . . whatever you can find.

The Driver/Putter Switcheroo Take your buddy's brand-new $900 Super-Duper-El Guapo driver out of his bag and hide it in yours, then replace it with an old beat-up persimmon from the lost-and-found barrel in the cart barn. Be sure to put the Super-Duper-El Guapo headcover back on the replacement. When it's unsheathed, your victim's heart will stop for as long as you can keep a straight face. This can also be done with a putter or—better yet—both.

Getting the Shaft This is the classic golf prank. Before you leave the course, take all the clubs out of your target's golf bag and replace them upside down—clubhead end first. Stuff as many as possible into the smallest opening and give each a twist. It's nearly impossible to pull the clubs out because they get so tangled. Hee-hee.

Shafted!

Pink Balls Remove all regular golf balls from your male buddy's bag and replace them with pink ones. Hopefully, he won't discover the gag until just before he's teeing off in a semi-serious tournament. Or even better, just before he's teeing off in a semi-serious tournament with a shotgun start, and he's as far away from the clubhouse as geographically possible. Now that's good humor.

Laura Davies One time I cut out a magazine picture of LPGA legend Laura Davies (about the same size as the top of my coworker's driver) and made copies. Whenever possible, I taped it to the top of his club so that when he removed the headcover, she was staring up at him. Use thick, super-adhesive packing tape so it doesn't come off very easily.

Your Mother Here's an advanced twist to Laura Davies. Tape a picture of your buddy's mom (or wife) to your own club. Then act surprised and blame somebody else. "Wow! Who taped this picture of my prom date to my driver?!!"

Call to Action

On every golf course in every corner of the world, after all of the players in the group have hit their tee shots on the first hole, someone in the group always says "and . . . we're off."

What a waste. You've got a split second to say something that everyone in your group, and possibly another, will hear. Make it memorable, comical, or totally irreverent—just be original.

Remember Mel Gibson as William Wallace in the movie *Braveheart*, face painted blue and shrieking wildly as he led his outmatched army of Scottish Highlanders across the field of battle to face the heavily favored legions of the English? Generations of oppression and tyranny released in a guttural barbaric yawp . . . FREEDOM!!!

As you depart the first tee, somebody (the host, perhaps) should say something similarly inspirational—but not necessarily as loud.

Birdies for breakfast—Eagles for dinner!

Four hours or less—Or else!

A ball in the pocket is worth two in the bush!

The only things we have to fear are three putts, rain clouds, and warm beer!

Chapter 13

Gas, Rent, and Beer Money

"Never bet against somebody you meet on the first tee with a deep suntan, a 1-iron in his bag, and squinty eyes."

—Dave Marr

It's important to understand the difference between wagering on a golf game and competing for prize money. As an amateur you're allowed to win money from a golf wager and retain your amateur status. However, you cannot compete in a golf event for prize money. You'll lose your amateur status. If you're ever in doubt—even a little bit—either consult the USGA or simply don't participate.

It's also important to understand that you don't, under any circumstance, ever have to gamble when you play golf. It's a part of the culture that appeals to many—but it's certainly not a universal must. When and if it comes up, however, it's essential that you understand the risks as well as the potential rewards.

Know Your Limits

It's taken me a long time to get comfortable playing for money, especially large amounts of money, probably because I paid out cash like an ATM at the start of my career. For me, it has become easier with time (and steady increases in compensation and ability).

Whatever your gambling preferences, be ready to answer the inevitable first-tee question: "What's the game?" Some people can play their best only when a paycheck's on the line. Others get vapor lock for a few pennies. It's important to know where you fall and to find others with similar gambling preferences as playing partners. Like Matt Damon's character said in the movie *Rounders*, "If you can't spot the sucker in the first half hour at the table, then you're the sucker." That thought applies to both the poker table and the golf course.

> "Don't be afraid to go out on a limb, 'cause that's where the food is."
>
> —Doyle Brunson

You need to know what amount of money you're comfortable gambling, or—more important—what amount you're comfortable losing. Playing for too much money can ruin your round, your day, your month, and perhaps your marriage and life. If you're worried about the loss, it will almost certainly distract you from the task at hand, which is to have fun, play well, and not lose your money, of course.

PEARLS FROM THE PRO

Whenever I tee it up in cash games, I estimate how much is at stake and consider that amount an immediate loss. I've played in far too many high-dollar games where the best player paid out the most cash at the end. Success is often a function of who you're paired with and how your opponents play, rather than your own game. If I happen to play well enough to win, I think of it as a bonus. Using this philosophy I'm able to concentrate on my game and not count the dollars every poor shot might end up costing me.

Many of the common money games have variations that escalate the financial risk. While some are played for a flat amount, others are played so the outcome of each hole determines the amount of money that exchanges hands. What's more, that amount can be doubled (or pressed) and then doubled again before you even leave the tee box. That's why it's important to have a clear understanding of the game you're agreeing to play before you tee it up. A two-dollar game can end up costing you hundreds. A five-cent game may sound like chump change, but in the end it can net you fifty dollars. Some guys play for singles and nickels, which means a dollar and five cents, respectively. Others play for singles and nickels that mean a hundred dollars and five hundred dollars. Everything—including risk, wealth, enjoyment, and stress—is relative, and all these variables require an honest self-assessment.

Everyone has a different level of gambling comfort, and it doesn't have anything to do with net worth or how much you can comfortably afford to lose. But when it does, it can be a very painful lesson . . .

FACE PLANTS

The season had ended in Idaho, and as many unattached assistant pros do, I had migrated south for the winter to San Diego to find work on the beach and in the sun. I had my TV in the front seat, my clothes in the back, and my clubs in the trunk. I'd been in town for only a week or two when a member from up north (let's call him "John") invited me to join him for a round at a very prestigious golf course. I was thrilled.

Two of the players in our group turned out to be professional golfers (not golf professionals—big difference), one of whom had competed in the Masters a year or two earlier. The third member of the group was a +2 handicap player—the defending men's club champion. John and I rounded out the fivesome. I hadn't played in weeks, and I was recovering from a severe softball (hamstring) injury. I was very rusty and nervous—a lethal combination in a cash game.

While we prepared to tee off, we discussed the amount of the bet and the game. Sheepishly, I announced that I was seriously wounded and had just $40 in my pocket, which was all I could afford to lose. John winked at me and held up his hand, almost like a pastor blessing his congregation, as if to say, "Don't worry about it, kid." So I didn't. The game was set and away we went. I had no idea what we were playing or for how much. It didn't really matter, did it?

The worst thing possible happened almost immediately when I made a birdie on the first hole. This apparently doubled every bet. As it turns out, it was the only birdie—or par for that matter—that I managed all day. I cruised to a smooth mid-90s round. It couldn't have been more humiliating. Or so I thought . . . Then we adjourned from the 18th green to the men's grill.

After a long silence, lots of erasing, and some high math, I was informed that I had just lost $515. Holy crap! All I had was $40. Not just with me, but to my name! That was my gas money, rent money, and beer money. It was all I had, and both my tank and refrigerator were empty. I looked at John for help. He didn't even make eye contact with me. He just kept his head down and shoveled popcorn into his mouth. Had I imagined his wink and wave on the first tee? I was sure he'd speak up and tell the boys that he had it covered. Wouldn't he? John? Help?!

The final result had me down $515, my host breaking even, and everyone else splitting my loss as their profit. I was the only loser at the table. When I explained my situation to the rest of the group, the biggest of the winners slammed a fist into the table and began cursing loudly. Apparently, the winnings were to be gas money, rent money, and beer money for him, too. I couldn't do anything other than hope he didn't reach across the table and beat the balance of the debt out of me. I offered my last penny and left with my tail between my legs—a beaten and broke young man.

A year or two later, while I was working at The Quarry, the same guy showed up as a guest one day. And, just my luck, he remembered me! Again, I dug deep into my pockets, and this time I had about half of the debt covered. He graciously accepted my offering and we shared a laugh about the incident. Sort of.

The moral: Always know *exactly* what game you're playing, how much it could cost you, and—maybe most importantly—who you're playing with. This knowledge can prevent a costly and embarrassing situation.

Shame on me for getting in over my head. Shame on John for not covering the debt as the hosting member. Shame on the tour player for taking my money ex post facto. We're all to blame. Learn from my mistake and you won't ever have to experience such a painful lesson for yourself.

Greg's Gambling Rules

These rules will help you realize your comfort level and set your limits when negotiating a money game. They've proven valuable on many occasions.

Understand the Game Find out if, when, and how much the amount of the bet can change. If you don't understand—ask questions. It's just like my grandpa always told me—"There aren't any dumb questions, just dumb people who don't ask questions." Or something like that . . .

> "He who asks is a fool for five minutes, but he who does not ask remains a fool forever."
>
> —Chinese Proverb

Consider the Amount of the Bet a Loss If you happen to win in the end, it will be a bonus.

Keep It Friendly When you're playing with someone for the first time, keep the bet friendly. (See page 195 for a list of non-fiscal alternative wagers.)

STORY TIME

At one of the nation's most prestigious men's golf clubs the members play against each other for only two dollars a round. Every member has so much money that it's pointless to play costly games. It's more about friendly competition than it is about fleecing their buddies.

Apparently, one day a brash young guest was trying to convince some of the members to play for higher stakes. This drew the ire of a patriarch of the club, who politely informed the guest of the modest two-dollar custom.

Undaunted, the "dot.commer" continued, insisting that his net worth was "several million dollars" and he wanted some real action. With that, the member presented a deck of playing cards to the loud guest and calmly said, "Son, several million, you say? I'll cut you for it." Ouch! Now that's real action.

Avoid the Sucker Punch If you want to play for a lot of money, do so only when you have a good feel for someone's ability and, most importantly, how it relates to that golfer's handicap. That's the nicest way I can think to say "don't get sucker-punched by a lying, cheating, stinking low-life sandbagger" (see chapter 11).

Stay in Your Comfort Zone If the amount of the bet is a distraction and adds pressure to your round, then you're playing for too much. Be confident enough to say so.

Beware of a Home Course Advantage Never gamble for large amounts at a golf course you've never played—especially if you're playing against others who have.

Opt Out Gracefully Rather than admit to not knowing the rules of common golf games or how to keep the scorecard, a good friend of mine usually tells his playing partners that he's forgotten his glasses and can't read the scorecard. The truth is he doesn't even wear glasses, but he's discovered this ploy throws the wolves off the scent.

Instead of making up excuses to avoid a money game, try this: Read *The Pocket Pro: Golf Gaming Guide* (a companion piece to this book, which is described on page 139). Then, suggest a new game that's specific to the size of the group, minus you. Teach them how to play it, if necessary.

When you can discuss golf games from an informed position, you've got the power. Your decision to decline is then based on an awareness of your preferences, which demonstrates experience, not made out of ignorance or fear.

Keep No Secrets Don't hide your gambling stash from your spouse. If you've got to keep it a secret, maybe you shouldn't be risking it in the first place. When (not if) you get caught, you'd better be ready to offer a quick explanation.

STORY TIME

Troy used to keep a massive bankroll, usually $3,000 or more, in a great big wad of sweaty cash that he lugged everywhere and hid from his wife. It was in the glove box of his car one day when she stumbled across it. When confronted, the first thing he blurted out was that he'd been secretly saving up to take her to Seattle for the weekend—an anniversary surprise! It worked, and she wasn't too mad at him, but he had to spend the entire roll in one weekend of fancy dining and shopping, not at the poker table or on the golf course.

Golf Gambling Customs

Here's how to act so you won't look or sound like a rookie golf-gamer or, worse, unknowingly offend someone by doing the wrong thing.

Winner Buys the Drinks

A universal golf custom is that the player who wins buys drinks or lunch. The purchase should be proportionate to the winnings. If you win big, buy the meal. If you win a little, just buy the first round of drinks. It's knowledge of the custom and adherence to the obligation that demonstrate experience.

The only allowable exception to this rule is if you're a guest at a private club and you're the winner. You can't buy the food and drink either because it's required to be charged to a member's account, they don't accept cash, or the host member simply won't let you buy. When this happens, make a token offer to do so, or offer the money as repayment of the caddie fees, perhaps, but don't make a big deal out of it. If the host says no, then it's no. Rather, send a prompt thank-you card, or maybe a bottle of wine, to acknowledge your host's graciousness.

PEARLS FROM THE PRO

If you're the winner and you're in a hurry to leave after the round, make every effort to leave some money with another player, or the bartender, to take care of the drinks. Don't be the person who takes the money and runs.

At many courses, public and private, when a player makes a hole-in-one it's customary for that player to buy a round of drinks for everyone in the clubhouse and on the course at the time. This can get expensive. Since it's a once-in-a-lifetime occurrence (if that), it's a risk you shouldn't be too worried about. If you do happen to be so lucky, and simply can't afford to buy that many cocktails, then don't do it. No one's going to bust your kneecaps or anything.

Pay Your Debt(s) Promptly

Fast pay makes fast friends. Enough said.

STORY TIME

I had the opportunity to play a very exclusive club one evening with a member and his two guests (one of whom was a sort-of celebrity in the golf industry—a putter designer for a prominent equipment company). I was thrilled to play with him, and was secretly hoping to score a new putter.

He and the other guest were playing a game with three bets on every hole: long drive, closest to the pin, and score. One guy would call out the value of the bets on the even-numbered holes, the other on the odd-numbered holes—any three amounts, for each bet, in order.

The putter-maker was having a bad day and losing his shirt, and the bets quickly escalated from $50-$50-$100 to $500-$500-$1,000 to $1,000-$2,000-$3,000. Why "friends" would play for that kind of jack was beyond me. In the end, the putter-maker had lost $22,000. As bad as that sounds, the worst was yet to come.

We changed venue from golf course to grill. There, I had the misfortune of watching the guy backpedal and ultimately welsh on the bet. He wouldn't pay—or more likely, couldn't. I've never seen grown men fight other than on TV or in a ring, and that was as close as I've been to two guys who almost did. I watched a friendship dissolve right in front of me over what started out as a friendly golf wager. It was awful.

Don't Get Caught Light

Only wager the cash you're carrying. Otherwise, the winner ends up feeling like a jerk. No gentleman wants to feel like they're putting the squeeze on someone.

If you forget this advice, and you're "light," make a commitment to pay the money promptly—then do so. If you don't, you're telling your playing partners you didn't take them seriously. Leave it in an envelope in each one's locker or make some other form of discreet repayment. Just be sure you do it.

> "Pressure is playing for $10 when you don't have a dime in your pocket."
>
> —Lee Trevino

Lose with Grace, Win with Humility

Don't whine, moan, pout, brag, crow, or gloat following a payout. Treat the rest of your playing partners with the same respect you'd want to be treated with if you had just shelled out or collected.

That doesn't mean you can't enjoy your hard-earned "struttin'" rights, because frankly, they're often more important than the monetary gain. But there's a big difference between letting your playing partners know you're proud of a win and rubbing it in their faces.

Round the Amount

If the win is an odd number of dollars or cents, offer to round the amount to an easier denomination to pay. It can be awkward trying to make change at the table to pay $6.70. Rather, round down to $6 if you're collecting, or round up to $7 if you're paying.

The Pocket Pro: Golf Gaming Guide

The Pocket Pro: Golf Gaming Guide was written to supplement *Golf, Naked.* To get your copy, go to www.pickituppublishing.com, and follow the prompts to place an order. For only $9.95 (less than a sleeve of balls), it explains the most popular side games played today, organized by group size. It also outlines the rules, explains key gaming concepts like the press, shows how to keep the score, and offers some strategy tips that will hopefully give you enough of an edge to recoup the cost next league night. *The Pocket Pro* even includes some of the newest games that are rapidly growing into favorites—like the New Nassau and Middle Man. Best of all, it has a water-repellent cover and is small enough to put in your golf bag, so you can keep the information with you on the course.

Here's an excerpt from *The Pocket Pro*'s explanation of the New Nassau.

Nassau (New)

This is a much simpler version of the old game. The New Nassau is 4 bets in 1—a front nine match, a 9th-hole match, a back nine match, and an 18th-hole match.

There's no more "overall" bet, which offers a couple benefits. One, it's not as confusing. Two, everything that happens on the front nine, stays on the front nine, and a lousy start isn't nearly as costly.

Like the Old Nassau, presses can be played, and can be made optional or automatic—it's up to you. Unlike the Old Nassau, and regardless of the standing of the match, or the number of presses, the final hole of each half stands alone as its own bet. The final hole also counts toward the outcome of all other bets—so it carries a significantly elevated importance.

When a bet is pressed, it begins as "E" in the column of the hole that was just completed.

Here's an example of a $2 New Nassau with auto 2-down presses:

Hole	1	2	3	4	5	6	7	8	9	Out
Black	375	209	611	407	556	428	233	602	201	3622
White	301	148	521	317	451	349	164	533	138	2922
Red	268	121	493	245	396	293	141	498	97	2552
Par	4	3	5	4	5	4	3	5	3	36
Starsky 8 » 0	5	5	5	4	4	4	4	5	3	39
Hutch 13 » 5	4	4	5•	5	6•	5	3	6•	3	41
Front 9	-1	-2	-3	-2	-1	E	-1	-1	-1	-$2
Front 9 Press		E	-1	E	+1	+2	+1	+1	+1	$2
Pressed Press						E	-1	-1	-1	-$2
9th Hole									E	$0
Handicap	11	13	1	9	5	7	15	3	17	

10	11	12	13	14	15	16	17	18	In	Tot	Hcp	Net
398	413	568	150	157	453	585	368	416	3508	7130		
307	329	483	112	130	376	497	286	344	2864	5786		
261	278	446	97	107	315	455	234	238	2431	4983		
4	4	5	3	3	4	5	4	4	36	72		
5	4	5	2	3	4	5	5	3	36	75	8	67
5	6•	6	3	3	6	6•	4	4	43	84	13	71
E	+1	+2	+3	+3	+4	+4	+3	+4				$2
		E	+1	+1	+2	+2	+1	+2				$2
					E	E	-1	E				$0
								+1				$2
12	2	6	18	16	8	4	14	10				

Starsky (an 8 handicap adjusted to 0) wins 4 bets for a total of $8: the Front 9 Press, Back 9, Back 9 Press and the 18th hole.

Hutch (a 13 handicap adjusted to 5) wins 2 bets for a total of $4: the Front 9 and the Pressed Press on the Front 9.

They tied the 9th hole and the Pressed Press on the Back 9.

Ultimately, Hutch hands over $4 at the end of this round.

A good money game can be a great way to test your abilities under pressure and get your heart pounding. Just remember it's your money you're gambling with, and you've worked hard to earn it. When you agree to gamble on a golf game, it's your responsibility to fully understand what you're agreeing to do. Don't hesitate to ask questions. Every game has many twists and variations—some regionally specific, others particular to the course—that should be clarified before the round.

My advice won't help you win more often. But it will make you more aware of exactly what you're up to out there. Avoid that moment when the thrill of competition is overtaken by the fear of losing your money. Above all else, enjoy the game.

The Club at Black Rock, Coeur d'Alene, Idaho—11th Hole.

Chapter 14

Lessons from a Dam Builder

"Golf is, in part, a game; but only in part. It is also in part a religion, a fever, a vice, a mirage, a frenzy, a fear, an abscess, a joy, a thrill, a pest, a disease, an uplift, a brooding, a melancholy, a dream of yesterday, and a hope for tomorrow."

—*New York Tribune* (1916)

My golf career started when I was just a kid. My grandparents loved the game, and my first forays came while visiting them on a nine-hole desert course in the tiny farming town of Wilbur, Washington. Playing golf with Grandpa wasn't easy. To him, golf was a game of respect, not an occasion for horseplay, and getting out of line would likely get my brother and me sent home. I still can't step across a putting line, replace a divot, or rake a bunker without thinking of my grandfather. As I grew older (and inevitably, so did he), one of the proudest—and saddest—days of my golf career was the first time I beat the old man.

Honestly, I don't know what kind of a player he was. I was too young to care when he was in his prime, and he was a shadow of himself by the time I was old enough to give him a run. Nonetheless, he was the inspiration for my career in golf. For many years I thought that he was a professional golfer. Since then, I've learned that many grandsons think their golfing grandfathers are professionals—because that's all they do. I realize now that golf is a reward for the retired, and he enjoyed that privilege daily. Lord knows he earned it.

His self-taught action wasn't pretty, but it was effective. It was quick and herky-jerky, part golf swing, part tomahawk chop. Blink, and you'd miss it. As it does for all of us, his golf swing reflected his personality. He believed in getting in, getting done, and getting on to the next project. He wasn't concerned with aesthetics, just the results. It was exactly the way you'd expect a fatherless, Depression-era high school dropout, World War II veteran, eastern Washington "dust bowl" farmer, and Grand Coulee Dam builder to play the game. Raw. With his guts and his massive hands.

I remember a yellowed newspaper clipping on their refrigerator—a photo of Grandpa holding his lucky hole-in-one ball. I remember the time he made an eagle on the 400-plus-yard blind dogleg second hole. We searched for that damn ball for hours, or so it seemed, and finally found it in the cup. I didn't understand the significance of making a deuce on such a long hole at the time, but I know that I'll never forget his Cheshire-cat grin (which was rare) and boyish embarrassment over the feat.

But, of all of the memories I treasure from my time on the golf course with Gramps, it's the lessons of etiquette and respect for others that still matter most. I hope those are the values I, too, am remembered for having passed on to my daughters and someday, perhaps, my grandchildren.

"Character, not circumstance, makes the person."
—Booker T. Washington

Respect Others and the Course

The behaviors you display on the golf course, and more precisely those that have nothing to do with your playing ability, will pointedly reveal your appreciation of the customs and subtleties of the game. Indeed, as Grandpa always taught me, most of these can be summed up in a single word—respect. Respect means demonstrating unwavering adherence to the principles of courtesy and etiquette, and respect means playing at a proper pace.

Etiquette and pace of play share an intimate relationship. Etiquette leads, pace follows. They're forever intertwined, each dependent upon the other. Golf has a rhythm. It's a dance. A grand production. It's the interaction of player to player, group to group, and all to the course.

To learn this rhythm, you must be aware of your surroundings at all times—like a defensive driver. Study and practice these principles of etiquette until they become second nature and you're acting on instinct.

> "We are responsible for what we are, and whatever we wish ourselves to be, we have the power to make ourselves. If what we are now has been the result of our own past actions, it certainly follows that whatever we wish to be in the future can be produced by our present actions; so we have to know how to act."
>
> —Albert Einstein

First, Do No Harm

Avoid any action that might have a negative impact on another player or on the golf course. Sounds simple enough, right? There might be more to it than you think . . .

Keep Up with the Group in Front of You Slow play is bad form for which there is no excuse.

Be Still When Others Are About to Swing It's okay to stand or park a cart where you're noticed; just stay still when it's "go time" for another golfer. Don't shift your weight, release or set the hill brake, turn your head, dig in your pocket, or move your shadow. It's okay to be seen. Just don't do anything to change your position once a player is in the act of swinging.

Be Quiet When Others Are About to Swing This includes talking, walking, making chimpanzee noises, slicing cheddar, spikes on concrete, clubs clanging together, cart starts and stops, cell phones, and bathroom doors. Anything that makes noise can be a distraction.

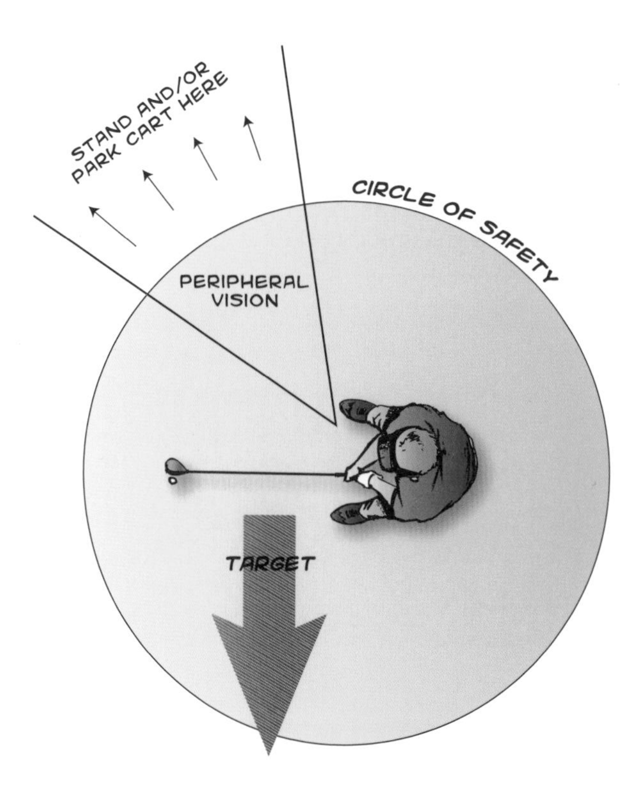

ROOKIE MISTAKES

Beginning golfers often slow the pace of play unnecessarily by taking the concept of noise way too far—in either direction. Remember that it's fine to walk and talk and make some noise, determine your yardage, choose a club and clean it, etc. Just don't do it in the short amount of time right before another player is ready to swing.

Of course you have to get from one point to the next, and you have to prepare for your turn while others are taking theirs. Just do so as quietly as possible. This is why it's important to pay attention to the other players.

When players are in their moment of focused concentration on the target and their next swing, either standing over the golf ball or approaching it, don't do anything to disrupt or distract them. But, until a player is in that moment, or if you're a reasonable distance away, out of sight and earshot, then continue to both quietly prepare and pay attention.

On the other hand, playing with someone who's too easily distracted by even the smallest noises is equally as frustrating. Some noise and distraction are inevitable. Learn to deal with them.

Don't Act Like a Meathead After a Bad Shot Your behavior can have a negative impact on the other players in your group and even players in other groups. That isn't fair to any of them, particularly if you damage the golf course as a result of your disgust. Throwing clubs, angrily digging divots, slashing branches, chopping flowers, or striking golf carts or your own gear should be punishable by ejection from the course and suspension of future playing privileges. Seriously.

A golf ball is like a perfect child—it always does exactly what it's told. In Communications 101, we're taught that most problems in the understanding of a message are the fault of the sender, not the receiver. So, rather than react brutishly after a bad shot, ask yourself how well you communicated your intent.

Truth is, only a few players in the world are good enough to deserve to get angry. Most likely, you aren't one of them. That's not intended to be mean or insensitive, but unless you've committed all of your time and resources to the game as a profession, you haven't earned the right to act like a jerk. And if you have, you'll likely reach a level of understanding that bad shots happen. You'll learn a respect for the game, the course, and your playing partners, which will likely prevent destructive behavior in the first place.

> "If profanity had an influence on the flight of the ball, the game of golf would be played far better than it is."
> —Horace G. Hutchinson

STORY TIME

The first time I met my little sister's jerk-doctor-fiancé was on the golf course. It seemed like the right idea, but it proved to be a rocky beginning. His etiquette was bad and his temperament was worse. At one point he made a practice swing while he was lined up in the wrong direction, and inadvertently jettisoned a muddy divot directly into the side of my wife's head. He offered no apology or attempt to replace the pelt. It was a disappointing first impression, and our relationship got off to a rocky start as a result.

To his credit, he realized that his perfectionist personality made it difficult for him to accept his mistakes and relax. He even quit for a few years. Nowadays, with a fresh perspective and more realistic expectations, he enjoys himself immensely while playing golf. Also, to his credit, perhaps he was somewhat nervous to have to play golf with his new fiancée's entire family, whom he'd yet to meet—including her really good-looking and overly protective jerk–golf pro–big brother.

Don't Throw or Break a Club—Ever! There are countless stories of serious injuries from thrown golf clubs, including lost limbs, eyes, organs, and even lives. I wish I could tell you that I've never done it, but that's not true. What I can tell you is that I'm ashamed of the times I have, and several years ago, I let one go for the last time.

I was playing with a country club member whom I respect—a several-time club champion and true gentleman. I stubbed a chip shot, after which I discreetly helicoptered my wedge toward the next tee box—so at least I wouldn't have to backtrack to retrieve it. After seeing the toss, he immediately gathered his gear, started walking for the clubhouse, and informed me that we'd never play together again. And we haven't. It was a very embarrassing lesson to learn, especially as the professional.

STORY TIME

Several years ago, while hosting guests, a club member got off to an unusually miserable start. He was 14 over par after 4 holes. On the fifth hole, a par 3, he announced to his playing partners that he was going to put the bad start behind him. He then proceeded to dribble his 6-iron neatly into the weeds just in front of the ladies tee—and exploded.

In a fit of rage, he slammed his club into the ground, and the shaft shattered to pieces. He said it didn't even seem like he'd hit it hard enough to cause such damage. While he picked up the pieces, he felt warm liquid in his mouth—blood. Looking in the restroom mirror he discovered he'd flayed his upper lip wide open and could actually see his teeth through the hole. Round's over, boys. Start the car.

He was lucky that a plastic surgeon was on duty at the emergency room and able to reconstruct his face. But sitting there, still in his golf cleats, surrounded by people with real injuries and illnesses, it became apparent just how stupid he'd been. No level of frustration or anger on the golf course should ever be worth serious injury. His outlook on golf has forever changed—and he has a good-size scar on his face to remind him.

Hopefully, it won't take such a painful or permanent reminder to convince you to keep your cool.

Don't Act Like a Meathead After a Bad Round It's a universal truth of the game that you'll never play your best. Just accept it. No matter what their ability or level of experience, nobody has ever finished a round of golf feeling like they executed every swing perfectly. Most golfers quickly forget about all the lucky bounces that may have saved them a stroke or two; they dwell on the bad breaks and unforced errors instead.

Many golfers tend to attach their play to their self-esteem. They allow a poor performance to affect their mood and the way they treat others. When you play poorly, leave it at the course. Bad play doesn't make you a bad person. It shouldn't influence your mood any longer than it takes to pay your debts and start your car.

> "It is very dangerous to have your self-worth riding on your results as an athlete."
>
> —Jim Courier

HER DIARY

Tonight he was acting weird again. We made plans to meet at the bar for drinks. I was shopping with my girlfriends all day and thought he'd be upset when I got dropped off late, but he made no comment.

Our conversation wasn't flowing, so I suggested we go somewhere quiet to talk. He agreed, but remained stoic. I asked him what was wrong; he said nothing. I asked him if it was my fault he was so upset. He said it had nothing to do with me, and not to worry.

On the way home I told him I loved him. He simply smiled and kept driving. He didn't even look over at me. I'm afraid I've lost him—he's distant and absent.

Later on, he did respond to my gentle caress, and we made love. But I still felt as though his thoughts were elsewhere. He fell asleep. I cried. I'm afraid he loves another . . .

HIS DIARY

Today, I shot the worst round of golf in my life . . . but afterward, at least, I got lucky!

Take Care of the Golf Course

You want to leave the course in better condition than when your round began. It's your obligation. You're paying for the privilege to play golf at a facility, not to have someone else pick up after you, rake your bunker messes, or repair your divots and pitch marks.

Really, this is just an extension of one of life's basic laws—to leave things better than you find them. It's what I was told by my folks growing up, and now what I ask of my kindergarten-age daughter when she goes to school or a friend's house. Pick up your mess before you leave.

Obey the Divot Policy

The traditional method has always been to replace divots, but it's not a universal procedure anymore. The sophistication of modern golf courses and hybrid grass types makes the standard "pick up, replace, and stomp" of the divot a sometimes thing. It's your responsibility to find out what the course policy is and, without exception, to obey it.

Obey the Cart Policy

Some courses don't even have cart paths and allow you to take their carts over hill and dale. Others require that the carts stay on the paths at all times. Just do what you're told. Leave and return to the cart paths at 90-degree angles when possible. It's important to keep the carts at least 50 yards away from all greens so that cart damage doesn't occur near the green. Tire tracks, skid marks, and other impressions will have a negative effect for the next golfer to hit a ball there.

PEARLS FROM THE PRO

Some people think golf carts are fun to drive—like amusement park bumper cars. The truth is that they're a nice way to get around the golf course, but fun they aren't. They're too slow to offer any real excitement. They can even be dangerous, especially when a golf course is wet.

If it gets wet enough, carts can spin out of control when driven at an angle up or down steep slopes. To prevent this, keep carts off the wet grass entirely, or make sure to go straight up or straight down steep hills.

If you do find yourself in a golf cart that's careening out of control, keep your limbs inside the vehicle. It's instinctive to put your foot out on the ground to try to stop the spinning. Don't. You're not heavy or strong enough to stop a cart that's out of control. The last thing you want is to catch good traction and find yourself underneath the cart, which could ruin a really good pair of silk pants.

Rake Bunkers with Purpose

Don't just go through the motions. Smooth the sand so there aren't any bumps or troughs that might create an inequitable lie and cause other players extra stress when their balls find the beach. I can tell you from experience that it's downright disgusting to be double penalized for a total stranger's rudeness. It only has to happen to you once, and you'll never leave your footprints in a bunker again. Always replace the rake where it was when you found it. Some courses prefer to place the rakes in the bunkers; others prefer to keep them out. Just follow the local custom.

Always lay the rake with the teeth down (another lesson from Gramps).

Discard Your Trash

Take care of your chewing gum, used Band-Aids, sunflower seed husks, and cigarette and cigar butts. Not only are they ugly and covered with germs; the butts can also be a fire hazard. If you smoke, don't be a smokin' butt-tosser. Instead, buy a canned beverage and use it as an ashtray.

> "Opportunity is missed by most people because it is dressed in overalls and looks like work."
>
> —Thomas Edison

Finesse the Short Game

Be a short-game Fred Astaire. When it comes to the green, your play must be light-footed and well choreographed. The reason is simple: most strokes come within 50 yards of the green, and mostly the ball travels across the surface of the ground rather than through the air. Thus, imperfections in the grass become more noticeable and have a greater potential for a negative impact on your score.

Greens cost more to maintain than the rest of the golf course, and their health is vital to the success of any track. That's all the more reason for increasing your alertness and responsibility when it comes to the short game.

Don't Step in Another Player's Putting Line

The Rules of Golf does not permit a player to smooth or repair spike damage in a putting line, which is the path on which a player intends to roll the ball toward the hole. Incidentally, damage caused by such other means as a pitch mark or an old hole plug can be repaired—one of the many quirky rules of the game that make it so complicated and charming. Here's how.

Once all balls are on the green, draw an imaginary line from each to the hole, and add a foot or two on each side of the lines to account for the possible break of the green. Remember where those lines are and avoid them. Step over or walk around them, but never on them.

If you accidentally drag a foot and leave a scuff mark, repair the damage yourself so it doesn't penalize another golfer.

ROOKIE MISTAKES

One of the most common procedures regularly butchered by beginners is marking, moving, and replacing a ball on the green.

Never use the small button on the golf glove to mark your ball. You might as well scream "rookie!" Carry two ball markers or coins in your pocket instead. You should always mark your ball on the green, and it may be necessary for you to mark the ball of another player from time to time. You mark your ball to get it out of your playing partners' way. It's a penalty to them if their ball strikes yours when they putt, and it's a distraction if it's in another player's peripheral vision. Make marking part of your normal putting routine, just like cleaning and realigning your ball before you putt.

To Mark a Ball

Place your marker flat on the ground behind the ball (opposite the hole), pick up your ball, then tap the mark down with the bottom of your putter. Don't pick the ball up until you place the marker on the ground. Mark, pick up, tap down, in that order, every time.

If you think your marker could be in another player's way, ask whether he or she would like you to move it. Don't wait to be asked.

- "Is that mark okay?"
- "How's my mark?"
- "Want me to move that?"
- "Which direction should I move my mark? High (uphill) or low (downhill)?"
- "Am I in your line?"

To Move Your Marker

Determine which direction to move it. Pick a landmark off the green (such as a tree, the corner of a house, or a street sign) that's perpendicular to your putting line (no nearer the hole). Place the head of your putter on the ground with the butt end next to the marker, toe end pointing at the landmark, and move your marker to the opposite end of the putter head (or vice versa if you've been asked to move your mark nearer to you). Stand back and let the other players each take their turn. Then, you *must* replace the marker prior to striking your next putt, by executing those steps in reverse order. If not, then it's a penalty on you for playing a ball from a wrong location.

To Replace Your Ball

Put the ball back down as close as possible to the front of the marker. Trying to steal an inch or two reveals inexperience, and some might even call it cheating.

Don't Lick Your Balls

Always use a wet towel to clean your ball after you've marked its location on the green. You'd be shocked at how many people regularly drag their tongue across a filthy ball—or pop the whole thing into their mouth—to clean it. I've even heard a couple of stories about players dying on the spot from anaphylactic shock, due to licking a chemically contaminated ball. Most courses will post a sign on the first tee to warn when a fresh coat of fertilizer has been sprayed. If not, they should. But as a hard-and-fast rule, don't ever lick your balls to clean them.

Shadow Boxer

Don't cast a shadow over another player's putting line or the hole. It's a distraction and makes the green more difficult to read. This isn't something to worry about at noon. But early in the morning or late in the evening it can be tricky to maneuver around a green without causing an eclipse.

Avoid the Putting Line

Don't stand on either end of another player's putting line while they're putting.

First, your partner (or your caddies) can't stand on your line because it could be construed as "assistance," which is illegal per the rules and a two-stroke penalty.

Second, don't stand on an opponent's line because it's distracting and really bad form.

Fix Two Pitch Marks on Every Green

A pitch mark is the dent made in the surface of the green by the ball when it lands. They're devastating to the condition of a green. Always fix two of them, even if your ball didn't make one. Inevitably, some cretins will have left theirs. An unrepaired pitch mark shows laziness and disrespect.

If you don't know how to fix a pitch mark, go ask your local pros. I guarantee they'll be glad to show you, since your inquiry will demonstrate your willingness to help take care of the course.

Tread Lightly

Avoid causing accidental damage to the surface of the green or the cup. If damage should occur, do your best to repair it promptly. Here are some common ways that it can happen.

- Leaning too heavily on the flagstick or dropping it
- Leaning too heavily on a putter
- Fishing the ball out of the hole with the putter head

- Damaging the lip of the cup when replacing the flagstick or stepping on, or too close to, it
- Downward gunfire and/or jackhammer use on the green (both can be distracting and destructive). If discharging of firearms is absolutely necessary, it's best to do so in a bunker.

Know Your Flag-Tending Responsibilities

Tending the pin is the act of holding on to the flagstick in order to promptly remove it from the cup after a player strikes a putt. It's a key aspect of keeping good rhythm to the game. A player so far from the hole that they can't see it has the option to putt with the flagstick in the hole. Should the ball actually go in while the flag is in place, however, it's a penalty. Hence the need for a flag tender, who should always offer to do it without being asked.

The player whose ball is closest to the hole, once all the balls are on the green, should assume all flagstick responsibilities. Before removing the flagstick, that player should ask all others if they can see the hole well enough to line up their putts. If the answer is no, then:

- Stand near the flagstick with one hand on it. Stay still and out of all other players' putting lines.
- Avoid casting your shadow over the cup or the line of the player who is putting.
- Loosen the base of the flagstick as soon as the putt has been struck, but leave the end in the hole. As the ball gets closer to the hole, remove the flagstick entirely.
- Lay the flag down on the fringe of the green in a location that isn't at either end of another player's putting line. Place it as near as possible to the cup to facilitate a quick getaway.
- The first player to hole his or her ball assumes the remaining flagstick responsibilities, which are to retrieve it and replace it once everyone has completed play of the hole.

PEARLS FROM THE PRO

If it's windy, grasp the cloth flag and pole at the same time. Then lay the flagstick on the ground so the weight of the pole is on top of the cloth flag. This will prevent the flag from flapping in the wind and causing a distraction.

Flag-tending etiquette is essential to the game. Study and practice it. Make sure you're in the right place at the right time in this delicate dance, and you'll quickly earn the appreciation of your playing partners.

Etiquette Is Not a "Sometimes" Thing

> "Golf is like a love affair. If you don't take it seriously, it's no fun; if you do take it seriously, it breaks your heart."
>
> —Arthur Daley

Good golf behavior begins long before the first golf ball is struck from the first tee and lasts well past the final putt. Commitment to the game and adherence to the fundamentals of fair play will take you far in golf—as well as in life.

Willingness to do the little things matters greatly on the golf course and in another of life's great endeavors—a successful marriage. After all, the secrets to success in both realms are much the same: a thick skin, a short memory, and a soft touch. Thoroughly raking the bunker is as considerate an act as squeezing the toothpaste tube from the bottom up. Picking up divots is like picking up dirty clothes, fixing pitch marks is like opening a car door, and tending the pin is like taking out the trash. And that makes keeping up with the group that's in front of you as good as an occasional back rub.

Commitment to the principles of etiquette, like a successful relationship, is a lifelong pursuit that requires consistency and integrity. It will take great effort, but you will reap great rewards when you always treat the game, the golf course, and your playing partners with the same respect that you'd appreciate receiving in return. I'm sure Gramps would be proud.

Chapter 15

Slow Play, Sunburn, and 7-10 Splits

"Have you ever noticed? Anybody going slower than you is an idiot, and anyone going faster than you is a maniac."

—Unknown

We all dance to a different beat. Some express effortless rhythm, fluidity, balance, and grace while others, like me, lurch pathetically, stagger, and flail—all knees and elbows like a high-speed waterskiing accident. All of the training and practice in the world can't save those of us cursed by such an unfortunate genetic predisposition. Thanks, Mom!

Just like our individual dance moves, we all play at our own pace. Some are ultrafast speedsters; others are glacially slow. Some have an innate awareness of their surroundings, with an instinct to adapt to conditions and change pace accordingly. Others remain oblivious, even when faced with the most blatant evidence of their own drudgery. Still others are totally aware, but unconcerned, and sometimes even angrily defensive, about their dawdling and deliberate tempo. It's not their problem, so why hurry? Many have the attitude that because they paid to play the course, they're going to play at their own pace, regardless of their impact on the rest of the golfers behind them—a very self-centered perspective.

> "It does not take sharp eyes to see the sun and the moon, nor does it take sharp ears to hear the thunderclap. Wisdom is not obvious. You must see the subtle and notice the hidden to be victorious."
>
> —Sun Tzu

The 3 Degrees of Slow Play

I've never understood why players get so offended when a group behind them is playing faster, or when the course marshal or golf professional asks them to speed up or let another group play through. It makes no sense. No one is saying that they're bad people or lousy golfers, just that the pace of their round is slower than that of others, causing congestion. I wonder if the same people who want to argue or fight with the faster group or the pro feel the same way about every passing motorist on the highway. Some people drive faster than others—and usually we'll move over to the right-hand lane to let them pass. It's no big deal—just common courtesy.

Allowing another group to play through should be seen as no less of a common courtesy. It isn't an attack on one's manhood or personal character, although the ridiculous defensiveness that sometimes turns to thuggery suggests otherwise.

HOMEWORK

Ask your local pro how many times they've been violently threatened by a group of golfers for telling them to quicken their pace, or how many times they've had to call the police to escort a group from the golf course as a result. I'm certain the answer will shock you.

It's important to understand that nothing can ruin a golf experience like slow play. Nothing. Bad weather, a poorly conditioned course, a man behind the wheel of the beverage cart, lousy play, or idiot playing partners all pale in comparison. Slow play trumps all. I read somewhere that most men would rather be known as a miserable lovemaker, an animal abuser, or a skilled knitter than a slow golfer. It's that bad.

I'm also convinced that pace of play has nothing to do with ability, and everything to do with awareness and adaptability. Every time you take to the course, your objective should be to keep up with the group in front of you. That's it.

When a course is busy, you'll either have to wait for the green or the landing area to clear as you reach the tee of the next hole, or you won't. If not, then you're out of position. This doesn't mean to risk hitting into another group. It does mean being ready to play as soon as the group is safely out of the way.

When there isn't a rabbit-group out in front, then your goal should be to play in as close to two hours per nine holes as possible. If necessary, ask the staff for the facility's desired time-per-round. They'll know, believe me, and be thankful that you've acknowledged its importance, because you might be the rabbit for others.

ROOKIE MISTAKES

Don't hit your golf ball into another group intentionally—*ever*. It's never appropriate to risk killing or seriously injuring another player because they've been playing slowly. As much as it feels like it should be, slow play is not punishable by death.

If you hit a ball that's headed directly for another group, yell "fore!" If you actually do hit into the group, then sincerely apologize promptly and make sure it doesn't happen again. Occasionally, a group can be out of sight around a corner, or you could nuke a 3-wood or make another such honest mistake. Just apologize as quickly as possible by walking or driving up to the group on the next tee, or wherever the most practical first intersection may occur. If they're angry, don't be confrontational. Just say you're sorry, make it clear that it was an honest mistake, and walk or drive away.

If you're playing in a group that gets hit into, give the guilty player or group the benefit of the doubt—once. If it happens again, you've got every right to be angry. This doesn't mean you can hit a player's ball back at him/her or stomp it into the ground. It does mean you should expect a prompt apology—and if none is given, perhaps a conversation with the golf pro or the course marshal is a practical course of action. Assume it was an accident, expect an apology, but don't seek revenge or justice. Always take the high road.

1st-Degree Burn: How to Keep Up

This is a fine pace of play—a nicely bronzed tan if you will. Here's how to keep it.

Stay Aware

Pay attention to the groups in front of and behind you at all times, and adjust your pace to theirs. You don't need to be obsessed to the point of distraction, just aware.

Be Ready to Play When It's Your Turn

That means completing all your pre-shot preparations before your turn. While others are playing you can set your bag down or get out of the cart, determine yardage and appropriate club selection, toss blades of grass to gauge wind strength and direction, read the green to choose a putting line, and take practice swings. When it's your turn, all that's left to do is swing.

ROOKIE MISTAKES

Interest in watching others, and ignorance of how to simultaneously prepare, causes the most drastic slowdown. It's necessary to be able to do both things at once. It's very common for rookie players to start their preparations when it's their turn, rather than have them done in advance.

Scorekeeping

Mark the scores at, or on the way to, the next hole—not at the green of the hole that's just been completed. The scorekeeper shouldn't have to ask for your scores on every hole. And don't assume that they've paid enough attention to count your strokes, either. At the completion of each hole as you're leaving the green, tell the scorekeeper your score.

Help Each Other Out

Be ready to pitch in with these and other opportunities:

Help others watch their shot to eliminate lost balls, or when necessary, join the search. Since *The Rules of Golf* allows up to five minutes for a search, this can be a huge time-saver, especially if someone in your group has poor vision.

Announce yardages to the other players when you're the first to determine yours. Even if their ball isn't exactly the same distance from the target, it can still help (unless you're in a tournament, since offering assistance does have rules implications).

Pull the cart up if another player chooses to advance on foot.

Grab clubs for others, by either picking them up off the ground or bringing a putter to the green, so they won't have to backtrack and waste time.

Rake a greenside bunker for someone if you're going to be the last to putt and they'll be the first. Or, hit your putt first, whether in the proper order or not, so they'll have time to rake properly and prepare to putt without feeling rushed.

Ask first, but be willing to mark the ball for another player if he has chipped or pitched from a distance away and you're already closer to the hole (or to where his ball ended up).

If there's an opportunity to help out, whether during a casual round or in competition, pitch in and do what you can. Most likely the favor will be gladly returned. It's a great way to score extra points with your playing partners, too. It's always nice to be popular.

STORY TIME

I read a story about a high school golf coach who had his team in position to win a major tournament. A player on the opposing team was searching frantically for a lost ball on the very last hole. As it happened, the coach was following that group, instinctively joined in the search for the opponent's ball, and found it. Talk about a dilemma! The coach informed the player without hesitation.

The player went on to save par, which, as you might guess, saved the day. The opponents won by a stroke.

When asked about it later, the coach said he hadn't even considered not helping out. It's what he'd been trained to do his entire life. It was a lesson he hoped his players would learn to accept and appreciate, although at the time they may not have seen beyond the short-term disappointment. I have a feeling that someday they will. Good for him.

Develop an Efficient Pre-Shot Routine

The length of your pre-shot routine should be directly proportionate to your scores. Now, I'm not saying that it's appropriate for a good player to take a long time, or that a beginner should hurry. I'm saying that it's bad form to grind over every swing as if your life depends on the outcome, especially if you're holding up the other golfers on the course—or in your group. There's a time and a place to be deliberate, and a busy course isn't either.

It's good to have a consistent pre-shot routine. It will certainly help to lower your scores. But when the routine becomes a cumbersome, time-consuming, PGA Tour wannabe production every time, it can be a real drag for everyone who's forced to endure it with you.

Gather information quickly, be decisive when it's your turn, and limit your practice swings to unique situations or uneven lies.

Don't Waste Time Between Shots

Be quick about everything you do between shots—from tying your shoe to replacing your divots to going to the washroom.

Park the cart or set your golf bag down between the green and the next tee box. That way you can get your equipment on the way to the next hole.

This same principle applies when setting extra clubs down on the side of the green. Set them down where they won't be forgotten and where you won't waste time retrieving them. Off of the green on your way to the next hole is a logical location.

PEARLS FROM THE PRO

To ensure that you never lose another wedge by leaving it on the side of the green, lay your extra club(s) on top of the flagstick once it's been pulled and laid down.

Limit Extra Trips to and from the Cart

Take the stuff you need with you when you leave the bag or get out of the cart.

- Take several clubs when your next shot is from an area where you can't reasonably predict the lie of the ball or the condition of the ground.
- Always take your putter when you're anywhere near the green.

- Carry the sand bottle to the tee box on par threes.
- Take three clubs to the tee of every par three. You may choose to play a specific shot type, or the wind might swirl and change direction, or any of a number of other factors may cause you to change clubs. Take the club you think you'll hit and the clubs on either side of it. Do this on the par 3s and not on the other holes because on most par 4s and par 5s, the goal is to hit the ball as straight and far as possible from the tee—usually with a driver or a 3-wood. On the par 3s, however, the distance the ball travels is the most important part of the equation. It's nice to have options with you, should factors that influence how far you might hit the ball change (wind, elevation, anger over a three-putt, blood alcohol content, recent HGH injections, etc.).
- Keep an extra golf ball in your pocket if you've already hit a few balls out of bounds. It's very painful to endure watching a playing partner repeatedly return to the cart (or the bag) to get ball after ball after ball—on every tee!

HISTORY LESSON

Slow play is the primary reason for the existence of private golf clubs. The members of such facilities have always been willing to pay for the privilege of playing golf with less congestion than is typical at most public golf courses. Over time, private courses began to compete against each other for the entertainment dollar, and they've morphed into the bait that lures would-be patrons to purchase a membership. But the genesis of the genre wasn't power, wealth, privilege, prestige, location, or course—it was avoidance of slow play.

It's no different really than paying extra for any amenity that isn't part of a standard offering. Usually the upgrade comes at a price.

2nd-Degree Burn: How to Catch Up

Here's where you'll notice that your golden tan has turned lobster-red and stings a bit. Perhaps it's even begun to peel. If this is the case, immediate attention is required to save your hide.

You should always take responsibility for your own pace of play and for that of your group. If you've fallen behind, you no longer have the privilege to play at your own pace. When you realize (or have been told by an authority) that your group is out of position, you have an immediate obligation to catch up as quickly as possible. Here's how to close the gap.

Hustle

Until you've caught up, double-time it. Hustle between shots. Walk swiftly to and from the cart and ball, tee box, and green. Quicken the pace of your pre-shot routine. Do whatever you can to play more quickly.

Play "Ready Golf"

Some would say you should always play "ready golf" to help maintain your position on the course, as well as proper timing and rhythm within your group. When a player is ready to go, he/she should, regardless of whether it's his/her honor on the tee or he/she is the farthest from the hole. Everyone should be on board with the decision to pick up the pace. Switching to ready golf is the easiest way to regain your position.

If you're engaged in a golf game that requires players to tee off in a specific order, plan accordingly and be ready to go as quickly as possible when you're up. Otherwise, the game should be temporarily abandoned if it's slowing your pace.

Tee Off When You've Finished Putting

There's nothing wrong with handing off your flag-tending responsibilities when you're the first to putt out, then going to the next hole and teeing off while the rest of the group putts. Just let another player know what you're doing, and ask them to put the flagstick back when all are done.

Change the Game

If hustle and ready golf don't seem to be closing the gap between your group and the one in front of you, then be willing to change the game a bit.

- Employ the "Lateral Rule": Treat all golf balls that might be lost or OB as if they went into a lateral water hazard. Add a stroke penalty to your score and drop another ball near the location where the original ball went out.
- Concede putts that are "in the leather": This means that if the ball is within the length of the bottom end of the putter grip and the hole, then it's good. The stroke is counted, but the putt isn't required to be struck.

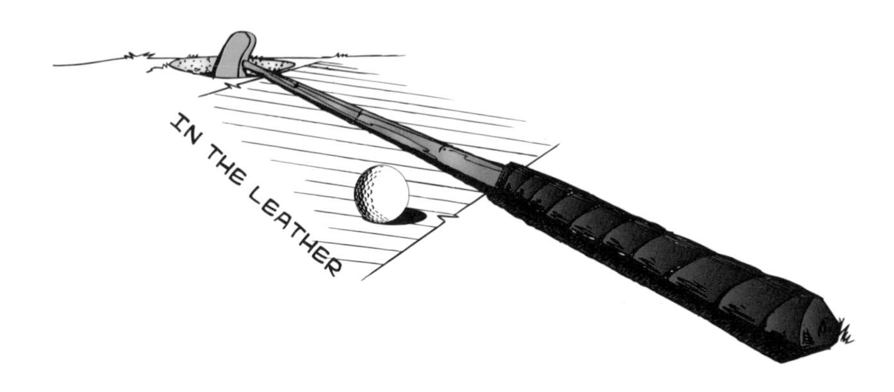

3rd-Degree Burn: Try Bowling

This is an all-out blistered and peeling mess of flesh. Get out of the sun, apply cream, and cool down immediately. Lengthy exposure to this kind of slow play can be carcinogenic. Seek professional help promptly.

If you ever notice (or are told) that you're more than an entire hole behind the group in front of you, it's time to take drastic measures.

Conventional instruction says to stand aside and let a group play through when you're unable to catch up and obviously slowing down the play behind you. But this isn't always the most appropriate course of action when a golf course is busy. Letting a group play through doesn't solve the problem, it just creates a new one. The best thing to do is skip a hole to catch up.

At this point it's your obligation to the rest of the players on the course to do whatever you must to maintain the proper pace for all. Considering that being behind has an exponentially negative effect on all the golfers that will play the course for the entire day, your round of 17 holes instead of 18 is a fair sacrifice.

If the course isn't busy, or there isn't a group immediately behind the group that's behind you (two groups back), then let the group play through. Sometimes groups fall behind. No big deal; it happens. Sometimes a group isn't behind at all; another group is just playing faster. In either of these situations, it's appropriate to let the group that's following play through.

How to Let a Group Play Through

While leaving the green, announce or motion to the group behind you (by waving your arm, as if to gesture "hey y'all, come on over here") of your intent to let them through on the next hole.

Proceed to the next hole and hit your tee shots. Wait for them to catch up and do the same.

Then follow the group to the fairway. You'll want to be there to begin the search for your golf balls, to ensure that the other group doesn't mistake your balls for theirs, and so you'll be in position should another group catch up during the play through.

How to Play Through

Clearly acknowledge the invitation to play through, and make it clear that you intend to do so.

Hustle to finish the play of the hole you're on—but not to the point that you risk sacrificing your performance.

Be polite, and thank the group for their thoughtfulness.

Don't take excessive time searching for lost balls. Temporarily revert to the lateral rule and concede putts in the leather.

IF I RULED THE WORLD

The Play-Through Tax

Any group that plays through another must purchase the played-through group a round of drinks, provided:

a. the players in the group that's being played through appear to be of legal drinking age, and

b. the group that's being played through is playing at a reasonable pace. No "drink poaching."

Note: If it's not possible to purchase drinks on the golf course, then do so after the round.

I think we'd all be more willing to let a group play through if it becomes customary to get a drink out of the deal. Let's do this! Let a group play through, get a drink. Play through a group, buy them a drink. Simple. Now it's up to you . . .

PEARLS FROM THE PRO

Getting stuck behind a slow group can be exasperating. How you handle those situations is important, especially when you're hosting guests. As the host, your attitude will be contagious, so do your best to remain calm and collected, which will go a long way toward making the most of the frustrating situation.

Here's a game the whole group can play that will help kill some of the downtime: it's called Poison. Play for dollars, drinks, or a mulligan when it's finally your turn to tee off. Poison takes place on the tee box; it is similar to croquet, without the wickets. The goal is to putt your ball, using your driver, and ricochet it off of the opposite tee marker, then back to the tee marker you're standing near, then back again to the other, and finally, strike another player's ball. The first player to hit all three tee markers and another's ball wins. Players get one shot per turn, unless their ball hits a tee marker or another player's ball, in which case they can go again.

Walk Another Mile in These Shoes

On behalf of golf pros everywhere, allow me to appeal to your inner slow player. Let's get one thing straight from the start—marshaling stinks! We're not cruising around the course monitoring each group's pace of play because we want to. It's not a good time. But it's an absolutely critical component to operating a successful golf operation, and to that end, we must do it.

It's a no-win situation. If a group is playing slowly, they'll get angry with the marshal for telling them to speed up. If a group is being held up, they'll get angry with the marshal for not doing anything about it. In either case, the course marshal is the bad guy.

Slow play is as challenging to manage as sandbagging is, for many of the same reasons. You (the pro) might really like the offenders. Slow players can be fun people—perhaps some of your favorites. They might be members of the board of directors or friends of the owner. They might buy lots of stuff in the golf shop and you might even give them lessons and profit handsomely as a result. The last thing you want to do is get some of your most supportive or influential patrons upset with you by telling them to play faster. They might decide to play elsewhere, or worse, decide it's time for you to work elsewhere.

All we ask is that you keep up with the group in front of you. If that's not possible, then do something about it. If you see a marshal or professional driving the course, let it remind you that your pace matters. If you're asked by an authority to speed up, don't get defensive or take it personally. We're just doing our job.

If a pattern of slow play persists, it might be time to consider changing your golfing habits. Maybe playing at a different time of day, or a different day altogether, is necessary. Or perhaps it's time to take up bowling.

Can I play through?

Chapter 16

Finish the Whole

"A whole is that which has a beginning, a middle, and an end."

—Unknown

Here's to the finisher, that rare breed of person who not only takes on a daunting task but also sees it to the end with grace and style. Good golf requires you to be a strong finisher. Follow these steps to making a positive and lasting impression when the game's over.

Keep It Classy

Take your hat and sunglasses off and shake hands with every player in your group before you leave the 18th green. Make eye contact and sincerely acknowledge the few hours you've just shared. Who cares if you just four-putted the last green and lost a few bucks because of it? Shrug it off and show some class.

Clean Up After Yourself

Just like good carpenters do with their tools, take care of your equipment before you put it away.

Clubs

With a wet towel or a scrub brush, clean the gunk off every club. It's nice to have fresh equipment when you start your next round, and it's better than trying to scrape off caked-on dead grass and dirt days later. Also, putting away wet clubs can cause them to rust. Dry them off. Pay attention, take the time, and respect your equipment.

Shoes

Dirt, mud, and grass on your shoes can stain the leather and cause you to replace them before their time. Cleaned and shined golf shoes should last for many years. Some courses offer the service, while others will make a brush or an air hose available for you to clean up your own kicks. Either way, take it upon yourself to keep your shoes fresh and clean.

Gloves

Strap your glove to the outside of your golf bag. This preserves its freshness by allowing it to dry out in a usable shape, rather than wadding it up and stuffing it into a random pocket. When a glove gets holey, wrinkly, slick, or crusty, it's time to replace it. Playing with a worn-out glove defeats the purpose and reveals inexperience.

Thank the Staff

Always stop by the golf shop when your round is done to say a quick thank-you to the staff. It's nice, and it also tells them that your group's no longer on the golf course, which might be important information. Perhaps the cart you used is needed for a group that's waiting. Maybe the superintendent wants to water some of the greens. Or maybe the pro will send some employees home to avoid paying overtime. Many things go on behind the scenes that the normal golfer probably wouldn't ever consider. Letting the staff know when you're done by thanking them is a great way to help out.

> "There will come a time when you believe everything is finished. That will be the beginning."
> —Louis L'Amour

The Art of Tipping

If tipping is permitted, and somebody does something for you that is tip worthy, then shell out. The shoe guy in the locker room who shines your kicks, the valet attendant who fetches your car, or the club scrubber kid who buffs your wrenches all deserve a buck or two here or there.

It's usually safe to assume that the staff "pools" their tip money at the end of the day, so each employee gets an equal share. Thus, tipping one person from each area is the same as tipping them all. For example, you should tip the valet attendant who retrieves your vehicle post-golf, but not the attendant who parks it upon your arrival.

Here's how to read the signals that tell you when a staff person is hanging around and expecting you to dig deep, instead of just going about his/her job:

Employee: "Hey, Mr. Member, how'd you play today?"
Translation: Please give me $2.
Employee: "Hi, Mrs. Member. I love those shoes. Are they new?"
Translation: Please give me $2.
Employee: "I've got your car pulled up to the front. Would you like me to put your clubs in the trunk, or will you leave them here?"
Translation: Please give me $2.
Employee: "I noticed that your grips are getting worn. Would you like me to re-grip them for you?"
Translation: Please give me $2.
Employee: "Can I clean those shoes up before you go?"
Translation: Please give me $5.
Employee: "Hi," "Hello," or "How are you?"
Translation: Please give me $2. Please give me $2. Please give me $2.

> "It's not tipping I believe in, it's overtipping."
> —Vinnie Antonelli (*My Blue Heaven*, 1990)

Knowing how it will be appreciated, what's the right way to discreetly hand an employee a tip?

Steering-Wheel Clip

The easiest way to leave a tip for the service staff is to clip a few dollars to your cart's steering wheel. That's as long as there's someone whose responsibility it is to clean your clubs and transport them to your car or bag storage. Believe me, they'll know who it came from.

Pass the Baton

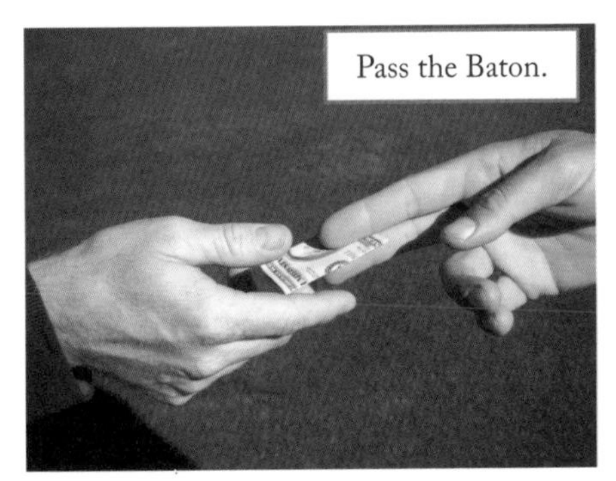
Pass the Baton.

Fold the money in half, then in half again, and put it between the first two fingers of your right hand. This conceals the amount, but not the money. You don't want to hide the money. Rather, make it obvious so the receiver can see it coming and will reach for it, instead of being fooled into thinking you're coming in for a handshake. It's like a sprinter passing the baton in a relay race.

Here are some tipping techniques to avoid.

The Shake

Although a tried-and-true method for generations, this isn't a reliable method for passing off a few bucks at the golf course. That's because most people don't shake hands with the service staff. So, when the cash-in-the-palm handshake is offered, the staff person usually isn't expecting it and doesn't know how to handle it, causing one of those awkward and uncomfortable moments. Admit it—you know exactly what I'm talking about.

The shake should be reserved for passing off much larger amounts. I regularly got those glorious handshakes during tournament weeks. Rather than tip each employee a few bucks independently (which wasn't permitted in the first place), many members gave me much larger handfuls of love to divvy up among the staff as I saw fit.

The Drop

I've seen members at so-called non-tipping clubs drop money on the ground and say something like, "Oops . . . you'd better grab that before it blows away." The sentiment is nice, and generally appreciated, I'm sure. But picking a tip up off the ground is degrading to the employee. Please refrain. Not only are you breaking a rule, you're breaking a spirit.

STORY TIME

I heard a ridiculous story along these lines about a new highfalutin private golf club—which I'll leave nameless. Apparently, on the first day of their big member-guest tournament all the employees were required to go down onto the practice range, and in front of several hundred participants, an airplane flew overhead and dropped a bunch of money for the employees to chase around and fight over. I can't imagine what the management was thinking, or why they agreed to such a disrespectful act, but that stinks. Hey, maybe next year they'll turn the sprinklers on, too!

Pickpocket

Don't *ever* (never, ever, ever) slide a few bucks into an employee's pocket—regardless of your gender or the employee's. Did I say never? It could be misconstrued as inappropriate, and you'll run the risk of getting in trouble for an otherwise innocent act of kindness. It's just not worth the risk.

Shiver Me Timbers

Unless it's from a sunken treasure, don't tip with coins. Enough said.

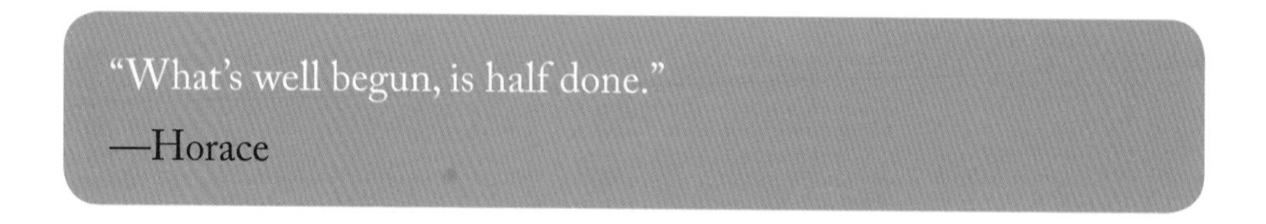

"What's well begun, is half done."

—Horace

Client and Guest Hosting (Part IV)

After the round, you must continue to be the director. Just because your round is finished, it doesn't mean your job as the host is. You've still got work to do.

Pay the Caddie

If you have a caddie, it's up to you to make sure he or she gets paid. Discuss this with your playing partners on the 18th tee (not green). If you intend to pay, you could say something like this, for example:

"Hey guys, when we get done I'll pay the caddie fee. If you want to kick in five or ten or twenty bucks each for gratuity, that's up to you, but I've got the base amount covered."

Pass the baton to the caddie as soon as possible following the round. Sometimes players forget to pay and adjourn to the grill—or worse, they leave altogether. The caddie will inevitably think they got stiffed and report it to the professional, who then will have to put the squeeze on the golfers. That's embarrassing for all, but especially for you, the host.

Direct Traffic

Send the players where they should go next: to the locker room to wash up, to the grill for some grub, or to the parking lot to drop off their gear at the car. Then, give the staff instructions such as putting the clubs in the cars or storage, or pulling the vehicles up to valet.

19th-Hole Etiquette

Post-golf chatter can get boring fast. Everyone wants to talk about themselves and their game and all the missed opportunities that would've turned their 95 into a 74. If you're the host, don't fall into the trap. Instead, make it a point to mention the great shots that everyone else hit. It shows that you paid attention. Your playing partners will appreciate it because they can answer your question, instead of shamelessly talking about themselves. Without even knowing why, your partners will have a sense that you're a fun person to play with.

PEARLS FROM THE PRO

While socializing after a round of golf, I always pose this question to my group: "What was the best shot you hit today?" Make sure you actually listen to their answers before turning the conversation back to yourself and your own game. It's a nice way to get your playing partners or guests to remember their good shots and finish the whole round on a positive note.

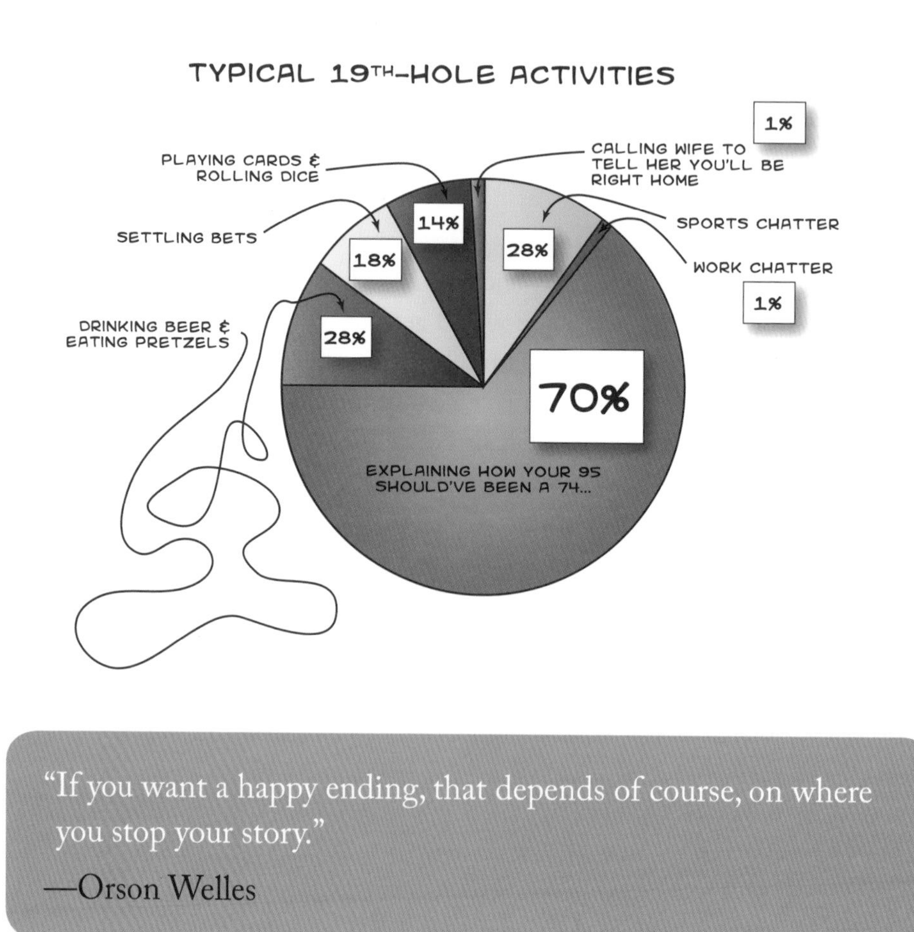

> "If you want a happy ending, that depends of course, on where you stop your story."
>
> —Orson Welles

Take a Final Inventory

Before you leave the property, take a thorough inventory of your stuff. Make sure you're leaving with everything you had when you got there, plus everything else you may have purchased or collected along the way.

Lost Clubs

It's very irritating to lose a club (most likely, a wedge). If you notice that it's missing before you leave the property and alert the staff while you're still there, the likelihood of recovering the stray club increases.

Check the Golf Cart

Cell phones, watches, sweaters, sunglasses, headcovers, and car keys are easy to leave behind. After you've checked your golf bag, make a complete inspection of the golf cart. It's a simple procedure that will eliminate avoidable panic.

Check the Trunk

If a staff person was supposed to get your clubs from the cart to your trunk, double-check to make sure they did. Once or twice every year at The Quarry and at Black Rock, a set of clubs would get put into the wrong "white SUV." On one memorable occasion a set of clubs was placed into the wrong vehicle, then went into the wrong airplane, which ultimately ended up on the wrong continent. Goofs like that occasionally occur. They can be incredibly frustrating and time-consuming to sort out, yet easy to eliminate by taking a quick glance at the gear in the back of your rig.

When you choose to play golf, take control of the entire experience, regardless of where you are or who you're with. At the end of the day, you'll earn respect and admiration for your effortless-seeming management of all the subtle nuances of this wonderful adventure we call golf.

> "Any man's finest hour, his greatest fulfillment to all he holds dear, is the moment when he has worked his heart out in a good cause and lies exhausted on the field of battle victorious."
> —Vince Lombardi

IMPACT (ĭm'păkt') v.
To affect or influence, especially in a significant manner.

Taking Your Game to the Next Level

Chapter 17

Tales from an Irish Rest Stop

"Golf is the cruelest of sports. Like life, it's unfair. It's a harlot. A trollop. It leads you on. It never lives up to its promises . . . It's a boulevard of broken dreams. It plays with men. And runs off with the butcher."

—Jim Murray

Men enjoy hanging out with other men, especially if they share a common interest in, or have a chance to beat each other at, something—anything. We thrive on the camaraderie that comes from friendly competition.

Hence the joys and adventures of one of golf's finest pleasures, the Men's Golf Trip, or MGT for short. It's much like one would imagine—stinky men who scratch themselves, play golf from dawn to dusk, drink responsibly, tell golfing-hunting-fishing stories, overeat, compete at everything, try to act like we're not competing at everything, and overeat some more.

Before departure, of course, we take the Golfhusbandocratic Oath, similar to the physicians' Hippocratic Oath but defined thusly instead: "An oath traditionally taken by married men pertaining to the ethical and rigorous practice of playing golf—oftentimes out of town."

A foursome makes a quorum. The guy with the lowest handicap can swear you in. Men, raise your right hand and repeat after me:

"We, men (generally), love our wives more than golf. We, gentlemen of leisure, do enjoy spending some time on the golf course with our families.

However, we, fellow links enthusiasts who understand the necessity of occasionally getting out of town and playing golf with the guys, do solemnly swear to uphold this sacred tradition. And we, fellow competitors of honesty and virtue, pledge to not say or do anything too stupid when we're gone, to be representative of our positions as relatively competent heads-of-household, and to think of our wives more than we can convincingly convey to them upon our return—so we won't even try."

If you haven't yet had the pleasure of experiencing a great MGT—you're missing out. A well-executed golf trip can be the catalyst to spark or renew your enthusiasm for the game and perhaps rekindle the fire of friendships lost.

There's something special that happens when like-minded people share a unique experience, especially on a golf course. Seeing familiar faces in new places is what makes memories. Golf is almost never about where you've been—only the memory of the experience that remains. So listen up, and start planning that trip!

DISCLAIMER:
Ladies, please forgive me for neglecting you here. Although I've heard they exist, I've never been on a Women's Golf Trip, or WGT for short. Nor do I feel I can speak intelligently on the subject. I would assume they are essentially the same as an MGT, but with noticeably less scratching.

The 10 Commandments of Men's Golf Trips

I. Thou Shalt Behave Accordingly

There are many reasons to schedule an MGT—tournaments, an early-season club dust-off in a warmer climate, or most commonly, semi-serious golf at a destination course or courses. Determine the reason for your scheduled excursion, and set your expectations accordingly. Then behave in a manner that supports those expectations. For example, you should get a necessary amount of sleep if you're competing, or stay up late to howl at the moon if you're out for fun and games with your buddies. The trip will be what you make of it.

STORY TIME

One time I let Troy talk me into going to Seattle, Washington, with him to compete in the Northwest Open Tournament. To him, there was potential for significant financial reward. For me, not so much. But I agreed nonetheless.

We hauled his dad's camper trailer several hundred miles across the state and easily spent what we were trying to save in airfare on gasoline. Oh well. Getting there is part of the process.

After the practice round, we threw a huge RV party and parking lot poker game. We were up really, really late—and we had to tee off really, really early. At some point Troy did a stage dive from the top step of the RV into the coolers and yard furniture below. Crash, bang, boom! The result was a broken rib and some painful bruising.

Needless to say, he didn't play very well, which was unfortunate because he practiced extensively to prepare, we drove quite a distance to get there, and we paid a lot of money to compete.

One good thing did come out of it, though. He played so poorly we were paired together for the final round, which was fun for me. For him, probably not so much.

II. Thou Shalt Be Organized

If reservations are required, confirm them—especially the ones for travel, golf, and lodging. You'll enjoy your trip a lot more without any avoidable delays. This includes pick-ups and drop-offs at airports, restaurants, and golf courses. If driving directions are needed, have them prepared ahead of time. Be efficient, and don't pass the burden of your disorganization or tardiness somewhere else, such as the busy golf course you're planning to play.

STORY TIME

During an amazing, all-expenses paid MGT to Scottsdale, the two friends of mine who threw the trip flew into town a day early to confirm golf and lodging reservations, pick up the rental vehicles, and do the grocery shopping ahead of time. When the rest of us arrived, everything was done. We were able to sit back, relax, and enjoy the company and the golf without a worry in the world. Job well done, guys!

Conversely, during my first trip to Ireland, after more than thirty hours of travel time, there was a mix-up at Knoch Airport with our reservation for two large SUVs. Instead, we ended up with a van and a tiny two-seater car. It was another two hours before everything was unsuccessfully sorted out, because we were still stuck with the alternative vehicles they offered us.

It was a lousy way to start a trip—sitting and waiting so close to the final destination, yet unable to get unpacked, cleaned up, and settled. Worse yet, shuttling the large group and equipment from hotel to golf course all week long became a significant chore.

III. Thou Shalt Be Flexible

Be willing to roll with the punches when the unexpected occurs. Hiccups such as delayed flights, road construction, or inclement weather are unavoidable, and the way you handle those disappointments will be contagious.

STORY TIME

One morning while at Bandon Dunes, I chose to ride to the golf course in one vehicle while my golf clubs went in the other. I assumed one of the guys in that rig would grab my sticks when they got to the course. I was wrong. Our chauffeur/masseuse/chef drove into town for groceries to prepare our crab feast for the night (are you feeling sorry for me yet?) with my clubs still in the back.

If you ask anyone who was on that trip, they'll tell you I was *hot* when I left to chase after my clubs. Unfortunately, my anger made the other guys feel awful. I'm sure I affected their enjoyment of the course for the first few holes. What's more, I made the staff feel terrible, too.

By the time I returned with my gear, I'd regrouped and realized that the error was really mine. I hadn't specifically asked anyone to take responsibility for my clubs. All in all, I missed only the first three holes, but I unnecessarily made the whole episode a great big deal.

Another key to flexibility is allowing time for the participants to have the option to do whatever they please. They might decide to rest, sightsee, or play more golf. They might go out or stay in. There will never be a consensus, so don't expect everyone to do everything together.

STORY TIME

During the downtime at Bandon Dunes, we enjoyed hiking to the beach, ping-pong, billiards, darts, naps, and backgammon. Evening poker games and backyard basketball were the primary alternate activities in Arizona. It's nice to enjoy post-golf entertainment that doesn't require money or driving anywhere.

Conversely, during my first jaunt abroad, we had a dominant alpha male in our group who required that we go where he wanted to go, eat where he wanted to eat, and sit where he wanted to sit. We ended up frequenting the same pub every night.

But on the last night of the trip, a stopover in London for a Van Morrison concert, I had wearied of pack life, smoke-filled European pubs, and lads with bad sweaters and worse teeth. I decided to go lone wolf and explore the city on my own. It was one of the best nights of any trip I've taken.

I had a pocketful of English currency I needed to spend or convert at the airport—so, of course, I spent it. But not as you might expect. I decided to feed as many homeless people as I could afford. For several hours that night I bought hot meals (cheeseburgers and french fries with vinegar) for the less fortunate who were stranded out in the bitter cold. It was an experience I'll never forget.

IV. Thou Shalt Stay Put

It's been my experience that staying in one place is better than constantly moving from course to course and hotel to hotel for two reasons. It's fun to play the same course multiple times, and it's also nice to unpack, feel organized, and have a home base.

Here's why I've enjoyed playing a smaller number of courses repeatedly. I find that I play better the second or third time as I become familiar with the track because there aren't any surprises on blind shots; because I get more comfortable with the turf and the way the club and ball react to it; and because I have a better idea of what club to use on a specific hole or a specific shot type that's unique to the terrain. If it's a good course, I'd rather play it multiple times from different tees to different hole locations rather than play a series of other courses just to add notches to my conquest belt.

In my opinion, the best possible scenario is a destination with multiple golf courses within walking or driving distance. You can stay in the same bed every night and play different courses during the day. As a bonus, you can play extra evening rounds on the courses you've previously played during the trip.

STORY TIME

The only complaint I heard from some of the guys on our tour of Ireland (my second trip to the Emerald Isle) was that we actually played too much golf. I have to agree. We spent most of our time on the motor coach and rarely had a chance to unpack our suitcases. We were always on the go (literally) to get to the next hotel or the next golf course. We played fantastic courses and stayed in amazing hotels. But it was a relief when we finally spent three nights in Killarney, where we were able to unpack, relax, and enjoy the local culture. It sounds silly to complain about such a once-in-a-lifetime trip, but next time I'll plan to slow things down a little.

An Irish rest stop

Two of my finest memories of that trip come from our stay in Killarney and have nothing to do with golf.

Late one evening we stumbled into the hotel bar, where we found a wedding reception winding down. The large family invited us to join in their tradition of singing to each other. Sitting in a circle, they took turns singing their favorite traditional Irish anthems. It was beautiful and inspiring. I even shed a tear or two, as did my mates. The voices were perfect and passionate, and the laughter, love, and sweet sounds of the country were intoxicating—until it was my turn to sing. Somehow each of my fellow Americans was able to decline the family's insistence that we each sing a solo of our own. But not me!

You might think I would have chosen the national anthem, a cultural classic, or perhaps even a sentimental love song. Sadly, I did not. With the entire wedding party watching, I belted out an old fraternity beer-drinking chant that was downright appalling. It wasn't one of my finer moments, but it was memorable nonetheless. Sometimes I wonder if that Irish family shares any fond recollections of the American baboon who crashed their party.

The very next night, while enjoying downtown Killarney, I was invited onstage to sing with the band—or so I thought. As I clambered happily up to join the musicians, two of the roughest rugby-playing bouncers I'd ever seen—or, actually, didn't see—collared me from the blind side and threw me into the street. Apparently I hadn't been invited onto the stage after all. As I politely commented about the bouncers' girly bow-ties, my travel mates had to restrain them from sending me back to the States in a body bag. I was told I was the first Yank to be tossed from a bar in Killarney in the last ten years. Maybe it's something I shouldn't be so proud of (and I realize I may have violated the Golfhusbandocratic Oath), but it was great!

As a general rule, if you'll spend more time in the car getting to and from the destination golf course than you'll actually spend on the golf course while you're there, plan to stay the night. For one-nighters or longer trips alike, here are your options.

- *Hotels.* This is the easiest and most common way to go, and someone other than your wife has to clean up after you, which is nice. But hotel lodging usually means eating a lot of spendy restaurant food and not having much room to hang out.
- *House rentals.* If everyone has their own bed, these are the preferred accommodations for a larger group. It might be more expensive than a hotel and require some preparation and cleaning. This way, however, you have somewhere to hang out that doesn't cost money, and it's really nice and significantly less expensive to prepare your own meals and pour your own drinks.
- *Camping.* It's the least expensive mode of lodging, but also the least likely to provide a good night's rest. If that's okay, then combining the two hobbies with friends is a great way to go. Camping does require setup and break-down time, so plan accordingly.

V. Thou Shalt Attempt to Build Camaraderie

Dish out only what you're willing to take. If your friends are anything like mine, you should expect to be made fun of for everything, on or off the course. Feel free to return the ribbing—but only in the same dose you're willing to receive. Nobody likes the sensitive guy with a sharp tongue.

PEARLS FROM THE PRO

To get you started, here are some golf-specific quick jabs you can throw. The rest of your verbal arsenal is up to you. These are things to say after the following occur:

- A poor drive: "Wow, long ball. Did you forget to take the headcover off?"
- A shank: "Holy cow! Did that hit the grip?"

- A lousy putt: Raise your hand, but don't say anything. When the player who hit the miserable putt notices and asks why your hand is raised (he will), then say, "Who else thought that putt was going in?"
- Another lousy putt: Just raise your hand. Nothing else needs to be said. (The rest of the players in the group should all raise their hands, too.)
- A stubbed chip that's left short (pick one): "Release." "Go." "Get up."
- A bladed chip that's racing across the green: "Sit." "Spin." "Pull a hammy."
- Sundown, to the bald(ing) guy: "Would you mind taking your hat off? I need some light."

Make sure that someone gets a nickname. This rule lies at the heart of everything right about an MGT. It will enrich the experience and make the stories afterward even better.

STORY TIME

In Ireland, one of the guys in our group was named Gwil—pronounced like "quill." Apparently it's Welsh. Another guy, Mike, just couldn't pronounce it. Mike tended to call him "Grill" or "Girl." Since this made Gwil quite unhappy, we all decided to call him Bob instead, spelled the same way forward as backward so Mike could say it. He's still called Bob to this day.

Play with every guy in the group. When you care enough to try, you'll learn more about a person in nine holes on the golf course than you can in twice that time at the airport bar.

VI. Thou Shalt Pace Thyself

Moderation in all things is a good motto to live by. But then again, a bunch of men on a trip indulge in a little immoderation from time to time. Just remember that most MGTs are more of a marathon than a sprint, yet most participants come out of the blocks at full speed with their hair on fire.

The biggest culprits for MGT overindulgence are too much drinky-drinky and too much golf. It's easy to ruin the trip for yourself and others by liquid overindulgence, particularly the first night. I understand the feeling of freedom and vacation; remember, though, that you may have to create a good first impression, get up early the next morning, and perform proficiently on the golf course. I speak from experience when I say you'll regret not being able to enjoy the day or be able to play at a level to be proud of because of a drink, or ten drinks, too many.

Believe it or not, you can also sabotage a trip by playing too much golf the first day. Playing until your hands and feet bleed and your back is torqued to exhaustion can cause you pain the rest of the trip. Avoid regrets and get your money's worth by staying in shape to play at your best.

If you must party like a college kid on spring break, do so in the middle of the trip. You'll have already made a good first impression and won't ruin the trip home by being sick in the car or on the plane.

VII. Thou Shalt Leave Thy Work Behind

Enough said. It'll be there waiting for you on your return, or it won't, but either way, don't drag the other guys into the boardroom with you.

Sometimes the line between work-related and recreational golf can get blurred. Sharing work stories or telling someone what you do for a living isn't the same as trying to close a deal. It's important to know the difference.

VIII. Thou Shalt Keep It Friendly

Unless you know all the other participants well enough to have played for money many times before, keep the wagering to a minimum. Here's why.

- The cost of the trip itself may be a financial stretch for some—and the added expense of gambling debt probably wasn't considered.
- Not everyone likes to carry large amounts of cash when they travel.
- Most guys, especially in a large group, won't have the *cojones* to say they can't afford the side action. It's a guy thing.

You can avoid betting by telling the game makers that

- You don't feel like you're playing to a level where you're confident enough to risk your cash.
- You don't want to ruin the experience for yourself and others by thinking about money rather than the golf course and their camaraderie.
- You're broke.

Sometimes it can be even more fun to offer an alternative to cash. For example:

- If you're staying in a rented house or camping, divide the group into teams that play for cooking and cleaning duties each night.
- If you're in a hotel, play for push-ups, sit-ups, a dive into an icy pool, a footrace around the building, a karaoke performance (winner picks the song), or anything that might cause embarrassment or physical exertion, but not cost money.
- Play for dinner, drinks, or appetizers after the round. At least if you end up losing you can put the tab on a credit card (no cash is required).
- Be creative and have a backup plan, or bite the bullet and tell the others that you're not comfortable gambling money you can't afford to lose. Most likely someone else will appreciate your honesty since it'll let them off the hook, too.

STORY TIME

In Arizona, one of the guys got in over his head in our money game and lost a few hundred dollars, mostly to me. I highly doubted that the debt was a comfortable amount for him to give away. The worse he played, the more he lost and the angrier he got. It was difficult to watch this downward spiral, and even more difficult to feel good about profiting from the disaster. Finally he broke down and pleaded for us to "Call off the dogs!"

I've been in those very uncomfortable shoes before, and on the 16th hole I pulled him aside and explained that I'd forgive the debt. To me the point of gambling on the golf course is for motivation, struttin' rights, and friendly competition—not financial gain from my friends or people who can't afford to lose.

When Troy and I traveled by RV to play in the Northwest Open we decided to compete for the privilege of sleeping in the bigger bed each night. Low scorer of the day got to sleep in comfort; the loser was on the fold-out couch. It was plenty of incentive for both of us.

On a golf trip to Florida with my former boss, Chad, we played for dances. Whoever lost the golf match had to find a girl to dance with that night in the hotel lounge. It was harmless, but embarrassing—since I lost and got shot down repeatedly.

A recent acquaintance taught me a game called "$5 Shirt" that I can't wait to play with friends. The monetary portion of the golf game is only $5. But the brilliant part is that the winner gets to pick the shirt that the loser *must* wear during their next match together. Usually it's a rummage sale classic, and hopefully it doesn't fit. Imagine the possibilities . . . hilarious!

IX. Thou Shalt Pack Properly

Take time to prepare, and make sure you have the appropriate gear along. It's quite a disappointment to show up at the destination and realize you've left behind something vital. It's just like my Grandpa always told me—"No matter what anyone says, you really don't want to end up in moose country without your coonskin cap." Or something like that . . .

STORY TIME

During a one-day trip to a warmer climate, a friend of mine learned the lesson of preparation the hard way. Instead of packing the night before, he just threw some gear together in the morning darkness. Upon our arrival he discovered he'd packed one golf shoe and one dress shoe. They were both black, both right feet, and apparently looked like mates earlier that morning. He was forced to buy a new pair of golf shoes, but the only pair in the golf shop wide enough for his massive feet cost $250 and came in electric-orange, white, and black. They were really ugly. He's yet to wear them again.

Gather your things the night before and study the weather before you go. You don't want to lug an umbrella and rain gear around on a sunny day, and you don't want to get caught in a deluge with little more than a windbreaker. Good rain gear is important. If you want to stay warm and dry, plan on making a bit of an investment up front; it will reap dividends every time you use it.

On multiday trips, try to pack as many things that can be worn together as possible. This way you can mix and match and wear a few pairs of pants or shorts multiple times each with a variety of shirts. Bring two pairs of shoes—if one pair gets wet, you can let them dry out while you lace up the other.

PEARLS FROM THE PRO

When packing for a golf trip, remember that few things matter more than having a really good pair of shoes. Bring shoes that you know are comfortable. Before you get blisters, take preventative measures by putting a strip of duct tape across each heel. Trust me, it works!

When packing your clubs into your travel case, wrap a beach towel around the clubheads. This will keep them from banging together and possibly getting damaged.

Don't forget to pack a proper MGT "first aid kit," which should definitely include sunscreen, bug repellent, aspirin, antacids, lip balm, Icy Hot, powder (for any areas that may be chafing), penicillin, sunburn lotion, and bandages.

X. Thou Shalt Try to Get Invited Back

Just like most things in life, what you get out of an MGT depends on what you put into it. Plan to have a great time. Prepare to have a great time. Expect to play your best, but consider the opposite as a possibility and don't overreact if you "take the gas." Be open to the idea of new or deepened friendships. Take some pictures of the places and lots of pictures of the people. But, more than anything, enjoy the process and behave in a manner that might earn you a return invitation.

Be the guy who

- Takes digital pictures, burns them onto CDs, and distributes them at the end of the trip.
- Helps with kitchen detail.
- Is funny, but doesn't seem like he's always trying to be funny.
- Volunteers to be the designated driver a time or two.
- Respects the other players in the group and the facility.
- Doesn't overreact after bad shots or holes.
- Compliments others on good shots, even if the opponents win a couple bucks as a result.
- Buys the on-course beverages, in turn.

Don't be the guy who

- Is an obnoxious drunk.

- Is always on the phone.
- Is a know-it-all, about golf or otherwise.
- Gladly joins in the consumption of food and drink, but never picks up the tab.
- Refuses to play with one, or some, of the other guys.
- Tells too many off-color bathroom jokes or has an excessively foul mouth. Unless, of course, everyone is using bathroom humor—then, don't be the prude.
- Always has a sensational or controversial opinion that's shared with or without invitation.
- Goes to bed early and complains about the noise when the majority of the guys are still up, or stays up really late and makes noise after the majority of the guys have gone to bed.
- Thinks it's funny to grotesquely pass wind.
- Pouts.
- Whines.
- Throws clubs.
- Complains about the condition of the course.
- Takes golf too seriously—and plays slowly as a result.
- Doesn't take golf seriously enough—and is a distraction to those who do.

Really, the best approach is to consider every trip a tryout. At some level, we're all just a bunch of kids on the playground hoping to make the team. Your actions should reflect that desire. Acting like a boob on the golf course, or treating the other guys like punching bags at the bar, is like asking to get sent back to the bench.

As I've said before, where you go is secondary to who you're with—and the best memories will likely not even happen on the course. Like the tortilla chip is to salsa, the french fry to ketchup, or the fish stick to tartar sauce, the golf course is usually less important than the good stuff that goes on top. These commandments will give you the tools to take a mediocre trip and turn it into something magical. Just call me Moses, leading you to the Promised Land . . .

Slieve Donard behind the 9th green at Royal County Down, one of the finer hotel accommodations that I've enjoyed.

Dromoland Castle, Shannon, Ireland—another fine example of humble Irish lodging.

Chapter 18

Gas Guzzlers, Grease Monkeys, and Golf Swings

"One minute you're bleeding. The next minute you're hemorrhaging. The next minute you're painting the *Mona Lisa*."

—Mac O'Grady

It's a good thing I'm a golf teacher instead of an auto mechanic. I have only a primitive knowledge of the way an engine works inside. And that's okay. Yet, I do understand the basics of fuel, spark plugs, pistons, and a carburetor enough to know that all must work together to produce an effective result.

Your knowledge of the golf swing should be similar—a general understanding of the movements required. It's not important to understand every microfunction of each body part. You do need to know how to get answers when questions arise, however, and you need to be willing to ask for help. This is where the twenty-eight thousand PGA members come in. We're trained to fix swings like auto mechanics fix engines.

Your job is to realize when something is wrong and be willing to take the car to the shop. PGA instructors can diagnose the problem and provide a solution. But rather than merely fixing the problem ourselves, we offer you the tools that allow you to repair your own swing for life.

PEARLS FROM THE PRO

I've learned not to teach my family. There's only so much instruction that my wife, parents, and siblings (including my jerk-brother-in-law) are willing to take from me. And honestly, there's only so much incompetence that I'm able to take from them without getting totally frustrated. You shouldn't try to teach your family either. Instead, let a professional handle it. They're trained to use the proper vocabulary, to determine each student's specific learning style, and most importantly, they don't have an emotional attachment that might cause them to be quick to anger if the objective isn't being met.

What Does a Teacher Really Do?

The function of an effective teacher might vary with every student. I prefer to be an adviser who waits for questions, then presents and explains new information, offers drills to help ingrain the desired result, and gives the student space to experiment and explore. The students' role is to take in this new information, challenge it, and make it their own.

A good instructor bridges the gap between the complexity of the motion of a golf swing and its verbal expression. No one will ever know what your swing feels like to you. Everyone will freely tell you what their swing feels like to them and assume that you can then integrate those thoughts into your own paradigm. But no one will ever know your swing. What do you think about? What do you feel? What fingers can you specifically feel in their correct locations when you take your grip? How does that relate to the clubface? How's your posture? How does that relate to swing plane? How's your balance? How does that relate to swing path?

This back-and-forth between student and teacher eventually leads to understanding. And understanding, applied with repetition, will unlock the secrets of your game.

PEARLS FROM THE PRO

Here are my thoughts on golf lessons.

Don't expect your teacher to tell you what you want to hear. If what you're doing isn't working, it needs to change.

Band-Aids don't fix bullet holes. There are no quick fixes, because under pressure or over time we all revert to our old habits. Swing changes take practice and patience.

Don't spend more money on equipment than instruction.

Treat a lesson like an investment. Take notes and write down key concepts so you keep the information. You paid for it!

Don't purchase a package of multiple lessons until you've taken a teacher for a test-drive. Make sure you believe in the method and the instructor before you spend your hard-earned money.

It's okay to take a lesson or two from multiple instructors to see whose philosophy best suits you. Don't feel that you're stuck with your first teacher out of unnecessary loyalty. We all understand.

> "We do not want to be beginners—but let us be convinced of the fact that we will never be anything else but beginners, all of our life!"
>
> —Thomas Merton

We're All Different

As you embark on this journey, remember that each of us looks and learns differently. We each have our own unique physical differences, as well as different expectations, goals, and learning styles.

ROOKIE MISTAKES

It's good to be thirsty for knowledge. But be careful of gathering too much, too fast. I've seen many beginners hang on every conversation with more experienced players to glean tips to help their own game. Remember that what's right for one player might be dead wrong for another.

I've given many lessons when it's become obvious that another player on the range, who isn't paying for the lesson, will eavesdrop on what I'm saying and then try to apply the information to his/her own game. This is dangerous for two reasons. First, if the swing suggestions are taken out of context, they can easily be misunderstood. Second, if the implementation of this advice isn't supervised, it can be incorrectly applied. The truth is that every lesson is intended only for the lesson taker and the student's own unique swing flaws.

So, if you've ever "poached" a lesson, and it didn't seem to help—don't hold the pro responsible for your lack of improvement!

What's Stopping You?

Now, more than ever, golf isn't just a game played by rich dudes in bad pants. It's the new national pastime, and anyone can play. I've taught hundreds of beginners of every gender, age, and size. I've taught Fortune 500 CEOs, five-year-olds, nannies, and neurosurgeons. Frankly, it's nice to be the first person to educate a player on how to grip the club and take a proper stance, rather than battle against incorrect prior knowledge or the old-school teachings of our fathers and grandfathers. The game has changed, and sometimes the hardest work is undoing bad habits rather than starting from scratch and creating good ones.

It can be scary, I know. Once you've made the decision to take a lesson, you're subject to feelings of humiliation and frustration. Believe me, those feelings will eventually lead to satisfaction and exhilaration. The most important things to take with you to a lesson or the practice range are an open mind and a resilient spirit. Be willing to learn and expect to be lousy for a while.

Most golf professionals repeatedly see certain groups of people who are reluctant to take lessons or give golf a try. Each group has these particular fears or unrealistic expectations in common.

The Self-Conscious Lady

> "In 1587 golf's first famous woman player (Mary Queen of Scots) was convicted and beheaded. Women's golf went into something of a decline after that."
>
> —Rhonda Glenn

My mom plays in the ladies league at a local public course. The other day she was paired with a woman who was teeing it up for the first time ever. During her first swing, the rookie accidentally let loose with a long, loud fart. The ladies lost it. Eventually they composed themselves and continued playing the hole. Then the beginner chipped in for a par—and laughed so hard she peed her pants and had to leave.

Apart from a spectacular outing like that, no one's ever going to remember anything you say or do on the golf course. That's because everyone is more worried about overcoming their own bag of golf insecurities.

Still, nobody wants to be lousy at anything, especially if it's as embarrassing as it is challenging. That's how the practice range and golf course feel for most female beginners, particularly because the golf stance doesn't feel very ladylike at first.

Myth All eyes are on you, as if every other person has stopped practicing and is laughing while you struggle. Even passing motorists pull off to the side of the road to mock you. News helicopters might even start to circle . . .

> "The reason the pro tells you to keep your head down is so you can't see him laughing."
>
> —Phyllis Diller

Truth You're going to be self-conscious, but nobody cares or pays much attention. Sure, someone may realize that a beginner is taking a lesson, or notice that you are inexperienced, but that's all it is—an awareness that you lack prior knowledge. But no one (with any class) passes judgment.

PEARLS FROM THE PRO

When you're taking a lesson or practicing, your position on the range matters. When you're in the middle of the range, you're more likely to be noticed and share interactions with those around you. If you're at the far left, everyone will have their back to you and won't pay any attention to what's happening behind them. If you're at the far right, everyone will be facing toward you, and have the opportunity to observe, but you won't be facing or distracted by them. They'll be out of sight and out of mind.

Inexperienced players should head to the left so no one will watch you; confident players to the right so no one will bother you; social players to the middle so you can make friends.

The Perfectionist Male

> "Our greatest glory is not in never falling, but in rising every time we fall."
>
> —Confucius

Men can be reluctant, or simply unwilling, to try new things when immediate competence is doubtful—especially when success comes easy in other aspects of life. Rather than suffer a slow learning curve and the risk of demonstrating total incompetence, we'll write the activity off as a waste of time, and even create some believable excuses to justify our position. By not trying something new, we can usually insulate ourselves from failure.

For me, it's dancing. I wish I could do it. It would make my wife and daughters very happy. But for now, the end result isn't worth the short-term demonstration of complete ineptitude.

Myth Golf follows the same predictable pattern of improvement as most other skills and/or sports:

Hard Work + Repetition = Success

Truth Golf just takes more time to get good at than any other sport (except maybe surfing). It's an equation that looks a lot more like this:

Practice^3 × Frustration + Trial and Error + Hard Work – Blood, Sweat, and Tears = Occasional Glimpses of Success

Take a deep breath and allow yourself to be a beginner. Understand this isn't like anything else you've ever tried before, and learn to laugh at yourself.

The Child (or a Child at Heart) with a Short Attention Span

> "Golf, like measles, should be caught young."
> —P. G. Wodehouse

At the Hayden Lake Country Club I was privileged to be a part of a junior program that's been in existence for more than seventy seasons—the Mughunters. It culminates at the end of July with the "Two-Ball on the Beach Tournament." Participants range in age from six to sixteen. An older kid is paired with a younger one, with one club each, and they play in the backyards of the homeowners who live next to the golf course on the lake. Some holes have decks, trampolines, barbecues, hammocks, and hot tubs as obstacles; another, in particular, has a tee box that's out on a boat dock and plays back to a green in a fire pit on the beach about forty yards, all carry.

Two-Ball on the Beach, Hayden Lake, Idaho.

It's one of the most magical golf experiences I've witnessed. Watching a hundred kids play golf in their bathing suits while they laugh, run, scream, and dive between homemade holes makes it clear what the purpose of the sport truly is.

Myth A kid's golf lesson is only a success when it improves the kid's golfing ability.

Truth There are kids who can't focus their attention on one thing for more than twenty seconds. A successful lesson doesn't need to accomplish anything that has to do with the specifics of the golf swing at all. I believe the only thing that matters is if a kid has fun at the golf course, and wants to come back again. Osmosis is inevitable.

A common theme among the great modern-day champions is that golf was always the reward for good behavior when they were kids, not an activity forced upon them. If kids are hungry to play, and deem it worth their effort to get good grades or do their chores, then a lifetime of fond memories is sure to follow.

I've been taking my young daughters to the practice range and golf course with me for quite a while now, but I've never asked them to, or made them, hold a club or attempt a swing. Every now and then they'll give it a try on their own, which is cool.

For now, they're much more interested in taking their shoes off and playing in the bunker, riding on the back of the cart, or chasing butterflies. So what? We enjoy our time together at the golf course. To them it's a fun place to go and hang with Dad, and if they're well behaved, they might get a snack before we leave. Who cares if their definition of golfing and mine aren't exactly the same?

Chapter 19

Whacking the Snake

"Reverse every natural instinct and do the opposite of what you are inclined to do, and you will probably come very close to having a perfect golf swing."

—Ben Hogan

Most of this book teaches you about the 99 percent of golf that has nothing to do with technique. On the other hand, a graceful swing can do wonders for your confidence. Understanding the swing will give you confidence. Build the right swing, and you're ready to take on the world.

During the countless hours of hard work I've put into my own game, I've made some surprising discoveries. Although at first glance the golf swing seems very complex, its essentials are few and well within your reach.

Another note: I believe self-discovery is the most important component to understanding the swing and improving your game. Analyzing golf on TV and reading complicated self-help books will take you only so far. It's up to you to do the rest.

"The answers are in the dirt."

—Ben Hogan

STORY TIME

I was a terrible player at the beginning of my career. Frankly, no one was more surprised than me when I passed the PAT. I've come a long way since then, and I've been fortunate enough to celebrate some real successes. I even set the course record at Black Rock (65). It was subsequently broken by the unstoppable Troy, and then again by PGA Tour star Rich Beem, but my name was on the board for a few months—something I'm very proud of. It's nothing short of a miracle when you consider the first swing advice I ever got from my dad. He told me, "Imagine the ball is a snake sticking its head out of a hole, and whack it."

The Pre-Swing Basics

You don't need to understand every muscle contraction, sphincter squeeze, and anatomical micro-movement of the golf swing to build a proficient motion. What you do need is a grasp of the basic pre-swing principles. This is the stuff your teacher will be talking about when you go take a lesson. Knowing the vocabulary—or better yet, understanding the fundamentals—will help you communicate more clearly and quicken the pace of your improvement.

Control the Controllables

It's very helpful to realize that most of the things that go wrong during your golf swing actually happen before the swing. You can greatly improve the outcome of each attempt by understanding how to control your attitude, center of gravity, posture, stance alignment, and most importantly, grip.

Attitude It's good to have lofty goals—but get real. Keep your expectations realistic. Understand the length of the improvement process, enjoy the challenge, and learn to laugh at yourself—because you will make lots of mistakes.

Center of Gravity Imagine a 16-pound bowling ball cradled in your pelvis. Your lower body should remain as stable as possible, while your upper body rotates around that bowling ball at the waist. During the swing, the bowling ball shouldn't move.

PEARLS FROM THE PRO

Remember your eighth-grade gym teacher? Polyester shorts a size or two too small and that whistle spinning around his finger. If the golf club is that whistle, then your center of gravity is the finger that drives it. While your center of gravity remains still, the speed of the golf club increases. Move the finger left, right, up, or down, and the momentum is lost.

Posture When taking your stance, let gravity dictate where your arms hang—which should be straight down from your shoulder sockets. Most people tend to reach out and get their hands too far from their body. This causes many swing flaws and compensations. If your swing looks or feels like you're pulling a dead cat out of a rose bush, it might be a posture problem.

Correct arm hang, straight down.

Reaching . . . This leads to many mistakes.

Get a Grip The grip is the most important aspect of the pre-swing fundamentals. After all, your grip is the only thing that attaches you to the club. For a right-handed player, the two most common mistakes are right-hand grip strength and left-hand anchor position.

Very few amateur golfers position their hands "strong" enough on the club. For a right-handed player, this means the crease made between the right forefinger and thumb must point to the right shoulder, not to the chin. This is critical because it keeps the radius and ulna bones of your forearms—and hence your clubface—from immediately over-rotating as you begin your swing.

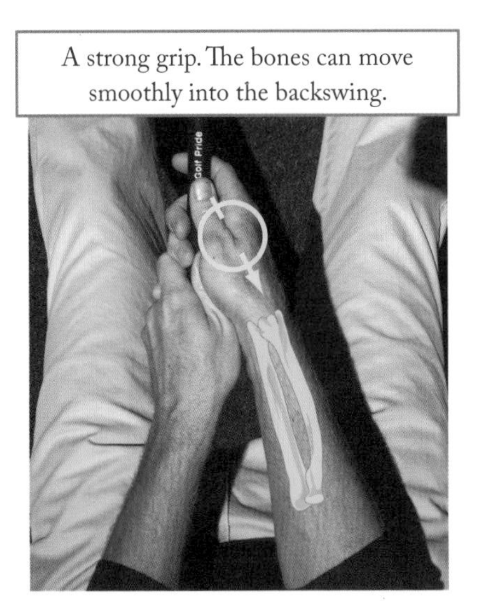

A strong grip. The bones can move smoothly into the backswing.

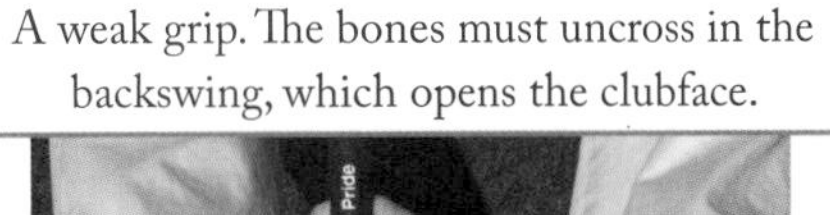

A weak grip. The bones must uncross in the backswing, which opens the clubface.

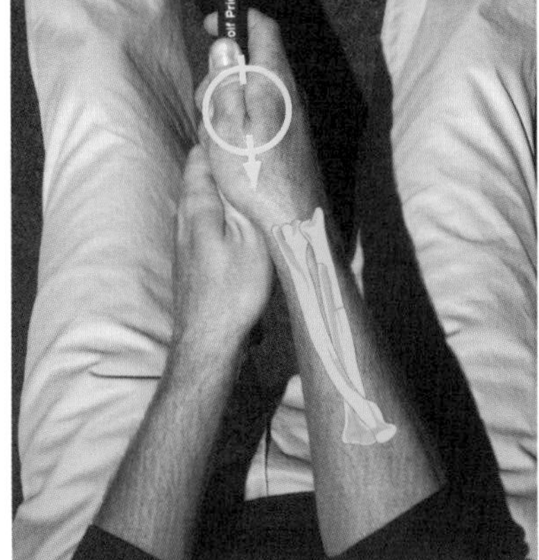

The other common grip flaw is a left hand that isn't anchored properly. With irons and woods, the thick meaty pad (the hypothenar eminence) at the base of the pinky side of the palm must rest on the top of the club. This creates leverage and an important angle between the club shaft and your arms.

An anchored grip . . .

should create an angle like this.

With the putter, the grip position of the left hand changes. The handle needs to be secured in the palm, which prevents the clubface from rotating and creates a straight line between the club shaft and your arms. This eliminates the tendency to break your wrists and promotes a more consistent stroke.

A proper putter grip . . .

should eliminate the angle.

> "If people gripped a knife and fork the way they do a golf club, they'd starve to death."
>
> —Sam Snead

Stance Alignment Be sure to consistently set up for each shot with your shoulders, arms, hips, feet, and knees all aligned parallel to your intended target. All too often, what feels correct isn't, and your properly executed swing might be heading in the wrong direction.

PEARLS FROM THE PRO

I ask my students to get in the habit of picking a two-foot target. I'll have them find a dead spot, a broken tee, a divot, or even a noticeable blade of grass two feet beyond the ball and in line with the target as a point of reference when they take their stance. Try it. You'll start hitting more shots on line.

These are the most common mistakes I've seen in players at every level. They're easy flaws to spot. Fix them and you'll go far toward having the swing of your dreams.

Ball Flight Laws

Here are the universal truths that dictate the outcome of every swing. You *must* know them.

1. Clubhead Speed

The distance the ball travels is chiefly a function of clubhead speed. The faster the clubhead swings, the farther the ball will go. Clubhead speed is influenced by several things, but the most important are the width and length of your arc.

The length of arc is the distance the clubhead travels during the swing. Generally, the longer the shot, the longer the swing. The width of arc is the distance from your center of gravity to the handle of the club. The farther your hands get from your center, the greater the circumference of your swing arc, and the greater the clubhead speed.

STORY TIME

During one particular lesson to a lady, I took great pains to explain the keys to clubhead speed. "Width of arc. Width of arc," I thought I heard her repeat excitedly. "Is that the secret?" Glad to hear my lecture was hitting home, I agreed it was a key component, for sure. Her next innocent question, however, brought the lesson to a halt. "But what's a 'vark'?"

2. Approach Angle

The depth of your divot is a sign of your approach angle. In simple terms, approach angle dictates the trajectory of the shot. It can be steep (high ball flight, deep divots) or flat (low ball flight, shallow divots).

3. Centeredness of Contact

Hitting the ball in the sweet spot of the clubface always feels better and goes farther. Sometimes slowing your clubhead speed will increase the centeredness of contact, which is why swinging slower can produce longer shots.

4. Clubface Position at Impact

Any curvature of the ball in flight is caused directly by the position of the clubface at the moment of impact. If the face is rotated to the left (closed), it will cause a hook. If it's square it will cause a straight flight. If it's rotated to the right (open), it will cause a slice.

5. Swing Path

Your divot indicates your swing path. The path can be left (pull), caused by an outside-to-in swing path; down the line, caused by an on-path swing; or right (push), caused by an inside-to-out swing path.

Here's how the two most important factors (4 and 5) combine:

Swing Path + Clubface Position at Impact = Shot Shape

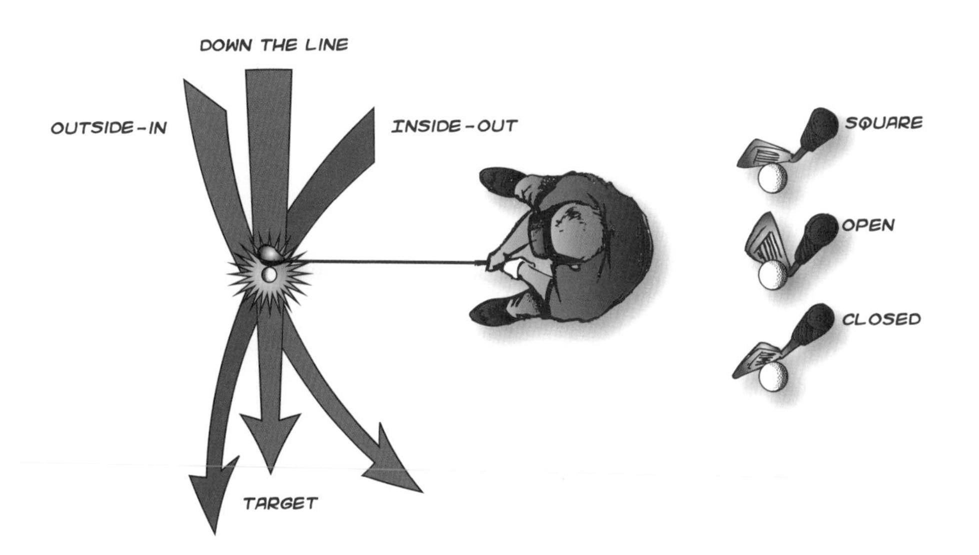

For a well-struck golf ball, the first half of the ball flight—the direction the ball immediately jumps off the clubface—demonstrates the influence of the swing path. The second half of the ball flight—where the ball spins after it's been in the air for a moment or two—shows the influence of the clubface position at impact. Understanding this is essential to becoming a more confident player. The ball flight of every shot is an observable fact, and the cause is an absolute. By placing the visual evidence of each shot into the equation, you can decipher what, if anything, went wrong during your swing.

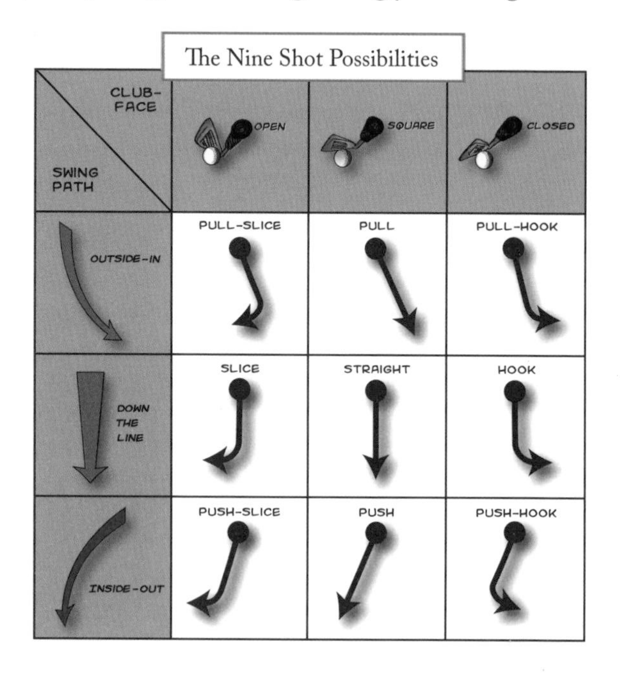

Building a good golf swing requires work. No one can honestly tell you otherwise. But grasping the things you can control prior to your swing, and deciphering the results every time, are the keystones to a respectable game. The frustrating thing about golf is that sometimes understanding doesn't translate to execution. When that happens, and all of your best efforts fail, just remember to rear back and whack the snake.

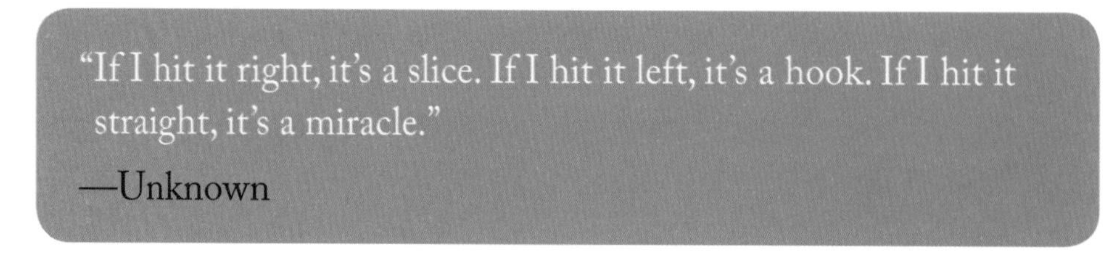

Chapter 20

Get Shorty

"If you knew how much work went into it, you wouldn't call it genius."

—Michelangelo

Nothing will lower your scores more quickly than a quality short game. The function of the three primary short-game techniques—putting, chipping, and pitching—is to control distance, and in the game of golf, distance is always more important than direction.

The fundamental concept to mastering the short game is the hinge, a motion that occurs during the backswing. The wrists cock to form an angle between the left arm and the club shaft, which ultimately adds velocity to the clubhead during the downswing. Controlling the hinge—or, when necessary, eliminating it altogether—is the key to a proficient short game.

Short-Game Shot Essentials

Here are four things to consider as you prepare to hit every short-game shot.

Grip

Once you've taken a proper grip, two variables guide the way you hold your club for the short game.

- *Firmness*: When chipping, grip the club firmly to make sure you don't unhinge your wrists. This enables the ball to roll across the ground. However, when trying to execute a high, soft pitch, the opposite is true, and a nice supple (loose) grip is better. The softer your hands, the less the ball will roll.

- *Location*: This refers to how high or low on the handle you place your hands. As a rule, the closer you grip to the butt end, the longer the club becomes and the farther you'll be able to hit the ball, but with less accuracy. The closer you grip to the shaft end, the shorter the club becomes, and with it the shorter the distance you'll be able to hit the ball, but with more precision. Think about which club you hit straighter. The driver or the putter? (I hope it's the putter, otherwise we've got some real problems!)

Alignment

When chipping and pitching, it's necessary to position your body's alignment slightly open to the intended target line. One, it allows for better binocular vision and sight of the target. Two, the club should sit on the ground slightly open to allow it to skip off the ground rather than dig teeth first into the turf right behind the ball—the dreaded "chili-dip." Have you ever hit that embarrassing shot?

Weight Distribution

For best results in the full swing, you stand with your weight evenly distributed for a balanced weight transfer. But in the short game, distribution of weight is different for each technique and isn't transferred at all.

Ball Position

The ball can be forward, middle, or back in your stance. Forward means toward the target, back means away from it. The trajectory of each shot is influenced by ball position. Forward makes the ball fly higher (pitching) and back makes it fly lower (chipping).

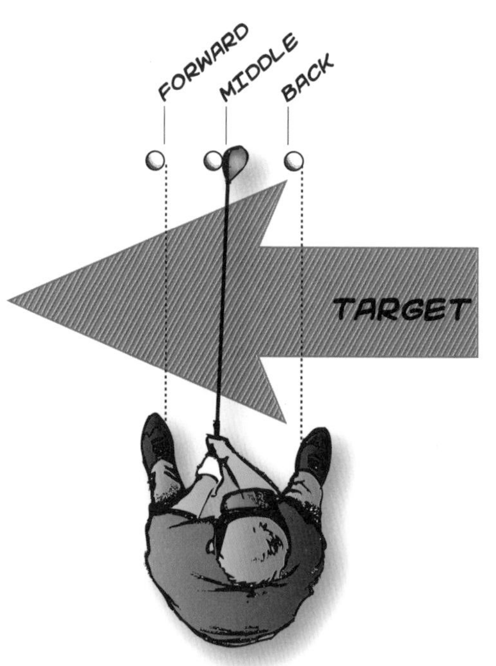

Notice that the first letters of these short-game essentials spell out a helpful mnemonic phrase—GAWB. Here's how the GAWB checklist works for each technique.

Putting

This is an attempt to roll the ball across the ground and into the hole using your putter. However, putting isn't limited to the green. You can putt from a reasonable distance off the green, as long as the terrain that the ball will roll across is fairly predictable, and the length of the stroke won't affect proper execution of the technique.

G Grip the putter firmly in the middle of the handle, with the back of your left hand facing toward the hole (see page 214).
A You should be aligned square to the intended target line.
W Keep your weight evenly distributed on both feet.
B Your eyes are directly over the ball.
Swing the putter with your shoulders—not your wrists! No hinge.

Notice how . . . the wrists . . . don't hinge.

When you set up to hit a putt, your eyes should be directly over the ball. To see if you do this correctly, next time you're on the practice green take your stance, then hold a ball up to the bridge of your nose and drop it. It should land on the ball you're about to hit.

Chipping

This is quite similar to putting, and the goal is basically the same—an attempt to roll the ball across the ground toward the hole. However, chipping occurs from off the green whenever the putter can't be used. A shorter club, such as a 9-iron or pitching wedge, is preferred.

G Grip the club firmly and choke down to make it slightly shorter.
A Align your body slightly open to the intended target line.
W Keep your weight forward, about 80 percent left foot, 20 percent right.
B Place the ball back in the stance, in line with the right big toe.

Like with the putter, swing your shoulders—not your wrists! No hinge. Keep your weight forward to ensure that you strike the ball before you hit the ground.

Notice how . . . the angle . . . doesn't change.

Pitching

Much like a slow-pitch lob in a softball game, a pitch shot should fly higher and land softer than the chip. This shot requires a backswing with a wrist hinge to produce enough clubhead speed to project the ball into the air—usually with a wedge. However, this backswing stops short of a full swing.

G Grip the club loosely and choke down to make it shorter.
A Align your body slightly open to the intended target line.
W Keep your weight slightly forward, 60 percent left foot, 40 percent right.
B Place the ball slightly forward of center, in line with the left heel.

Stop the backswing when your left arm is parallel to the ground, making sure weight stays on your left foot throughout. The length of the follow-through should match the length of the backswing.

No Hinge | Hinge | No Hinge | Follow-Through = Backswing

Beach Bummin'

For many, getting a ball out of a greenside bunker can be a hopeless proposition—a real bummer. It doesn't have to be. Understanding this simple technique will reap immediate rewards on your next trip to the beach.

The ball position, weight distribution, and swing technique for greenside bunker play are exactly the same as for pitching. There are, however, a couple of modifications to the setup. The clubface and stance must both be significantly more open. This is important because an open clubface adds loft to the club, which makes it fly higher and land softer. It also exposes the "bounce" of the sole of the club, which allows it to plow through the sand, rather than dig into it. Because an open clubface causes the ball to fly to the right of the target, you must adjust your stance and aim to the left.

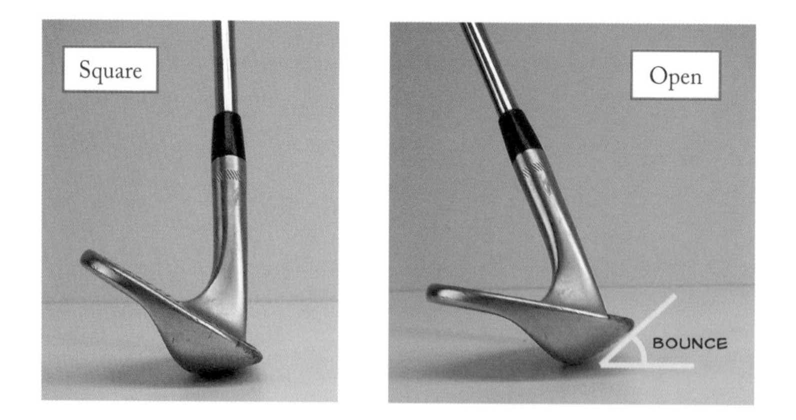

Then, swing the club along the adjusted target line and land the clubhead on the ground, bounce edge first, an inch or two behind the ball. The farther behind the ball the clubhead enters the sand, the harder you'll have to swing, and the less it will spin.

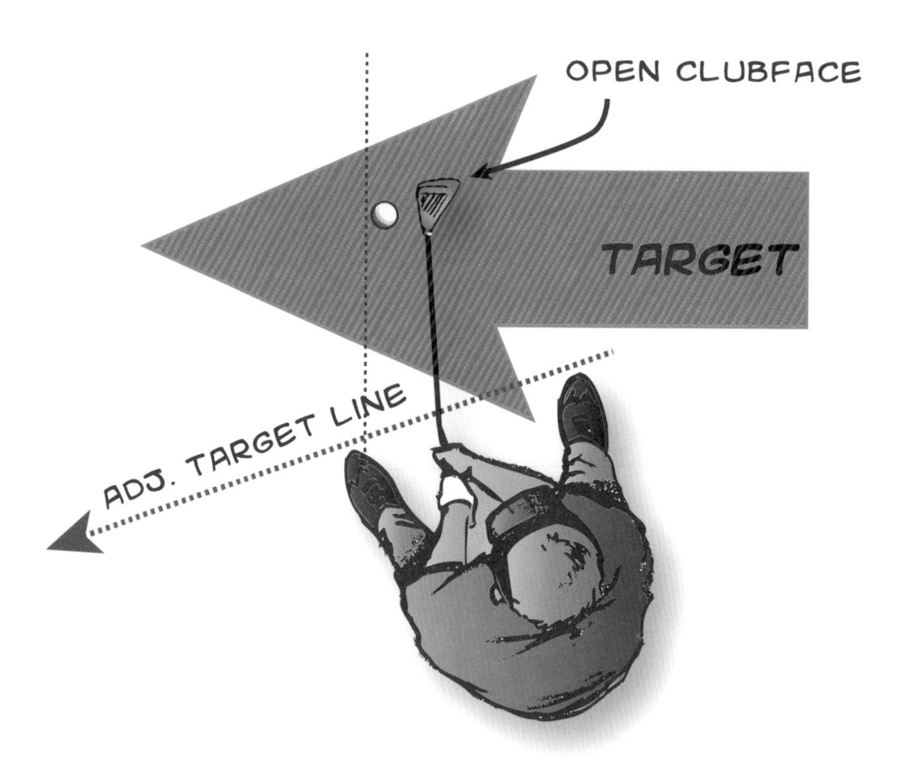

What to Do When?

> "Everything should be made as simple as possible, but not one bit simpler."
> —Albert Einstein

Not only is it crucial to understand how to putt, chip, and pitch, it's just as important to understand when to use each technique.

The rule to live by, coined by PGA Tour legend Tom Watson, is "Putt whenever you can, chip when you can't putt, and pitch only when you have to." So keep the technique as simple as possible. The fewer the moving parts, and the shorter the backswing, the higher the likelihood of success.

It's common to see beginners using the wrong technique at the wrong time. They might, for example, attempt to pitch the ball from areas around the green when it isn't necessary. I realize it's much prettier to see the ball fly high and land softly on the green. But it's also potential for disaster if you're too close. Have you ever skulled one and sent an ankle-rocket screaming across the green, only to be faced with a similar shot from the opposite direction, or worse? Me, too. It's completely avoidable by choosing to putt or chip rather than pitch.

Be Athletic

When you play catch in your yard or shoot a basketball at the gym, do you think about wrist hinges, arm angles, muscle tension, and proper exertion of force? Or do you catch the ball, look at your target, and throw it in that direction? Most of the time, I bet it comes pretty close to its intended destination without excessive analysis or effort.

Acting instinctively on the golf course is important, too, especially in the short game. When you're putting and chipping, think of athletically executing a natural motion. Putt the ball to the hole. Chip the ball onto the green.

Don't turn the technique into a series of "if-thens": If I take the putter back to my right big toe, and if the green speed is approximately a 12 on the stimpmeter, and if the elevation of the golf course is 2,500 feet above sea level, and if I exert a small amount of additional force at impact, then I might make this putt. I prefer: See target; hit ball to target.

Trust your instincts, training, and natural athleticism. It's a much easier way to play the game.

> "It is not the mountain we conquer, but ourselves."
>
> —Sir Edmund Hillary

Just like the power pitcher in baseball who uses only two pitches—the fastball and the curve—a good golfer's short-game arsenal should also be simple. Develop a trustworthy putting stroke and understand how and when to chip and pitch. That's it. Keep your short-game techniques boring and basic. Your scores will immediately reflect the more experienced approach.

The Idaho Club, Sandpoint, Idaho.
Photo provided courtesy of The Idaho Club

Chapter 21

Horses for Courses

"Golf is an awkward set of bodily contortions designed to produce a graceful result."

—Tommy Armour

I've heard people describe themselves as great range players with lousy scores. They hit the ball well on the range, but it doesn't translate to the course. This is because the course offers a different set of circumstances for every shot—including the lie, wind, sun, shade, turf, stance, pressure, and natural obstacles—while the range remains the same. I've developed some principles to help my students take their games from the range to the course, any course—and ultimately to the next level.

I've been privileged to share in the satisfaction of many success stories, including professional golfers, men's and ladies' club champions, high school state champions, and to date, almost a dozen juniors who've earned full-ride Division I scholarships. Over time, we've found these common themes for long-term improvement.

Embrace Your Tendencies—Don't Fight Them

If your tendency is to hit a cut, then hit a cut. If you naturally hit a hook, then hook it all day. Embrace it and rely on it. Don't try to change it on the course. The range is for working on technique. But when you're done working, leave it at the range. Whatever your particular habit, at game time you should be ready to accept it, expect it, and play it.

The Best Thought Is No Thought

> "Man is an animal. I am an animal. I respond naturally to a situation. This natural response is not intuitive; it is conditioned by the number of times I've been in a situation, and what I've learned from thousands of mistakes and a few successes. I no longer have any power over my reactions. I simply let my mind run. My body can only follow."
>
> —Unknown

Keep your swing thoughts to a minimum. There's nothing wrong with having a mantra that reminds you to key in on something—but keep it simple and consistent. Using your brain during the swing is impossible. Reserve it for strategy, not execution.

Don't let "paralysis by analysis" happen to you. One minute you're thinking about plane, face, path, rotation, turn, transfer, and tempo, and the next thing you know it becomes impossible to swing with any confidence. Just let go, wipe the slate clean, relax, trust your preparation, pick a club, make a swing, and play the basics of the game—get this ball into that hole. Nothing more, nothing less.

Understand Uneven Lies

This is an area of the game that very few people take the time to learn, or have the opportunity and patience to practice. However, knowing the tendencies of ball flight based on an uneven lie is essential to lowering your scores.

Imagine that on a level lie, the loft of the club is designed to project the ball perpendicularly upward. When the horizon is shifted, the loft will still project the ball perpendicularly upward, but from the new orientation. Here's what the ball will have a tendency to do as a result.

- *Uphill*: When playing up a hill, the slope adds loft to the club. Thus, the ball tends to fly higher and shorter and to roll less than normal. Play the ball forward in your stance and take more club (less loft).

- *Downhill*: The opposite is true on downhill lies. The ball will fly lower and roll more than normal. Play the ball back in your stance, take less club (more loft), and lower your left shoulder to match the angle of the slope.

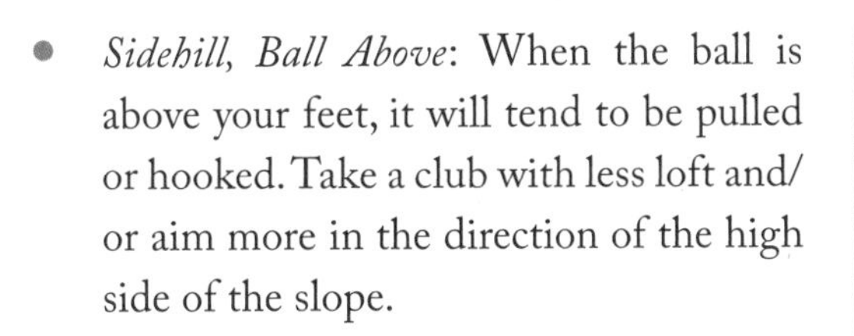

- *Sidehill, Ball Above*: When the ball is above your feet, it will tend to be pulled or hooked. Take a club with less loft and/or aim more in the direction of the high side of the slope.

- *Sidehill, Ball Below*: When the ball is below your feet, it will tend to fly away from you like a push or slice. Take a club with less loft and aim more in the direction of the high side of the slope.

Eliminate Compounding Mistakes

It's difficult to admit defeat, I know. But when you hit a bad shot or get a bad bounce, don't make things worse by trying to pull off the impossible. The discipline to take your lumps can turn quadruple bogeys into bogeys—and end up saving lots of strokes.

There's a time and place to try for a miracle, but if you're seriously trying to lower your scores, think twice about when those attempts are really appropriate.

Assess the Value of Risk

I'm not suggesting we shouldn't ever take risks on the golf course. I realize that the thrill of executing a challenging shot is one of the reasons we all play the game. I know an aggressive play can be advantageous at times. What I'm saying is that you need to consider the ramifications of risk when determining your target and club selection.

- What's the best-case scenario? Eagle? Birdie? Par?
- What's the worst? Hazard? Out of bounds? Lost ball? Trees? Bunker? Rough?
- What are my potential relief options, should I fail to execute?
- Am I working with or against my tendencies?
- Can I actually hit the shot—or am I hoping to hit the shot?

Sometimes low-percentage shots are worth the attempt. However, it's critical to train yourself to take a more analytical approach when determining the risk and potential reward.

Realistic Improvement Requires Patience

My golf students often express frustration when they don't improve as quickly as they'd like. When they ask me for solace, I typically say: "Adjust your expectations. You'll get out only as much as you're willing to put in." It's not always a popular response, but I think it's a necessary point. If your work isn't producing the reward you expect, honestly assess the quality and frequency of your input. Perhaps you'll need to step it up a notch, to focus and direct your efforts in order to achieve real improvement.

Golf offers a rapid rate of learning at first, which slows down over time. You're asked to stand sideways in an orientation that isn't aligned toward your target like every other sport that you've ever played, then bend over so your eyes are no longer aligned with the horizon like they have been every day of your life. Finally, you're required to propel a very small ball into the air with equipment that seems more appropriately suited for yard work or ritualistic torture. On your first day, simply swinging without falling over is a remarkable success. As your game progresses, however, new behavior can only be attained through experience, repetition, and massive trial and error. It can be a very frustrating paradigm. The expectation of the same pace of continued improvement remains, but the impossibility thereof is undeniable.

Better Bad Shots

The easiest way to gauge improvement is by the quality of your bad shots—not your score. When a group of PGA Tour players were asked how many perfect golf shots they hit per round, the average answer was just three. Even at its highest level, golf isn't a game of striking pure shot after pure shot. It's a game of managing all the others.

Hang in there long enough and your bad shots will improve, followed by your score. When your miss-hits get closer to the center of the clubface, your shot results will get closer to the hole. Better bad shots lead directly to better scores. If, a year ago, your volley of terrible shots broke three windows and knocked out two people, but today you only maimed a duck and lost a clubhead, it's time to celebrate!

> "I know I'm getting better at golf because I'm hitting fewer spectators."
>
> —President Gerald Ford

PEARLS FROM THE PRO

We all have five different swings. The goal is to make them as similar as possible.

1. Our swing on the practice range when we're alone.
2. Our swing on the practice range when it's crowded.
3. Our swing on the golf course when we're alone.
4. Our swing on the golf course when we're with others.
5. Our competition swing.

By changing internal and external factors, getting comfortable when we play with others, or gaining confidence in our own ability, we can narrow the gap that inevitably exists between the first and fifth of these swings.

Engage in the Process

You can and will improve every time you undertake a golf experience. Competing, taking a lesson, or simply playing solo on a Sunday afternoon all present the same opportunity to learn. The process never ends.

There's a difference between form and function. I've seen players with gorgeous golf swings who can't get it airborne, and I've seen players who look like a swinging convulsion who routinely break par. I've seen players with great golf swings who don't seem to enjoy themselves, and people with downright awful action who absolutely love the experience. At the end of the day, ability shouldn't matter. The goals of the game are to learn, have fun, and eventually get the ball in the hole.

Definitely consult your local PGA professional to help make more sense of these concepts. Your pro can help develop a lasting partnership designed for appropriately paced long-term improvement.

Oh, and one more thing. It's simple, really.

Just keep your head down and your eye on the ball and keep your left arm straight, but not locked stiff, and in your backswing keep your right knee bent and your weight on the balls of your feet, but not too far toward the toes, which could cause a hook, and remember to tighten your inner leg muscles, kind of like you're pulling your knees toward each other to engage your pelvic floor muscles, and try to exhale just before you start your takeaway, and when the club is parallel to the ground, make sure the clubface is slightly closed, keep the toe in the air and the shaft pointing down the target line, and keep your chin up away from your chest to facilitate a more fluid turn away from the ball by giving your left shoulder space, and keep your left heel on the ground for increased torque, a move that will increase the x-factor of your backswing, but don't, under any circumstance, ever let your left wrist hinge go beyond 90 degrees, since this could cause you to re-grip the club in the last two fingers of your target-side hand and cast it at the start of the downswing thus pre-releasing the club, resulting in a major power leak, and initiate the downswing with an aggressive hip rotation and hold the left wrist hinge-angle as long as possible to create maximum velocity through centrifugal force and leverage manifesting itself in the whip of the release, and finally, stick the landing by posting up onto the target-side foot without spinning your toes toward the target. Got it?

Giddyup!

Gozzer Ranch, Coeur d'Alene, ID—16th Hole.
Photo provided courtesy of Gozzer Ranch

Chapter 22

Found in Translation

"Running through the Rules are the underlying principles that, like the steel rods which lie below the surface of reinforced concrete, serve to bind together the brittle material and to give it strength."

—Richard S. Tufts

Most golfers will never play with an official walking the course and monitoring their moves, or with TV cameras taking close-up video of every step and swing. Most are left alone to locate their own ball and play it as it's found or to determine the proper course of action should it be lost, out of bounds, unplayable, in a hazard, or in some other situation. There's no referee, no stopwatches or tape measures, and no judges. This is what makes the game so special and its rules so different from most other sports—the participants are expected to call infractions and penalties on themselves.

To demonstrate experience on the golf course, you need to know what to do. This is important when you're playing with others who know what they're doing. It's even more important when you're playing with others who pay attention to what you're doing. You don't want to be the topic of locker room chatter for the wrong reasons.

You should commit a handful of the basic rules from *The Rules of Golf* to memory, since they regularly apply during the course of normal play. All other questions can be answered by referencing the rules book. But that's not as easy as it sounds. The rules can be confusing—and filled with italicized definitions that slow the reading and muddle the message. Sometimes, the important information gets lost in translation.

The first step is to get the rules book out of your golf bag (where it should be) and familiarize yourself with the definitions. The rules won't make much sense if you don't learn the specific terms used throughout. Next, I want you to dog-ear the following pages as I translate them here, which will help you eliminate those frantic on-course searches.

> "Study the rules so that you won't beat yourself by not knowing something."
> —Babe Didriksen Zaharias

The Rules You Need to Know

Certainly, the following translations are not intended as CliffsNotes®. You still need to read the USGA's *The Rules of Golf.* These are just my interpretations of the rules I've seen most questioned and misunderstood.

The Ball Must Be Played as It's Found (Rule 13)

This is the fundamental premise of the game. The ball must be played as it lies, and the player isn't permitted to improve that lie, the area of the intended stance or swing, or the line of play. This creates incentive to hit good shots and keep the ball in the fairway and on the green. Rough is rough for a reason.

The most common breach of this rule is when players move their ball to a better location or a fluffier lie, the ever-popular "foot-wedge." But it also means that you can't alter the condition of the ground near your ball so it can be struck more easily.

Have you ever pressed down tall or thick grass behind your ball? Have you ever repositioned, or even removed, tall weeds or branches so you could more easily take your stance? Have you ever taken a "practice swing" with the intention of chopping down some of the brush near your ball? If you answered yes to any of these, you've broken the rule. You're only allowed to hit your ball, find it, and hit it again. As I tell my daughters: You get what you get and you don't throw a fit.

STORY TIME

One time during a ladies' member-guest tournament shoot-out, I called a penalty on one of the participants. At the top of her practice backswing, she clipped a branch off a nearby tree. She continued her routine, unaware that what she had done was an infraction. I had to inform her, along with all the other competitors and hundreds of spectators, that she had incurred a penalty. The act of breaking the branch could've provided her club safe passage through the barky gauntlet, thus improving her area of intended swing.

The rule states very clearly that anything "fixed" can't be altered or broken.

My decision made a few people pretty angry. One drunken female spectator even got in my face to challenge the ruling and loudly called me a handful of slurred expletives. But the rules are in black and white and I saw it happen. What was I supposed to do? The rules require integrity from the player and the official. Not enforcing what I saw would have been unfair to the rest of the competitors.

Had the competitor known the rule, I'm sure she would have called it on herself and saved us all the embarrassment that day.

> "There is no surer nor more painful way to learn a rule than to be penalized for breaking it."
> —Tom Watson

Grounding Your Club (Rule 13, cont.)

You can't "ground" your club in a water hazard, lateral water hazard, or bunker. This means you aren't permitted to touch the ground with your club (or your hand) prior to the start of your swing. Doing so is considered "testing" the condition of the ground—and that's not allowed.

How and When to Drop (Rule 20)

Rule 20 discusses the proper procedure for taking relief and dropping a ball, when permitted under a rule (such as moving your ball off a cart path), and for doing the same in a situation where the ball may be lifted and dropped as a result of a penalty (such as dropping out of a water hazard).

When you're required to drop a ball, do just what it says: stand tall, hold the ball at shoulder height and arm's length, and drop it. The underhanded toss, the hip-high chuck, the side-armed fling, and the drop-and-prop are all illegal. When you drop a ball, do it the right way.

No rule says a player has to take relief—it's just an option. Sometimes it might even be better to hit the ball where it is rather than drop it and risk having a worse stance, lie, or view of the target.

For example, you can choose to take relief from an immovable obstruction—such as a cart path—if it interferes with your stance. The rules permit free relief. However, if you choose to take relief, you can't change your mind if it doesn't help as much as you'd hoped.

Should you decide to take relief, it's critical to understand that dropping a ball into play comes with some stipulations, and at times, depending on where the ball comes to rest, the ball must be re-dropped.

> "If there's one thing golf demands above all else, it's honesty."
> —Jack Nicklaus

Removing Loose Impediments (Rule 23)

Mother Nature's litter (officially known as "loose impediments"), such as pine needles, twigs, branches, dead animals, rocks, snow, or other such things sitting on the surface of the ground and not sticking to the ball, may be removed anywhere on the course—except in a hazard. But, in doing so, you cannot cause your ball to move. For this reason, take extra care when walking on or removing loose impediments near your ball. Again, this is part of the penalty for hitting your ball off the beaten path.

STORY TIME

During my most recent jaunt to Ireland, one of the lads in our group drew a particularly crappy lie. While playing Ballybunion, his ball came to rest on a small pile of dung from an unknown mammal. Not knowing the rule, and frankly, not caring, he chose to move his ball from the steamer and clean it.

As Rule 23 explains, dung can be removed without penalty unless it's adhering to the ball, which it was in this case. In a competition, he would have been required to play the ball from its fecal perch, or declare it unplayable and take the corresponding penalty. Nice, huh?

> "Golf is not a game, it's bondage. It was obviously devised by a man torn with guilt, eager to atone for his sins."
>
> —Jim Murray

Man-Made Obstructions (Rule 24)

According to the rules, an "obstruction" is anything man-made. However, sometimes a natural object is used as a specific feature on the course: for example, a retaining wall constructed from several logs. This is clearly not "nature's litter" and should be treated as man-made. There are two types of obstructions: movable and immovable.

Movable: If the obstruction can be moved, you can do so without penalty, even if it's in a hazard. If the ball moves as a result of removing the obstruction, you can drop and play your ball without penalty.

Immovable: If you touch an "immovable obstruction" (bleachers, an outhouse, or a scoreboard, for example) with any part of your body when you take your stance, or your club will touch it during your swing, you get relief. If the immovable obstruction is in your way, but your body or club won't touch it before or during your swing, then you're not entitled to relief (unless you're on the green).

To take relief from an immovable obstruction, first determine the nearest spot (to the ball) that affords you complete relief when your stance is taken. Then measure one club length from the spot but no nearer to the hole, and drop your ball within that club length.

Ground Under Repair (Rule 25)

Abnormal ground conditions (usually called "ground under repair" and marked by white paint lines on the course) are treated just like an immovable obstruction. Interference occurs when your stance or swing will touch the specific area of the course, and free relief may be taken.

PEARLS FROM THE PRO

When playing a course for the first time, always take a minute to read the local rules on the scorecard. You might discover a twist to the rules that will come in handy and maybe even save you a stroke or two.

For example, at Black Rock I made a local rule that damage caused by nonburrowing animals was considered an abnormal ground condition—and free relief could be taken. We frequently experienced significant damage to the course caused by herds of elk and deer that lived in the nearby forests.

Embedded Ball (Rule 25, cont.)

If your ball plugs into the soft soil of closely mown grass "through the green," you're also entitled to free relief. The phrase "closely mown" is important. It's defined as "any grass cut to fairway height or less." You're not entitled to relief in longer grass—such as the shag surrounding the fairway. Again, this creates incentive to hit good shots.

IF I RULED THE WORLD

If I could change just one thing in *The Rules of Golf*, I would allow relief to be taken from a ball that comes to rest in a divot, just as is already allowed for an embedded ball. I've seen countless quality shots end up rolling into a divot and costing a player a stroke or two as a result of the bad lie. If relief is given for an embedded ball, I don't understand why relief isn't given for a ball in a divot.

Here's how my new rule would read:

Free Relief from Divot Damage

A ball that has come to rest in or upon any condition that appears to be damage caused by another player in taking and/or repairing a divot in closely mown grass may be cleaned and dropped, without penalty, as near as possible to the spot where it lay, but not nearer the hole.

Seems reasonable, doesn't it?

Water Hazards and Lateral Water Hazards (Rule 26)

Commit this one to memory. If your ball goes into a "water hazard," you have three options. You can

- 1. find it and hit (no penalty);
- 2. replay the shot (one-stroke penalty);

- 3. drop a ball anywhere on an extension of an imaginary line connecting the flag and the point where the ball crossed the margin of the hazard, no nearer the hole (one-stroke penalty).

If your ball goes into a "lateral water hazard," you have five options: the same three as for a water hazard, plus two additional options.

A player may drop within two club lengths (no nearer the hole)

- 4. from where the ball crossed the margin of the hazard (one-stroke penalty);
- 5. from a point equidistant to the hole on the opposite side of the hazard (one-stroke penalty).

PEARLS FROM THE PRO

Remember:
Water hazard = Yellow = 3 options.
Lateral water hazard = Red = 5 options.

The Coeur d'Alene Resort, Coeur d'Alene, Idaho—14th Hole.

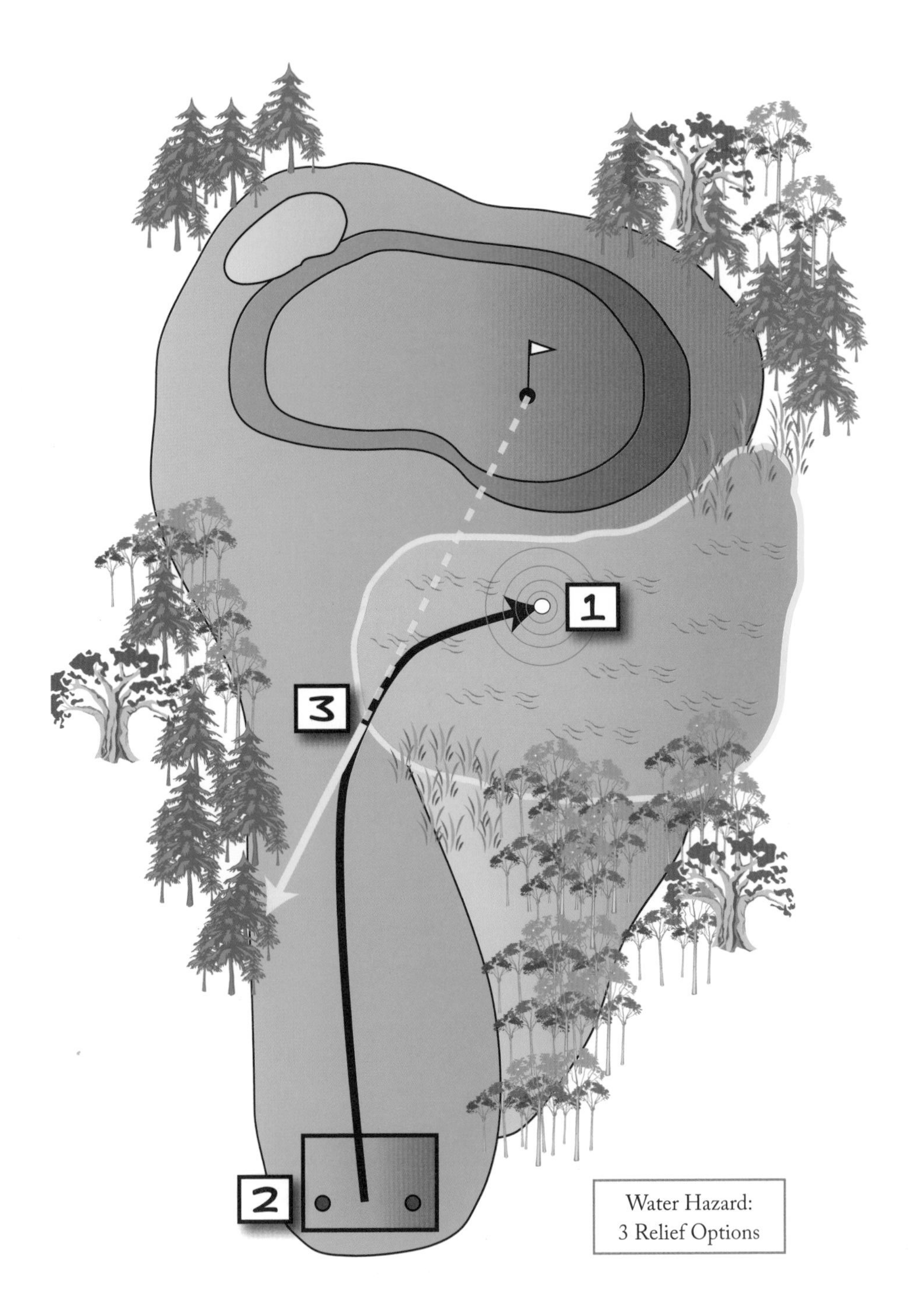
1
3
2
Water Hazard:
3 Relief Options

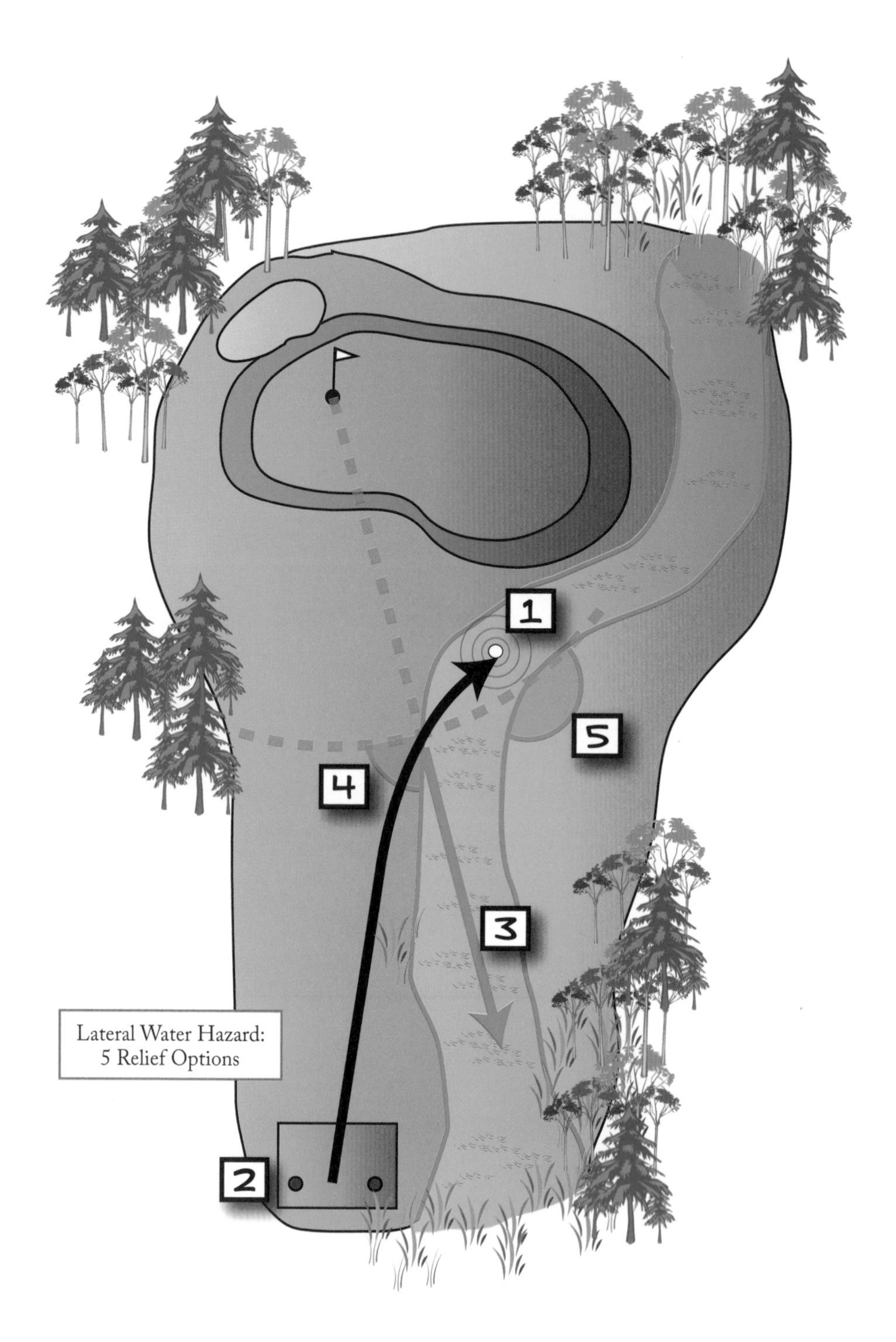
1
5
4
3
Lateral Water Hazard:
5 Relief Options
2

Lost and Out of Bounds (Rule 27)

This rule penalizes a player one stroke plus the distance the original ball traveled—known as a stroke and distance penalty—when a ball is lost or hit out of bounds. You must "replay" the stroke from the original location, and add a one-stroke penalty. For example, after hitting a drive out of bounds, your next stroke (from the tee, again) would be your third.

PEARLS FROM THE PRO

Remember:
Lost Ball or OB = Replay the stroke + one-stroke penalty.
Lost Ball or OB = Bad. Very bad.

Provisional Ball (Rule 27, cont.)

The "provisional ball" is designed to speed up play by saving you a return trip to the original location. If a ball is thought to be lost or out of bounds, you can play a provisional until you get to the place where the other might be, look for it, and then proceed accordingly.

To do so, a player must declare a ball a provisional prior to hitting it. If it isn't announced as such, then the original ball is immediately assumed lost or out of bounds, the penalty applies, and the provisional ball becomes the ball in play. Be sure you mention it to the group.

Also note that you can make an infinite number of strokes with a provisional ball until the place where the original ball is thought to be located. You can then abandon the provisional, and any strokes made with it, if the original ball is found in bounds.

As it happened, I learned an unforgettable lesson about the provisional ball during my third attempt to pass the PAT.

FACE PLANTS

There I was, cruising along nicely through the first fifteen of thirty-six holes, right around par and definitely well-positioned for a passing score. Then I stepped up to the sixteenth tee.

I boomed a high draw down the left side of the long uphill par 5. It appeared to come close to the out-of-bounds markers. I was certain it was in bounds, but for formality's sake I declared I would hit a provisional ball should the original be out. The second ball followed a similar path, but it snapped a wee bit more and clearly sailed out of bounds. The third did the same.

The fourth time, I angrily scraped the ball way to the right. I needed a ball in play! Per *The Rules of Golf*, I continued to play the fourth drive. I misshit it one more time and reached the place where my first ball was (I hoped!) still in bounds. But it wasn't. Oh no! Now I laid eight, still more than 250 yards from the green. OUCH!

Things quickly went from really bad to even worse. With my very next shot I hooked a 3-wood left of the green into a dense thicket of juvenile pines. Again I declared a provisional should that ball be lost, and again I hit the exact same shot. Frustrated, I decided not to hit another provisional and hoped I'd be able to find at least one of those two.

As luck would have it, I found them both. They were actually touching each other. My caddie said, "I haven't seen two balls so close together since I was in the locker room this morning." (One of the all-time great one-liners, although I didn't appreciate the humor at the time.)

As I went to determine which ball was the original and which was the provisional, I discovered I had hit two identical balls—each with the same number and the exact same markings. Neither had a distinctive scrape or scratch, nor even the yellow color a ball turns when it hits a pine tree. It was impossible to tell the difference. DOUBLE OUCH!!

Fuming and totally unsure of what to do, I picked up both balls, bid adieu to my co-competitors, and marched directly to my car in the parking lot, where I threw my clubs in the trunk, sped off, and didn't look back. A few days later I received a ninety-day suspension letter from the PGA for walking off the golf course during an event. TRIPLE OUCH!!!

What should I have done? I've only recently learned the proper procedure. Since both balls were found in bounds, but were indistinguishable, I could pick either of the two balls, play it as the provisional, and abandon the other. I would've then been hitting my twelfth shot.

The moral: Know the rules, take your provisional ball attempts seriously, and use a different numbered ball so you can differentiate it from your original ball. And don't ever walk off the course in the middle of a competition. It was truly bad form, but yet another great learning experience.

Unplayable Lies (Rule 28)

If you ever decide that your ball is "unplayable"—which is the prerogative of the player at any time—you're given three relief options. Each is a one-stroke penalty.

- 1. place the ball two club lengths from the spot;
- 2. drop a ball anywhere on an extension of an imaginary line connecting the flag and the ball, no nearer the hole;
- 3. replay the shot.

PEARLS FROM THE PRO

One club length or two? Well, as a rule of thumb, whenever a player is permitted to move his/her ball as part of a free relief procedure, one club length from the nearest point of relief is given. If the ball is unplayable, under penalty of one stroke, a player may move the ball up to two club lengths from where it lay—not from the nearest point of relief.

As a golfer, you've been trusted to uphold these sacred tenets. It's your obligation. Learn the rules and be willing to call a penalty on yourself, regardless of the circumstance. This is our code, indecipherable as it may be, and a true understanding of the game can be found only when we translate that code to our very own play.

Bandon Dunes, Bandon, Oregon—4th Hole.

Chapter 23

A Roadblock or the Fast Lane?

"The moment one definitely commits oneself, then providence moves too. All sorts of things occur to help one that would never otherwise occur. A whole stream of events issues from the decision, raising in one's favor all manner of unforeseen incidents and meetings and material assistance which no man could have dreamed would have come his way. Whatever you can do or dream you can, begin it. Boldness has genius, power, and magic in it. Begin it now."

—Goethe

I believe that golf is best when shared. It's been my privilege to learn that the real value of golf is not in mastering the swing or the short game, but in making friends for life. I've found lasting satisfaction in sharing time with my playing partners, and in the inevitable exchange of thoughts, ideas, and memories. That's what counts, not what's written on the scorecard after the round—unless it's a phone number or an e-mail address.

So why don't we spend more time playing with those we love most? Over the course of my career, I've seen countless golfers who don't play with their family—at all. Certainly, I'm not suggesting that you forsake all other opportunities and only play with your immediate family and relatives. And I'm not talking about how to teach your loved ones to swing a club or educating them in the *Rules of Golf*. I suggest leaving that to a trained professional. But I believe there are ways to awaken someone's interest so they'll want to be taught those things, and ultimately choose to take that next step on their own.

Getting a Loved One Excited (About Golf)

There's a secret to successfully introducing the game to your loved ones. It's a way that gracefully allows them to be in control of the process. Interest leads to excitement, and excitement to integration. I've seen it with my own eyes.

Let's examine the best approach, through the eyes of a man who wants to interest his wife or girlfriend in the game.

Suggest Ways to Share the Experience

Tell her you'd like to spend more time with her—and mean it. Explain that you also really like to play golf, and if there's any way to combine the sport with more time spent with her it would be very meaningful to you.

Non-golfing significant others often feel as though they compete against the game for attention and affection. Golf becomes the rival. In the hope that golf can instead become a memory-making machine for both of you together, try something like this:

> Honey, I'd like to spend time with you and play golf. Maybe we can hang out at the (range/golf course/private club) and talk more about (your day/work/the kids/an upcoming event), or you can bring your (book/iPod/laptop), while I (practice/play).
>
> I won't, under any circumstance, bother you about trying it. I just want to have you there with me. If you feel like you want to give it a try, that would be great. Just let me know.
>
> Maybe we can grab a bite in the clubhouse when I'm done so we won't have to hurry home and cook. The point is that I'd like to spend more time with you.

> "Not everything that is faced can be changed, but nothing can be changed until it is faced."
>
> —James Baldwin

Demonstrate Pleasure, Not Pain

Convincing her to join you on the golf course and then throwing clubs, pouting, and shouting obscenities isn't likely to convince her that you're enjoying yourself. She might even think that's the way golfers are supposed to behave. She might question why you play the game at all.

To demonstrate the pleasure of golf, stop in for dinner or a drink at the clubhouse on a busy evening. Being surrounded by the sights and sounds of the usual post-golf revelry should break the ice. It might just be enough to convince her to come back sometime soon.

Explain the Basics, But Don't Make It Intimidating

Don't overwhelm her by keeping score, telling stories of your love for the game, or lecturing on respect, tradition, history, and the rules. Even attempting to show too many swing techniques can do more damage than good. All that stuff is intimidating—and causes reluctance. Respect for anyone, or anything, is always earned. Over time, it might happen, but not until an investment in the game is deemed to be worth the cost, paid in effort.

Rather, make the game as simple and approachable as possible. Think of the golf course like a giant playground to navigate in any way she wishes. You can play golf by the official rules, keep your score, and attempt to make a technically perfect swing—or not. Who cares? As long as you're spending time together at the golf course, you've crossed the first hurdle.

> "Golf tips are like aspirin. One may do you good, but if you swallow the whole bottle you will be lucky to survive."
> —Harvey Penick

Be Patient, Positive, and Persistent

Think about how long you've been exposed to the game and its culture. You simply can't expect your loved one to learn it all at once. Some things take time, and assimilation into the golf culture can only occur at a certain pace. This includes the ability to swing a club and play the game, as well as all the little things such as where to stand, when to speak, how to dress, and the myriad other details. Realize that all these things will come in time.

Be patient, explain things thoroughly, and demonstrate when needed. If you lose your cool and show frustration, you become a roadblock, not the fast lane.

> "Of course we all have our limits, but how can you possibly find your boundaries unless you explore as far and as wide as you can? I would rather fail in an attempt at something new and uncharted than safely succeed in a repeat of something I have done."
>
> —A. E. Hotchner

Bribe Her If Necessary

Women like cute shoes and new clothes. Didn't you know that? To encourage participation, buy your lady a pair of super-cute golf shoes or a coordinated outfit. She might want to get started just to wear the new gear.

PEARLS FROM THE PRO

Intentionally buy her an outfit that's too small from the golf shop where you'd like to get her to start playing. She'll have to exchange the items for the correct sizes—which secretly forces her to go to the course—and you'll flatter her socks off when you buy her a pair of shorts that's a size or two too small. Just be sure to *never*, and I mean *never*, buy a size that's too large. Always miss small.

Admit Defeat Gracefully

Believe me, I know what it's like to have my mind made up about something. For me, it's hunting. I just don't have any interest in it. It seems like it requires lots of expensive equipment, clothes, licenses, and permits just to get started. What's more, you're required to tromp around in the wilderness by yourself with elk, moose, or deer urine sprayed all over your body, hide in bushes and trees, and try to kill large, horned animals. The only thing worse I can imagine would be succeeding. Then you would have to gut the beast, clean it, cut it up, and lug it back to your vehicle before the carcass either rots or you're attacked by some other opportunistic carnivore. No thank you!

Similarly, golf just won't appeal to some. At that point, there's really nothing you're going to say or do to change her mind. When a loved one has no interest, then what? Accept defeat gracefully, and love her anyway.

For better or worse, in sickness and in health, with golf or without . . . I do.

Ace the Smell Test

What about those of us who love the game and still have a bad day? Sooner or later, it's bound to happen. Sometimes it's due to internal factors such as a miserable performance, unrealistic expectations, or a bad attitude; other times it's external influences such as lousy weather or the bad attitude of another player. The more time that passes following a bad experience, the greater the chance our frustration or even resentment will grow. For this reason, it's essential to make a prompt and honest assessment of what went wrong, then get back out to play again as quickly as possible.

For every new golfer who chooses to begin the journey, there's always another who calls it quits. Those who drop out apparently decide that the frustration and anger of learning just aren't worth the investment of time and effort required to improve. Believe me, I know the feeling well. Sometimes it seems like the best thing to do is chuck the clubs, bag and all, into the nearest water hazard, or donate them to junior golf, and call it a career.

When your golf game doesn't hit the mark, consider exactly what went wrong. Use your gut reaction to compile a smell test of the experience. Then, work to increase the good and eliminate the bad. After every golf experience, determine what worked and what didn't. Ask yourself these questions:

- Did I have a good time? Did the rest of my group?
- What should I do differently next time?
- Is my liver still intact? Is anyone in jail?
- Did I play as well as I'd hoped? Were my expectations realistic?
- Does it really matter?

The beauty of this game is how it shows us glimpses of our greatest potential; then, just when we think we have some control, it strips us naked and keeps us humble. As soon as you understand that truth, and ultimately embrace it, you'll make your golf game a lot less frustrating and a lot more fun.

> "Experience is not what happens to you. It is what you do with what happens to you."
> —Aldous Huxley

What Makes Golf So Special?

It can be just you and the course, or it can include hundreds of people competing in an open tournament. It can be casual, convenient, and low-key, or it can be pressure packed, intense, and terrifying. Sometimes you'll have complete control of the situation; other times you'll just be along for the ride.

The benefits of the game stretch well beyond camaraderie and a good time, or even the respect earned with an occasional (and timely) proficient performance. There's a realm of personal satisfaction that can only be known by experiencing genuine challenge and by demonstrating mastery, even if for only fleeting glimpses of brilliance. The pleasure is sweeter because of the pain. When that sense of supreme pleasure and hard-earned success is found side-by-side with family and friends, you, too, will be hooked forever.

In one of my favorite books, *Golf in the Kingdom*, Michael Murphy's main character, the mysterious guru Shivas Irons, offers this marvelous description of the game in the unique vernacular of the Kingdom of Fife (which lies between the Firth of Forth and Firth of Tay in Scotland):

> . . . Fascination is the true and proper mother of discipline. And gowf is a place to practice fascination. 'Tis slow enough to concentrate the mind and complex enough to require our many parts. In that 'tis a microcosm of the world's larger discipline. Our feelin's, fantasies, thoughts and muscles, all must join to play. In gowf ye see the essence of what the world itself demands. Inclusion of all our parts, alignment o' them all with one another and with the clubs and with the ball, with all the land we play on and with our playin' partners. The game requires us to join ourselves to the weather, to know the subtle energies that change each day upon the links and subtle feelin's of those around us. It rewards us when we bring them all together, our bodies and our minds, our feelin's and our fantasies—rewards us when we do and treats us badly when we don't. The game is a mighty teacher—never deviatin' from its sacred rools, always ready to lead us on. In all o' that 'tis a microcosm o' the world, a good stage for the drama of our self-discovery. And I say to ye all, good friends, that as ye grow in gowf, ye come to see the things ye learn there in every other place. The grace that comes from such a discipline, the extra feel in the hands, the extra strength and knowin', all those special powers ye've felt from time to time, begin to enter our lives . . .
>
> . . . Devoted discipline and grace will bring ye knowin's and powers everywhere, in all your life, in all your works if they're good works, in all your loves if they're good loves. Ye'll come away from the links with a new hold on life, that is certain if ye play the game with all your heart . . .

One positive golf experience leads to another, and so on in a self-perpetuating, momentum-gathering chain of events. If you've ever been sucked into golf's wonderful vortex, you know exactly what I'm talking about. One great shot is all it takes. Then it's a personal best 9-hole score. Next, some quality time with your spouse or close friends who've found similar golf momentum. And on and on and on . . . It's truly been my pleasure to witness so many people, young and old, experienced and new to the game, get swept away for a season—or a lifetime.

If you're new to the game, I hope I've inspired you to pursue the lifetime of memories and relationships that are born from hitting a little white ball around a big green field. If you're learning this fine sport, I hope I've helped you bring more fun and less worry to your game. If you're an experienced player, I'm sure you'll agree with me when I say that many of the deepest and most meaningful relationships in my life are the result of my countless golf experiences. I hope and pray that you, too, might be so blessed.

I have an itch that can only be scratched with an 8-iron. Actually, it's the opposite of an itch—it's more like a tickle. "Itch" implies nuisance, and this is anything but. No matter how I contort and tangle, I can't quite reach it, and I'm not sure I ever will. It just might be impossible to successfully quell the sensation that's always calling me back to the course and compelling me to play yet again.

Into the Sunset.

Glossary

"Have you ever noticed what golf spells backwards?"
—Al Boliska

As I mentioned way back in chapter 1, there's a big difference between the "official" language of golf and the "real" language of golf. These definitions should help you with the real language.

Any terms listed in italics also have an official definition that can be found in the USGA's *The Rules of Golf*, but these will get you going in the right direction.

"A" player: A method for identifying golfers by ability and/or handicap in league competitions. Low handicap to high; A-B-C-D.
"Heck no, we didn't win. The 'A' player in our group shot 117!"

Abnormal ground conditions: Any standing water, ground under repair, or damage caused by an animal or bird.

Ace: See "Hole-in-one."

Adjusted score: A manipulation of a player's score prior to officially posting it to the handicap computer.

Adolf Hitler: Slang term for taking "two shots in a bunker."
"I Adolf Hitler'd it on number 13, and made a double bogey."

Aim: An effort to align your body and your golf club to most effectively hit a ball toward your target.

Albatross: A score of three under the par of a hole. An albatross is a very rare bird indeed.

Alignment: The position of your body in relationship to your intended target line.

Backswing: The motion of the golf club as it swings away from the ball.

Bag drop: The area where players can drop off their golf clubs near the clubhouse prior to parking their car.

Ball in play: A ball is "in play" from the time a player tees off until they hole out, or the ball is substituted, lost, or hit out of bounds.

Ball marker: A coin-like item used to mark the position of a golf ball on the green when it's lifted to be cleaned and/or moved out of another player's putting line.

Ball position: The placement of the golf ball in relationship to your feet when you take your stance.

Bellied wedge: To intentionally putt the ball using the blade of a lofted wedge.

Big dog: See "Driver."
"I know it's risky, but I'm going to hit the big dog here, and hopefully I'll be able to get home (reach the green) in two (strokes) on this par 5."

Birdie: A score of one stroke under par on a hole.

Blade: See "Thin."

Bogey: A score of one over the par of a hole. If the score is worse, then a prefix is added to bogey to describe the score: double-bogey, triple-bogey, quadruple-bogey, etc.

Break (green): The slope of the green that a player must estimate when putting.
"That putt had no chance of going in because I didn't play enough break."

Breakfast ball: See "Mulligan."

Buggy: See "Golf cart."

Bunker: A collection of sand strategically positioned about the golf course intended to stop the forward movement of the golf ball and cause a player difficulty playing their next stroke. Also known as beach, kitty litter, sand trap, or trap.

C.C.: Country Club.
"Thanks for calling Snorting Moose C.C. How can I help you?"

Caddie: A person who carries the bag, walks with the golfer, and assists an individual or a twosome in the play of the course. This person offers advice on club selection, strategy, and putting. A good caddie can improve your score by several strokes, particularly on a course you haven't played before.

Capped: A tie in a skins game.
"Inconceivable! My ace got capped!"

Cart rental: Paying a golf course for the use of a golf cart.

Cart staging area: The area near the clubhouse where the carts available for rent are ready and waiting.
"Why don't you guys go to the locker room and change your shoes, then I'll meet you at the staging area."

Cash game: Playing golf with the specific intent to gamble for money.

Casual water: This is a fancy term for temporary, standing water that is not an official "water hazard." Snow and ice can be treated as either casual water or a loose impediment. Also known as a puddle.

Chariot: See "Golf cart."

Chief: See "Driver."

Chili dip: See "Chunk."

Chinos: See "Khakis."

Chip-in: To chip the ball into the hole from off the green.

Chunk: Hitting the ground behind the ball.

Closest to the pin: A common tournament contest where the player who hits their tee shot closest to the flagstick on a par 3 wins a prize.

Conversion chart: The table specific to each golf course that converts a golfer's handicap index to a course handicap.

Course conditions: The quality of the surface of the golf course. Course conditions are subject to change based on many factors, such as weather and maintenance schedules.
"The course conditions were tough today. The windstorm last night really did some damage."

Course handicap: A player's converted handicap index.

Course rating: An assessment of what a scratch player would score at a particular course.

Cuban: Slang term for a putt that's left short. (It needed one more revolution.)

Cut: Term that describes a left-to-right ball flight (for a right-handed player). A cut is not as severe as a slice.
"I had to hit a cut around that big tree in front of the green."

Deuce: A score of a two on a hole.
"That was the only par 3 I made a deuce on all day."

Dimples: The indentations on the surface of the golf ball. Serious engineering goes into dimple design, and shape, depth, density, and pattern all influence its aerodynamics.

Divot: Is the divot the hunk of grass and dirt that's removed when you take a golf swing and strike the ground—or is it the hole that's left behind? Hmmm . . . (It's the pelt that's removed.)
"Always replace or discard-and-fill your divots."

Dogleg: A golf hole curved in shape.
"I tried to cut the corner of the dogleg, and ended up in the pond instead."

Dots: Marks on the scorecard that indicate where a player gets strokes in a net game.

Downswing: The forward movement of the club toward the ball.

Draw: A mild hook.

Driver: The 1-wood.

Driving range: See "Practice range."

Dub: See "Chunk."

Duff: See "Chunk."

Eagle: A score of two under the par of a hole.

ESC: Equitable Stroke Control. An adjustment made to a player's score prior to officially posting it for handicap purposes.

Etiquette: The expectations of proper behavior to be demonstrated on the golf course by every golfer.

Even par: A score equal to all pars during a round of golf.

Fat: See "Chunk."

Field: All the competitors in a golf event.
"There are so many strong players in the field this year, I'll be happy just to make the cut."

Flagstick: You know what? If you don't know what the flagstick is, raise your hand and I'll come hit you on the head with one.

Flight: A grouping of players (or teams) by ability.
"Hooray! I won the consolation bracket of the Net Flight in this year's Club Championship."

Follow-through: The continuation of the forward movement of the golf club after impact.

Forecaddie: A person who works for an entire group to watch for wayward shots, manage the housekeeping chores, and help them maintain an acceptable pace of play. Don't expect a forecaddie to improve your performance. Instead, a forecaddie should enhance your enjoyment of the course by handling most of the on-course etiquette responsibilities, so you don't have to.

G.C.: Golf course or golf club.
"Thanks for calling Nimble Yak G.C. How can I help you?"

G.I.R.: Green-in-regulation. Hitting your ball onto the green in two strokes under the par of any hole.

Give away the hole: An expression that means to not aim a putt outside of the edge of the hole.
"It breaks a little, but I wouldn't give away the hole."

Golf ball: The ball that's specifically designed for use when playing golf.

Golf cart: The vehicle designed to transport golfers around a golf course.

Golf clubs: Tools designed to project the ball into the air or roll it across the ground toward the intended target.

Golf course: The field on which the game of golf is played.

Golf experience: An all-encompassing term describing everything that goes into playing golf—from preparing to play, to post-golf wrap-up.

Golf professional: See "PGA professional."

Golf shop: The building or room(s) at the golf course where the professional staff work. It's here you'll check in and/or purchase equipment.

Golf swing: The motion intended to strike a golf ball while using a golf club.

Green fee: The fee charged by a golf course for the permission to play.

Green speed: The speed that the golf ball will roll across the surface of the grass on the green.

Green-reading: An attempt to correctly predict the speed and break of an upcoming putt.

Grind: When a player is very deliberate on short-game techniques in an effort to make the best possible score.
"It looked like you were grinding hard out there today."

Gross score: A player's actual score (without handicap adjustment).
"You shot 65? Gross???"

Ground under repair: Damage to the course, usually marked by white lines.

Guest fee: Green fee at a private course.

Handicap (hole): Rank of difficulty of each hole on a course.

Handicap (player): An average of a player's ten best scores out of their twenty most recent, it's the number subtracted from a player's gross score to derive a net score. The handicap allows players of all skill levels to fairly compete.

Handicap index: A number with a decimal point that converts to a course handicap differently at every golf course.

Hazards: A defined land feature you don't want to hit your ball into. These menaces come in three variations: water hazard, lateral water hazard, and bunker. Water and lateral water hazards can exist without water in the case of a ditch, canyon, or gully. See page 34.

Headcover: The protective sleeve fitted over the head of a golf club—usually made for a wood.

Heavy: See "Chunk."

Hole: See "Flagstick."

Holed: A ball is "holed" when it is completely in the cup.

Hole assignments: The hole a player is required to begin their round on during a shotgun start.
"Great. Our hole assignment is number 12. At least we'll get the hardest hole out of the way first."

Hole location: The exact location of the flagstick. At times, it can be important for strategic consideration such as club selection.
"I chose to hit an iron off the tee on the short par 4 because I wanted to have a full wedge (with spin) into the front-of-the-green hole location."

Hole-in-one: The rare act of hitting the ball into the hole in the first stroke from the teeing ground.

Honor: The first person to tee off on a hole, usually with the best score on the previous hole, is said to have the "honor."

Hook: A right-to-left spinning shot (for a right-handed player).

Horse: Slang term a caddie might call his player, or a weaker partner might call a stronger partner.

Horserace: See "Shoot-out."

Housekeeping: Proper care for the course including, but not limited to, replacing/discarding divots, raking bunkers, and fixing pitch marks on the green.

Hybrid: A cross between an iron and a wood club.

Impact: The precise moment the golf club strikes the ball.
"You sliced the ball because the clubface was open at impact."

In the leather: The distance from the bottom end of the putter grip to the hole.

Irons: The classic-looking golf clubs designed to project the ball into the air from the ground.

Jock: See "Caddie."

Khakis: See "Chinos."

Lateral: See "Shank."

Lateral rule: A modification to *The Rules of Golf* making it easier for a group to maintain proper pace of play.

Lateral water hazard: Typically, a body of water a player must play alongside parallel to the intended direction of play. Lateral water hazards are designated by red stakes or lines.

League: A conglomeration of like-minded folks who've agreed to play golf at a specific course at a recurring day and time. Fun competitions and camaraderie generally abound.

Lip: The edge of the hole.

Local rules: A modification to *The Rules of Golf* to account for an unusual condition or circumstance specific to a particular golf course.

L.O.F.T.: Lack of Friggin' Talent.
"Well sir, in my professional opinion, you've clearly got a L.O.F.T. problem."

Loft: The angle between the clubface and the ground.

Looper: See "Caddie."

Loose impediments: Mother Nature's litter, such as pine needles, twigs, branches, dead animals, rocks, snow, or other such things sitting on the surface of the ground, and not sticking to the ball, which may be removed anywhere on the course—except in a hazard.

Lost ball: A ball is deemed "lost" when it is not found within five minutes of searching.

Lumber: See "Driver."

Mercerized: A process in which cotton fabric is soaked in an acid bath to remove the tiny fibers that might make the garment look "fuzzy." This gives the fabric a nice lightweight and shiny appearance.

Moosehead: A score of 10 on a hole. Put your thumbs into your ears and fan your fingers out like antlers. Get it?

Mulligan: A do-over.

Municipal: A city-owned public golf course, also known as a "muni."

Net score: A player's actual score, less handicap.

"It's just not mathematically possible to shoot two net scores of 65 in back-to-back rounds."

O. J. Simpson: Slang term for hitting a lousy shot, but still "getting away with it."
"I really hit an O. J. Simpson on number 5 today—it rolled the entire way there, but ended up 10 feet from the hole for birdie."

Obstruction: Anything man-made, or man-placed as a feature, on the golf course. Obstructions can be movable or immovable.

Open stance: For a right-handed player, a stance that is aligned left of the intended target line.

Out of bounds: All golf courses have parameters usually defined by white stakes or white lines, fence posts, or the inside edges of paved roads that might border the course. The area outside of these markers is out of bounds. Also known as OB, Obi-Wan Kenobi (from *Star Wars*), or Oscar Bravo.

Pace of play: The speed that a player or group plays the golf course.

Pairings: A list of players in a tournament field, usually by hole assignment or starting time.
"Did you see the pairings yet? We get to play together! Wanna share a cart?"

PAT: Playing ability test that an apprentice professional must pass in order to become a PGA member.
"It takes the average professional about six or seven attempts to pass the PAT."

Penalty stroke: A stroke, or strokes, added to your score for various infractions including hitting it into the water, hitting it out of bounds, having too many clubs in your bag, etc.

PGA: The PGA of America is the world's largest sports organization, with twenty-eight thousand men and women golf professionals who are the recognized experts in growing, teaching, and managing the game of golf while serving millions of people nationwide. Since its founding in 1916, the PGA of America has enhanced its leadership position in a $62 billion-a-year industry through premier spectator events, world-class education and training, philanthropic outreach, and award-winning golf promotions. Visit PGA.com.

PGA professional: Today's PGA professional is the public's link to the game, serving an essential role in the operation of golf facilities throughout the country.

Pin sheet: A sheet that depicts the hole location on all 18 holes.
"I forgot to check the pin sheet and ended up hitting the ball way past the hole, which left me with no chance but to make the severely downhill putt."

Pique: A cotton fabric commonly used for golf shirts.

Pitch mark: The small depression left by a golf ball in the surface of the green.
"It's a requirement of the game that every player fixes their pitch marks."

Play through: Standing aside on the golf course and allowing a group immediately behind you (and playing faster than you) to go on ahead.
"It's good manners to allow a faster-moving group to play through."

Play-through tax: A show of appreciation by purchasing an on-course beverage for any group that allows you to play through.

Playing partners: The other golfers in your group.
"Hey pro, thanks for the pairing today. I really enjoyed my playing partners."

Practice range: The area at a golf facility dedicated to practice.

Pre-shot routine: The process by which players prepare to hit their next shot.

Press: The act of doubling a previously agreed-upon golf wager.

Private golf course: A golf course requiring purchase of a membership to join and play.

Pro-Am: A common golf tournament type with one professional and four amateurs competing together as a team.

Pro shop: See "Golf shop."

Provisional ball: A secondary ball that is played until the location or condition of the original ball can be determined.

Pull-cart: Two- or three-wheeled vehicles that allow a player to push or pull their clubs as they walk the golf course.

Putting green: The area of very short grass that surrounds the hole. Also known as dance floor, hardwood, or carpet.

Putting line: The imaginary line you intend to roll your next putt on toward the hole.

R&A: The Royal and Ancient Golf Club of Scotland. The R&A is the oldest governing body of the sport.

Range: See "Practice range."

Range balls: Golf balls intended to be hit exclusively at the practice range.

Ready golf: A decision to play whenever ready, regardless of whose turn it is, in order to maintain an acceptable pace of play.

Regular: Someone you see at the golf course just about every time you go there.

Regular group: A handful of golfers who routinely play together at the same day and time each week.

Rock Hudson: Slang term for a putt that "looks straight but wasn't."

"S" word: See "Shank."

Saddam Hussein: Slang term for a golf shot that goes "from one bunker straight into another."

Salman Rushdie: Slang term for a putt that's "an impossible read."

Sandbagging: To cheat by misrepresenting one's ability.

Save par: To miss a green-in-regulation, but make one putt or chip in to make a par.
"I'm exhausted. I was grinding all day and only managed to save a few pars."

Scorecard: The card on which score is kept for a game of golf.

Scramble: A common format in which all players in a group compete as one team and hit all their shots from the same location after choosing the best shot each time.

Scratch golfer: A golfer with the ability to shoot even par or better.

Shank: A really, really, really bad golf shot that glances off the hosel, rather than striking the clubface.

Shoebag: A cloth or plastic bag in which you carry your golf shoes to and from the course.

Shoot-out: See "Horserace."

Shop: See "Golf shop."

Shot shape: A term used to describe the visual result of a golf shot.
"Wow, I didn't like that shot shape at all! I was trying to hit a cut, and hooked it 40 yards left instead."

Shotgun start: A common method of starting groups of golfers on every hole at the same time. A loud sound signals the beginning of the round to facilitate proper pace of play and ensure spacing between the groups.

It's a useful way to maximize play on busy days—or during a tournament. When all players start at the same time they'll finish at the same time, which makes it easier to schedule post-golf social activities.

Skinny: See "Thin."

Skull: See "Thin."

Slacks: See "Trousers."

Slice: For a right-handed player, this is the dreaded left-to-right spinning banana ball.

Slope: A numerical assessment of the difficulty of a golf course.

Smother: See "Hook."

Snowman: A score of eight (8) on a hole.

Son-in-law: Slang term for a lousy but usable golf shot—"it wasn't what you were hoping for, but it'll do."

Spike marks: Damage caused to the surface of the green by the spikes on the bottom of golf shoes.
"It's important to pick up your feet when you walk on the green to prevent spike mark damage."

Spit the bit: A slang term for falling apart under pressure.

Square (1): Delivering the clubface to the ball in proper alignment to the swing path and target line.
"Hallelujah! I haven't hit the ball with a clubface that square all day."

Square (2): In match play, when two sides are even.
"How does our match stand? Are we square?"

Starting time: See "Tee time."

Stimpmeter: The tool used to measure green speed.

Strategy: In golf, strategy consists of determining club selection based on the probable outcome and risk versus reward of every shot.

Stroke: An attempt to strike the golf ball.

Stub: See "Chunk."

Sweet spot: The middle of the clubface.

Swing speed: The speed, measured in miles per hour, that the clubhead travels during the golf swing.

Swing thoughts: The mental preparation for a golf swing.

Target line: The imaginary line on which you intend to hit your golf ball.

Tee: A device used to raise the ball above the ground in preparation for hitting your drive. It may be used only on the "teeing ground."

Tee time: A reservation to play golf at a particular course at a specific time.

Teeing ground: This is the level area of short grass from where play of each hole begins. It's also known as the tee box, tee, box, bump, or mound.

Teeing it up: Slang term for playing golf.
"Are you teeing it up this evening after work?"
"Yes. I told my wife I've got a meeting. That should give us a couple of hours."

Tending the pin: The act of holding the flagstick while another player takes a putt.

The Majors: The four most prestigious and important tournaments of the PGA Tour calendar: the Masters, the U.S. Open, the British Open, and the PGA Championship.

The Rules of Golf and the Rules of Amateur Status: The book of official rules that govern the game; editions are published annually by the USGA.

Thin: The opposite of chunk. Hitting the top half of the golf ball, which can send it racing across the surface of the ground.

Through the green: The entire golf course, with two exceptions: the tee and green of the hole being played and all hazards on the course. Through the green does not mean "beyond" the green. It's a noun, not a preposition.

Topped: When the ball is hit at the very top, driving it into the ground and only advancing it forward a few feet.

Track: Slang term for a golf course.

Trolley: See "Pull cart."

Trousers: See "Slacks."

Turn: The transition between the front and the back 9.

Undulation: The subtle mounds of the golf course.

USGA: United States Golf Association. The governing body of golf in the United States and Mexico.

Water hazard: A body of water a player has to go over or around perpendicular to the intended direction of play. Water hazards are designated by yellow stakes or lines.

Wedges: The shortest and most-lofted irons.

Whiff: A total miss when attempting to strike the golf ball.

Winter rules: A determination to allow players to move their golf ball to better grass. Typically employed in the early spring or late fall when the course is excessively wet and/or muddy.

Woods: The longest and least-lofted golf clubs. They have large hollow metal heads.

Wrong ball: Any ball that is not the original "ball in play."

Wrong putting green: Any green that is not part of the hole being played. "You get free relief off a wrong putting green."

Acknowledgments

They say it takes a village to raise a child. It took a small army to help me raise this baby.

I've had a chance to see and do some pretty cool things in my career as a Golf Pro. Most meaningful, however, have been the personal relationships I've developed over the years. Frankly, there are just too many people—colleagues, employers, and members—to mention here, and you'd lose interest if I tried. But those who generously contributed their time and energy to this book deserve some recognition, and there's one person who it simply couldn't have happened without.

If the Six Million Dollar Man has a younger brother, I bet he looks just like Denny Ryerson. Denny is a Hollywood-handsome, extremely successful businessman and founding member of the Club at Black Rock in Coeur d'Alene, Idaho. When we opened in 2003, he was recovering from a recent bypass surgery. After his first round he staggered into the Golf Shop, looking like he'd packed a refrigerator on his back all day, sweating profusely and gasping for air. After my initial concerns that I'd have to perform CPR, or worse—that we'd lose a member on opening weekend—subsided, I admired his stubborn determination to finish the round and our friendship was sparked. Now fully recovered, he's actually gotten younger every year since.

A couple years later, over a glass (or four) of Merlot, we began to discuss the idea for this book. Independently of one another, we had formulated a plan for the exact same topic. My interest was to promote the game—a modest form of repayment for all it's given to me. His point of view was that of a new golfer who'd struggled with, stumbled over, and blundered through many of the subtleties of the game and that of a frustrated husband and father who'd futilely tried to teach his family to play. We immediately shared the same vision. Yet the likelihood of me ever having the time (let alone the talent) to do this, however, was doubtful at best.

Another year or two after that, shortly after I'd hung up my Golf Pro spurs, Denny approached me and offered to make this endeavor my new full-time occupation! At that point in my life, the only thing I'd ever written was a Christmas letter. To steal a line from the movie *Tin Cup*, "You have extra large *huevos*, my friend."

Denny—Thank you! You've changed my life. Your generosity and support mean the world to me and my family. *Did I tell you I have an idea for another book . . .?*

The two guys that brought this whole thing together deserve most of the credit, my big brother Jeff and my editor David Kilmer. I simply started with an idea and some incoherent ramblings on paper. Together, they turned it into something we're all pretty proud of.

Talk about taking a chance—Jeff quit his job as an engineer and relocated eight hours away from his beautiful family (fortunately, they've now joined him) to work full-time with me on this book. He's solely responsible for the proofreading, typesetting, graphics, and layout of every page. Jeffy, thanks for your hard work. It's been fun to reconnect.

David was quick to sink his teeth into this project—and can take full credit for it reading like a *real* book. I'm not sure how he sifted through my verbose rough draft and unearthed a legible manuscript, but he managed. David, you're an archaeologist-poet. Thanks for your expertise and enthusiasm.

Thanks to Jeremy Deming at IMGX in Coeur d'Alene for your incredible artwork. My favorite is the sandbagger dude. When I first sat in your boardroom and asked if you could help me with this, you took me seriously. At that point, not many did. You da man, and you delivered.

Thanks to my review team. Your input most definitely helped. I hope you all recognize your suggestions and personal touches—they're in there. Greg Ross, Craig Sullivan, Paul Leonard, John Richards, Chad Stoddard, Pastor Mike Rima, Janet Andrews, Mom, Dad, Amy, and even my jerk brother-in-law, Jason. Thank you all for the gift of your time. Believe me, nobody understands its value more than a Golf Pro. I'm humbled by the willingness with which you all agreed to assist.

To the PGA Member Golf Professionals in the trenches who've supported and promoted this book, thanks millions. I hope I'm able to say the things to your members that you can't. Continue your noble efforts, try to spend more time with your families, and let's grow this magical game together.

Thanks to the golf courses that contributed photos: Black Rock, Gozzer Ranch, Circling Raven, StoneRidge, the Idaho Club, and the Coeur d'Alene

Resort. Thanks to Bill Morrow, Kendale Trahan, and Derek Lane at the Quarry for allowing me to use your fine facility as my photo studio. Thank you, my friends, Kelly (pinky-out) and Sonny (pinky-in), for your pretty poses. Thanks to my self-appointed "promoter," Rusty Reyes.

Finally, to my inspiration—my beautiful wife, Sweet Jillian, and my chicks, Taylin Mae and Marin Grace—thanks for surviving the Golf Pro phase of our journey. You are the reasons for all I do. Sweetie, thanks for your support and perseverance. This would be pointless without you.

God answers prayers. I'm living proof and have been undeservedly blessed beyond measure. For that, I can only hope to reflect some of the Light. May God bless you too—and may you all discover what's *really* important, on and off the golf course.

Art on pp. xiv, 40 (bottom), 159, 182, 209, 233 by Greg Rowley.

If you're interested in any of the work you've seen throughout this book or any of the golf courses that I've pictured, here are links to the corresponding websites.

Pick It Up Publishing
www.pickituppublishing.com

Imagination Graphics—
Jeremy Deming
www.imaginationgraphics.com

Blue 541—David Kilmer
www.blue541.com

The Club at Black Rock
www.blackrockidaho.com

The Coeur d'Alene Resort
www.cdaresort.com/golf

Gozzer Ranch
www.gozzerranchclub.com

Hayden Lake Country Club
www.haydenlakecc.com

The Quarry at La Quinta
www.quarryinfo.com

Bandon Dunes Golf Resort
www.bandondunesgolf.com

Play Golf America
www.playgolfamerica.com

PGA of America
www.pga.com

United States Golf Association
www.usga.com

Circle Raven Golf Course
www.circlingraven.com

StoneRidge Golf Course
www.stoneridgeidaho.com

The Idaho Club
www.theidahoclub.com

About the Author

Greg Rowley, a PGA member, has worked at and managed some of the finest golf facilities in the United States. The Club at Black Rock, where he was the Director of Golf, was named *Golf Digest's* "Best New Private Course" in 2003. In 2004, Greg was named by *Men's Journal* as having one of the "50 Best Jobs in America." He serves on the Board of Directors for the Inland Empire Chapter of the PGA and has won several awards for his innovative programs, including the 2008 President's Award for Growing the Game of Golf. Greg has played with and taught men, women, juniors, seniors, celebrities, professional athletes, PGA Tour players and beginners. *Golf, Naked* is his first book.

Greg is a graduate of the University of Idaho, where he majored in lots of things and eventually graduated with a degree in Psychology. He minored in varsity volleyball, intramural basketball, fraternity antics, and barroom activities—including, but not limited to, beer-pong, billiards, foosball, shuffleboard and darts.

He lives in Coeur d'Alene, Idaho with his wife, Jillian, his daughters Taylin and Marin and two big black dogs. He can usually be found relaxing on Hayden Lake, driving over things in his Jeep, competing in local Pro-Am golf tournaments, or playing co-ed rec-league volleyball and softball. He plays third base.

Order your copy of *The Pocket Pro: Golf Gaming Guide* today!

You may either fill out this order form and mail it to us along with a check for $9.95 made out to Pick It Up Publishing, or simply go to www.pickituppublishing.com and place your order online.

Name: ____

Address: ____

____

City: ______________________________ State: __________

ZIP: __________

E-mail: ____

Send to:

THE POCKET PRO
c/o Pick It Up Publishing
PO BOX 3667
Coeur d'Alene, ID 83816